Rome Seizes the Trident

Rome Seizes the Trident

The Defeat of Carthaginian Seapower and the Forging of the Roman Empire

Marc G. DeSantis

Pen & Sword
MILITARY

First published in Great Britain in 2016 by
Pen & Sword Military
an imprint of
Pen & Sword Books Ltd
47 Church Street
Barnsley
South Yorkshire
S70 2AS

Copyright © Marc G. DeSantis 2016

ISBN 978 1 47382 698 4

The right of Marc G. DeSantis to be identified as the Author of this Work has been asserted by him in accordance with the Copyright, Designs and Patents Act 1988.

A CIP catalogue record for this book is available from the British Library

All rights reserved. No part of this book may be reproduced or transmitted in any form or by any means, electronic or mechanical including photocopying, recording or by any information storage and retrieval system, without permission from the Publisher in writing.

Typeset in Ehrhardt by
Mac Style Ltd, Bridlington, East Yorkshire
Printed and bound in the UK by CPI Group (UK) Ltd,
Croydon, CR0 4YY

Pen & Sword Books Ltd incorporates the imprints of Pen & Sword Archaeology, Atlas, Aviation, Battleground, Discovery, Family History, History, Maritime, Military, Naval, Politics, Railways, Select, Transport, True Crime, and Fiction, Frontline Books, Leo Cooper, Praetorian Press, Seaforth Publishing and Wharncliffe.

For a complete list of Pen & Sword titles please contact
PEN & SWORD BOOKS LIMITED
47 Church Street, Barnsley, South Yorkshire, S70 2AS, England
E-mail: enquiries@pen-and-sword.co.uk
Website: www.pen-and-sword.co.uk

Contents

Preface		xii
Part I: Breaking Carthage		1
Introduction		3
Chapter 1	Sources	9
Chapter 2	The Contestants	14
Chapter 3	Sicily: Theatre of War, History of Blood	28
Chapter 4	War at Sea in the Age of the War Galley	33
Chapter 5	Breaking Athens: A Case Study	42
Part II: The First Punic War		49
Chapter 6	Trouble at the Toe of Italy	51
Chapter 7	Opening Moves	63
Chapter 8	Mylae, 260 BC: Rome's Fleet Sails in Harm's Way	73
Chapter 9	After Mylae	81
Chapter 10	Ecnomus, 256 BC	86
Chapter 11	The Battle of Cape Hermaeum, 255 BC	99
Chapter 12	Rome Tries Again	104
Chapter 13	Drepana, 249 BC	110
Chapter 14	The Debut of Hamilcar Barca	120
Chapter 15	Endgame: The Battle of the Aegates Islands, 241 BC	122
Chapter 16	Peace	130
Chapter 17	Was Seapower Worth The Cost?	133

Part III: Conflicts Between the Wars — 139

Chapter 18	Illyria and Gaul	141
Chapter 19	The Mercenary Revolt 240–238 BC	146

Part IV: Strangling Carthage — 155

Chapter 20	The Second Punic War, 218–202 BC	157
Chapter 21	A Second War with Carthage	162
Chapter 22	Hannibal in Italy	167
Chapter 23	Holding the Line in the Adriatic: The War with Macedonia	171
Chapter 24	Sicily and Sardinia	175
Chapter 25	Carthage's Spanish Ulcer	184
Chapter 26	Africa	189
Chapter 27	Seapower in the Second Punic War	198

Part V: Destroying Carthage — 205

Chapter 28	Roman Naval Operations in the East	207
Chapter 29	A Third War with Carthage	215

Conclusion	223
Notes and References	228
Bibliography	242
Index	246

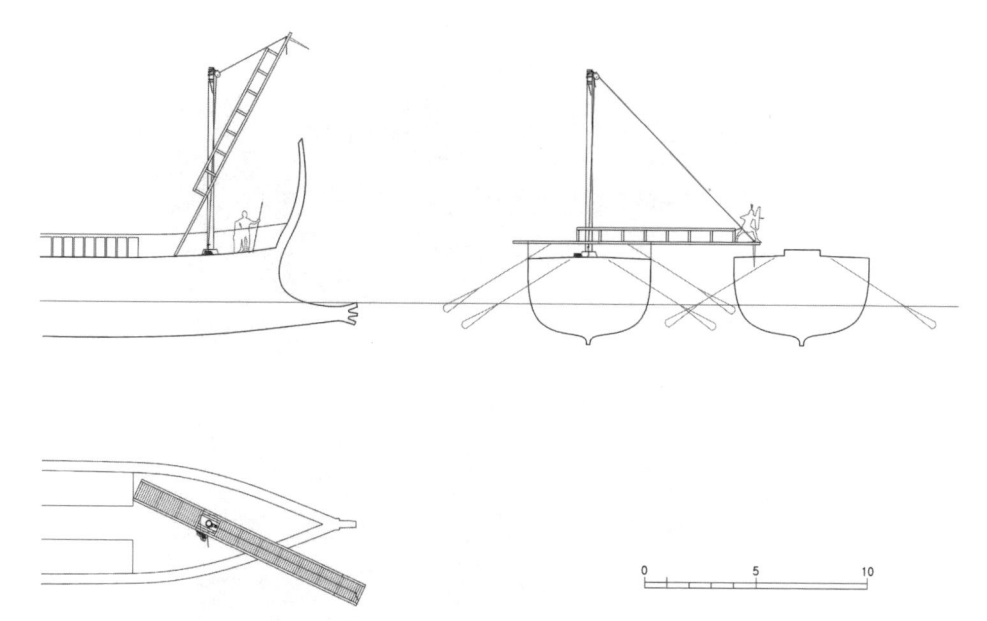

The Corvus Boarding-Bridge. (*Illustration by Julia Lillo*)

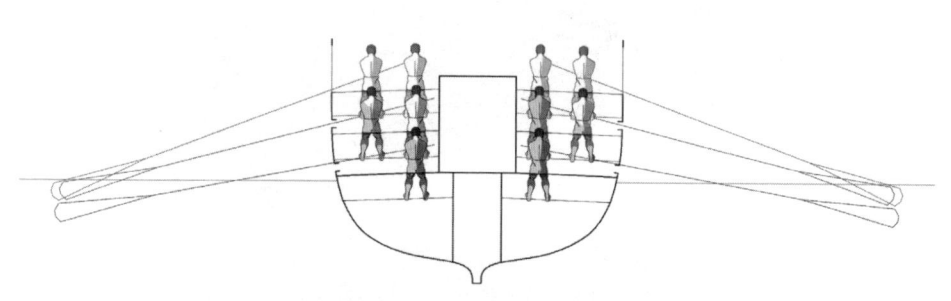

Seating Arrangements of Rowers in Quinquereme. (*Illustration by Julia Lillo*)

The Battle of Ecnomus, 256 BC.

Key:
1: Roman First Squadron (Vulso)
2: Roman Second Squadron (Regulus)
3: Roman Third Squadron and Cavalry Transports
4: Roman Fourth Squadron (Triarii)

A: Carthaginian Left Wing
B: Carthaginian Centre (Hamilcar)
C: Carthaginian Right Wing (Hanno)

(*Illustration by Julia Lillo*)

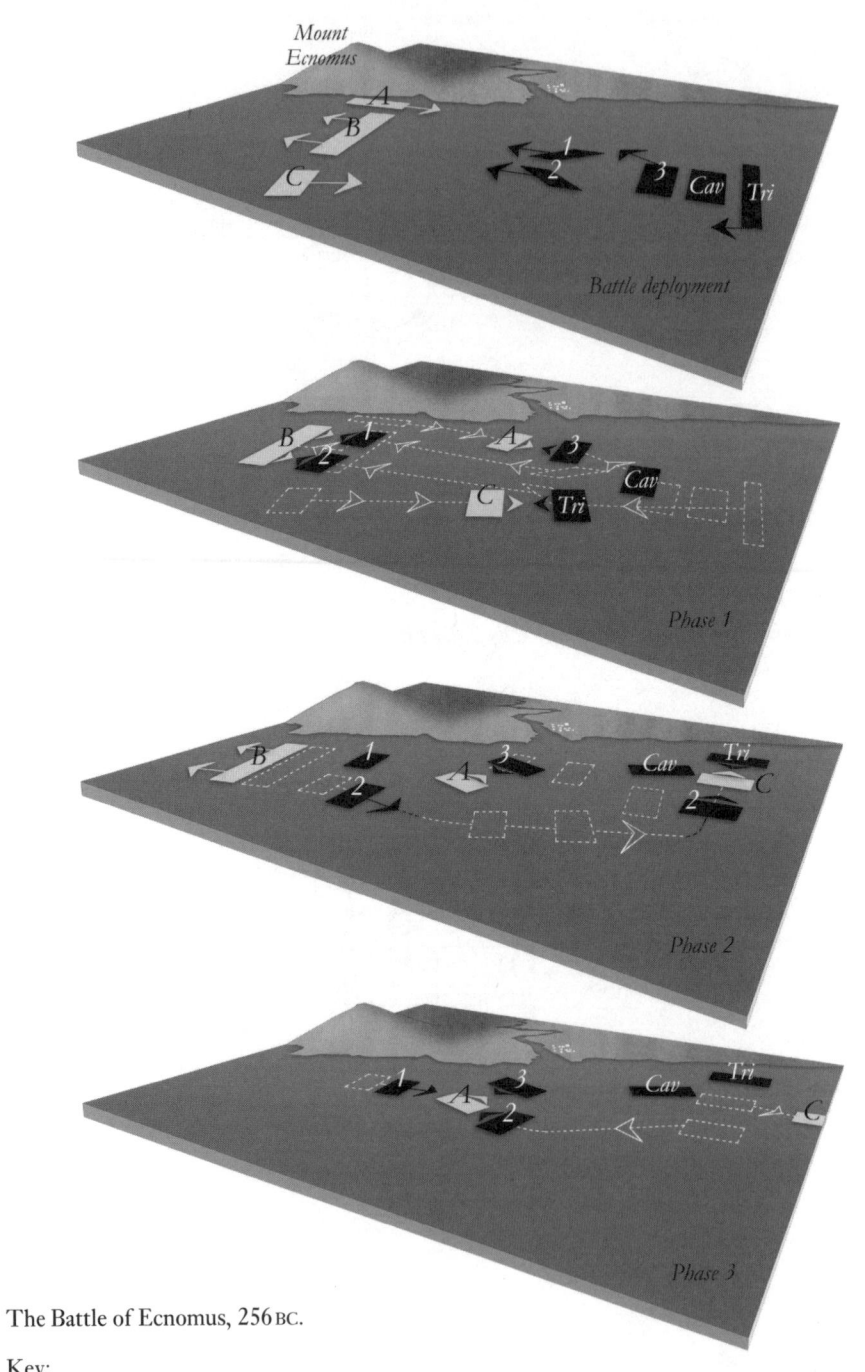

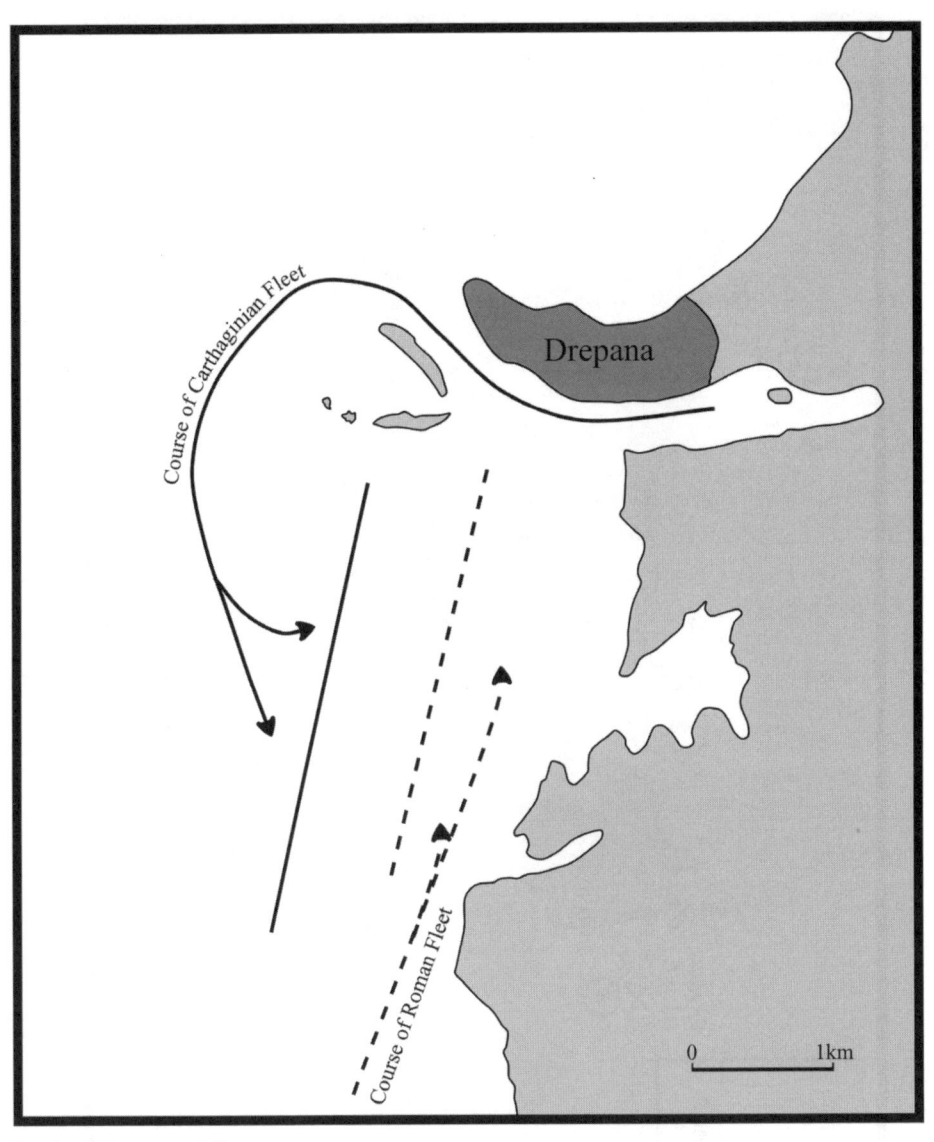

Battle of Drepana, 249 BC.

① Battle of Mylae, 260 BCE
② Battle of Ecnomus, 256 BCE
③ Battle of Drepana, 249 BCE
④ Battle of Aegates Islands, 241 BCE

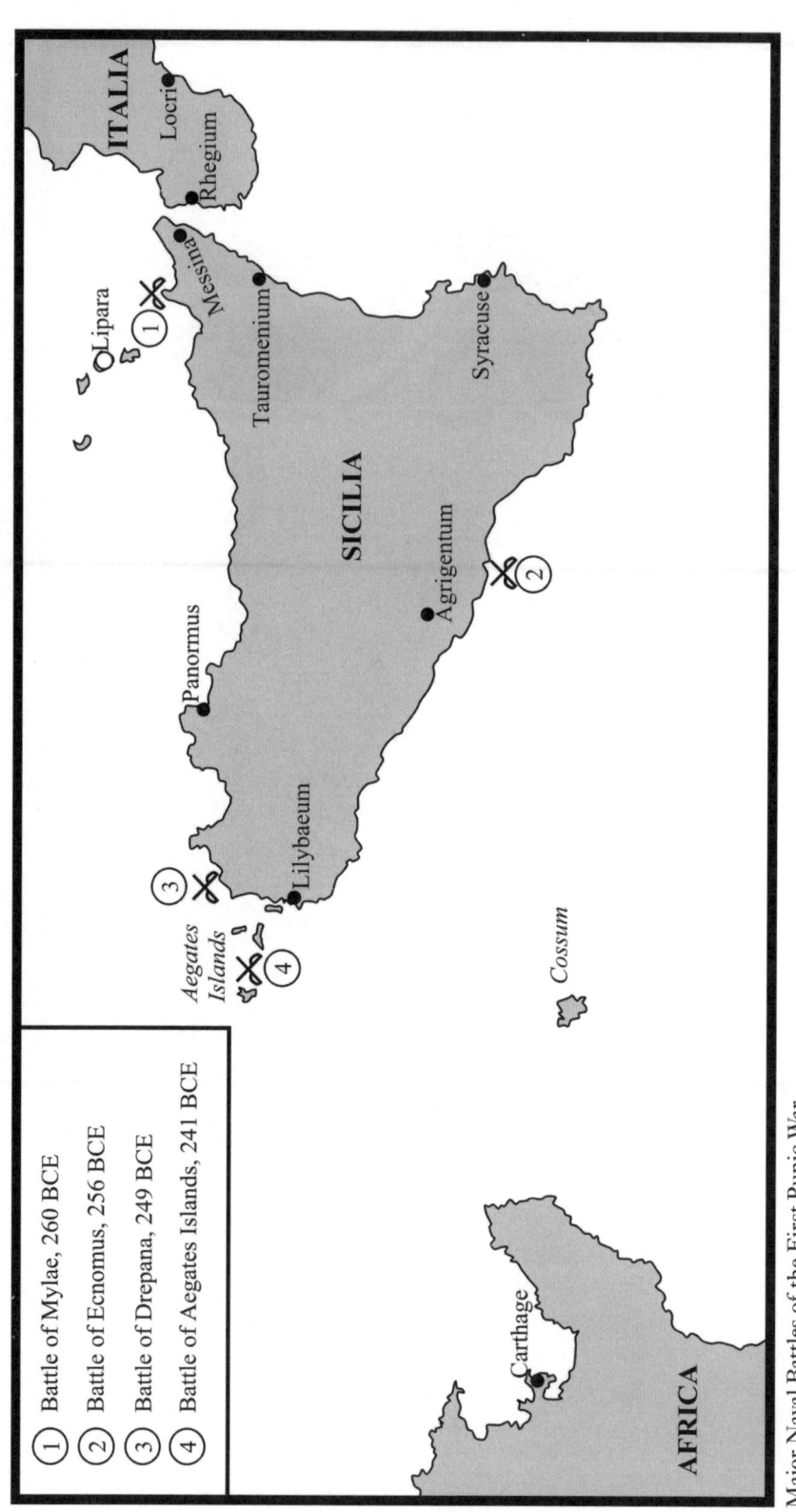

Major Naval Battles of the First Punic War.

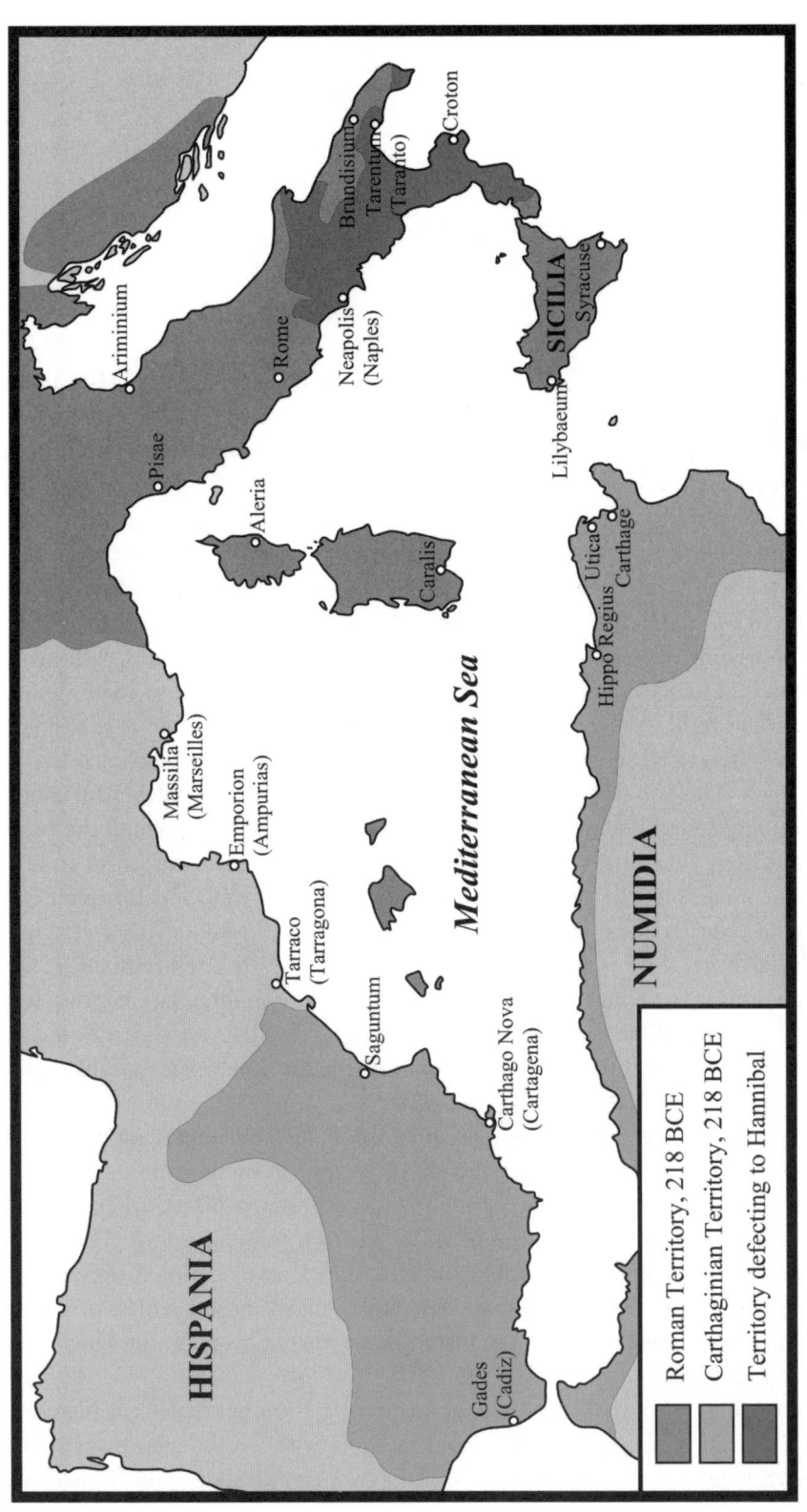

The Western Mediterranean at the Time of the Second Punic War.

Preface

When I was still attending university, a fellow classmate told me a joke that sums up the difficulties of modern historians of the ancient world: Two such scholars were talking together as they walked down a quiet hallway in their university's department of history. They strode past the open door of one of the large lecture halls. Inside, a throng of academics was listening attentively to a speaker at the lectern. 'What is going on in there?' one asked the other. 'It is a conference on medieval history,' came the reply. The first historian snorted in derision as he peered through the doorway. 'Journalists!'

The writing of the history of ancient matters presents historians with many problems. The nature of the source material is always subject to some doubt, even when mild. Many important events are known to us from just a single source, often itself written centuries after the fact. There is no choice but to rely upon it for the sake of the narrative. There is also the problem of trusting a surviving source too much. Has it survived because it was deemed the best? Or was there luck involved, and did this particular text just happen to endure into the modern era in the safe confines of a monastery while less fortunate but superior texts perished? With regard to ancient sources for Rome's death struggle with Carthage, there is also the issue of the silence of the Carthaginians. It is a commonplace to say that victors write history. It is a commonplace because it is true. What would the Carthaginians have to say about their wars with Rome? It can only be expected that they would not cast the Romans in a favourable light. It is our loss that such sources do not exist.

Such is the difficulty of our reliance upon material emerging from the ancient world. In addition, the writing of history in modern times does not ensure exactitude. No historian is free from interpretative biases, and every last one will read a text through the prism of his own understanding. There is a marked tendency among historians to discount stories or events if they derive from a late-in-time source, one that is therefore judged suspect, unless of course the story is welcome, and aids the historian in proving his point, in which case it is then counted.

Where historical writing is scant, or unedifying, the other tool of the historian is the shovel. If history, at times, can't be done with words, then there is the hope that the archaeological remains of the past can fill such gaps. Sometimes this is sound, at other times less so. By their very nature, objects can only give mute testimony to the past. Interpretation is just as consequential in the study of physical objects as it is in the reading of texts, perhaps more.

With regard to military history specifically, we do not have in our possession anything from ancient times that would today qualify for that description. Ancient historians wrote extensively about the Punic Wars, but not from the standpoint of how the operations were conducted or with the multiplicity of details that we would doubtlessly prefer to have. So in many instances, battles are said to have taken place, but the tactics and terrain are left undescribed. Important matters, such as numbers or the disposition of troops on the field, are given no attention at all.

Ancient military history must necessarily contend with a host of unknowns. The tools that we have at hand are careful attention to the details provided by the source material, what is left unsaid, and the use of reason. There will be many words and phrases in this book such as *likely*, *may*, *probably*, *possibly*, *reasonable*, *could have*, *might have*, *must have*, and so on. Though I make use of them as sparingly as possible, I need them at times to signal that I am speculating. The limits of knowledge are always present, and in many instances certainty will never be had. The task of writing a history of the ancient world must be approached with humility. I try also to keep my own speculation to a minimum, and only indulge in it when I think that I have evidence that will support a reasonable interpretation that sheds some light on the subject.

Since this is primarily a naval history, the sea fights must be examined in as much depth as can be achieved. Unhappily, determining how ancient sea battles were actually fought is especially troublesome, because they are typically described in only the briefest manner. Even the lengthier accounts pose their own problems. We must reconstruct these engagements without the aid of reports of any of the direct participants. The numbers and types of ships involved are uncertain, the dates are inexact, and the histories were written long after the events under study. These too are all Roman histories, with the Carthaginian side of the story left untold, though in a few instances pro-Carthaginian sources emanating from the Greek world were used by later authors, such as Polybius.

It may seem that there is not much method to this madness. That, however, would be the wrong lesson to draw. We must make do with what we have. Judgment is a necessary tool to employ when seeking to understand events from so long ago. So what follows is not *the* military history of Rome's naval wars with Carthage, but *a* military history of the conflicts. It is the author's own interpretation of what happened.

Part I

Breaking Carthage

Introduction

The Great War for the Middle Sea

For millennia, the Mediterranean, or 'Middle Sea', was the central stage in which the drama of Western history played itself out. The Mediterranean, and the lands surrounding it, or those connected to it by trade and culture, was the grand avenue through which flowed the wealth of the world, along with ideas both religious and philosophical that would profoundly shape the way that humanity would think and live for centuries.

The search for the origins of the struggle between Rome and Carthage is a long one. At root, there was fear of the other, and the apprehension of the power of a potential adversary. In terms of geography, both states were centrally located in the Mediterranean, on the north and south shores respectively. In between them was the strategically vital island of Sicily, a jewel set amidst the glittering sea, with wealthy cities and rich farmland. It was a prize beyond measure. For centuries the Greeks and Carthaginians had vied for control of the island. War was not a new thing to Sicily.

The potential rewards of dominion over the Middle Sea do not explain the length and bitterness of the conflict. The First Punic War, fought between 264 and 241 BC, in particular was noteworthy for its extreme span. Both sides would be left exhausted by their exertions. What had begun in 264 BC as a war between two states that had no prior history of battle was transformed into a hatred that would impel hundreds of thousands to their deaths over the course of more than a century.

The seemingly interminable First and Second Punic wars would recall the massive bloodletting of the First World War, another struggle that lasted far longer than anyone would have reasonably expected. Both sides would display immense courage and extraordinary stubbornness, and a concomitant willingness to expend blood and treasure in profligate amounts even though grinding stalemate was the result. Even when Rome had assured itself of superiority by winning these first two wars, 'Carthage must be destroyed!' was the merciless cry in the Senate by those who hated and feared the ancient enemy in equal measure. At the end of more than a century of warfare, Carthage was demolished and Rome was embarked upon a course of empire the likes of which has never been seen again in the Mediterranean world.

4 Rome Seizes the Trident

It is an understatement to say that Roman victory in the wars with Carthage had profound consequences for all future history. Roman law would prevail as the source for most European legal codes, even until the present day. Greek philosophy would be ensconced as the dominant mental model for understanding the world. Indeed, not least among Rome's accomplishments was that it made the world safe for Hellenism even as it would eventually conquer, and be conquered by, Greece.

The subsequent history of Europe, after the fall of the empire, was influenced strongly by the memory of Rome. Justinian and Charlemagne both attempted to put the empire back together from the many broken pieces left behind in its wreckage. The Holy Roman Empire, rightly said to be not much of an empire, or holy or Roman, for that matter, was still an expression of this longing for a return to the unity of the Roman era. The formation of modern European states and their offspring elsewhere in the world owes much to Roman legal and political thought. The Romans did not invent the idea of a voting assembly with enforceable political power, but their Senate became the model for many successor bodies, with the upper house in the American Congress taking its name from it.

Roman dominion of the Mediterranean was decisive in religion too. Jesus of Nazareth would be born a subject of Rome. St. Paul was a citizen of Rome. St. Augustine, Bishop of Hippo, was a native of Roman North Africa, hailing from the territory of once-mighty Carthage, the city in which he would eventually study. The language in which he wrote his seminal works, however, was not Punic (Phoenician), but Latin. Augustine's conceptions of sin, redemption, the notion of a just war, and the relationship of man to God became pillars of medieval Christianity, and still resonate strongly among modern Christian denominations.

The outcome of the vast struggle between Rome and Carthage is thus not a matter of mere historical curiosity. The modern world as it exists today owes much of its character to the survival of Rome and the defeat of Carthage. How Rome won those wars at sea is the subject of the present work.

Control of the Sea

Among the most remarkable developments of the struggle was Rome's decision to challenge Carthaginian dominion at sea. Rome is today famous for its legions, but not so much for its navy. Yet a powerful fleet was indispensable for Rome's imperial expansion. The empire would not have been possible without a navy. History as we know it would have been vastly different.

In the early years of the First Punic War, Carthage was supreme at sea, and she exploited that dominance to the full. After years of frustration, Rome decided to take the fight to the Carthaginians on the waves. Rome would have to have a great navy of its own. The Greek historian Polybius, himself living as a remarkably well connected political prisoner in Rome several decades after it had built its first large fleet, wrote about this extraordinary decision in his *Histories*. He explained Roman thinking at the outset as being one of practicality and unswerving determination.

> But so long as the Carthaginians held unchallenged control of the sea, the issue of the war still hung in the balance. In the months that followed many inland cities came over to the Romans for fear of their army now that they were in possession of Agrigentum, but at the same time many of the coastal cities deserted them because they were overawed by the Carthaginian fleet. So when the Romans saw that the balance of advantage continually oscillated from one side to another for this reason, and that while the Italian coasts were repeatedly raided and devastated those of Africa suffered no damage, they were filled with the desire to take to the sea and meet the Carthaginians there. It was this factor among others that persuaded me to describe the war at greater length than I would otherwise have done. I was anxious that my readers should not remain ignorant of an important initiative of this kind: that is, how and when and for what reasons the Romans first ventured upon the sea.[1]

That this was to be Rome's first usage of warships was not strictly correct. In 311 the Romans had organized two squadrons of ten ships each.[2] Echoing the practice of having two men (the consuls) in charge of the army, the fleet was headed by two naval commissioners.[3] These men were the *duoviri navales*.[4] But the record of the early Roman navy was not impressive. In the mere two instances in which it was active, it suffered defeats. By far, Roman naval strength was enhanced more by its alliance with Greek Neapolis (Naples) of southern Italy, which it had captured in 326, than by its native efforts.[5] Ironically, Rome's small navy fell into disuse after 278, when it entered into a treaty with none other than Carthage. By its terms the Carthaginians were responsible for providing ships to fight Pyrrhus. Later, as Rome brought other Italian Greek maritime cities into alliance, it became their duty to provide naval support in wartime.[6]

Yet the odds against Rome at sea in the First Punic War, though long, were not insurmountable. The way forward had been demonstrated over a century before during the Peloponnesian War by the Corinthians who had developed prow-to-prow ramming tactics to overcome the highly-trained Athenian navy's advantage in rowing and manoeuvring. The goal of the Corinthian tactics was to turn battles at sea into boarding engagements more akin to fighting on land.

They succeeded in doing this, and the Romans, who used the same tactics, succeeded also. That is not the whole of the story. In conjunction with the Corinthian-style tactics the Romans used a remarkable and mysterious device known to history as the corvus. This was a boarding-bridge set at the prow of a Roman war galley that was dropped upon the deck of an enemy ship when contact had been made. Once down, Roman marines, really their legionaries at sea, would hurry across and overwhelm the Carthaginians. The Romans made their best weapon on land, their infantrymen, their most powerful asset in sea battles too. Though the Carthaginians had a long headstart in mastering the intricacies of naval warfare, they proved incapable of defeating the Romans at sea except in exceptional circumstances.

The Second Punic War was in many respects a continuation of the First Punic War, with one crucial difference being that the Romans held control of the sea from start to finish, and the main threat from Carthage came from the land. Roman maritime supremacy was never seriously challenged, even though it was extremely hard-pressed in many theatres by the enemy. This naval dominance did not win Rome the Second Punic War, but its possession did prevent it from losing.

Why War?

Much has been said about causes of the wars with Carthage, not merely in the immediate sense of what events precipitated the fighting, but in the fundamental sense as why two such powers came to blows at all. Relations between the two states had been comparatively good even into the third century. But some at least foresaw the coming conflict. Pyrrhus, who had campaigned in Italy on behalf of the Greek states in the south, and was still smarting from his costly battles with the Romans, said of Sicily: 'What a cockpit we are now leaving for Carthaginian and Roman to fight in.'[7]

We can discard the notion that the conflicts were ultimately attributable to cultural or 'racial' differences between the parties. These differences did not cause the Romans and Carthaginians to fight. Conversely, cultural, linguistic, and religious similarities have never prevented wars among rival states. The religious and cultural similarities of the Lutheran Swedes and Lutheran Brandenburgers did not prevent them from fighting several wars in the seventeenth century. Latin, Catholic France fought Latin, Catholic Spain in vicious wars too. The Japanese were at war amongst themselves for almost the entirety of their history until unification in the early seventeenth century. Even while Rome and Carthage fought tooth and nail, the Hellenistic Greek empires of the East engaged in their own wars. One would expect that if differences somehow provided an impetus to war, then wars between similar nations would be correspondingly less frequent. The examples adduced above (there are innumerable others) would seem to indicate otherwise. Thus, if similarities were no obstacles to fighting, then it must also be admitted that there is no evidence to suggest, and thus no reason to believe, that the Romans and Carthaginians would inevitably come to blows because of their *dissimilarities*. There must be a more logical explanation for why these two states warred.

Polybius tells us that Rome and Carthage entered into three treaties in the centuries prior to the First Punic War. In Rome he saw the texts of these treaties inscribed upon bronze tablets set within the Treasury of the Quaestors which stood next to the Temple of Jupiter Capitolinus. The first treaty dated to 508–7, the very beginning of the Republic. The Carthaginians, ever-conscious of the need to safeguard their mercantile interests, saw to it that the trading rights of Roman merchants in Libya and Sardinia were seriously circumscribed. The Romans obtained for themselves trading privileges in Carthaginian lands in Sicily. The second treaty, which may be dated to 348, reiterated the terms of the earlier treaty. Though the terms were essentially the same, it is probable that both sides felt it useful to repeat the earlier accord so as to avoid any misunderstanding about each other's sphere of influence. Rome at this time (the mid-fourth century BC) was only concerned with Italy, while Carthage astutely sought to curtail the access of outsiders to her maritime trading empire.[8]

The primary cause of the wars would seem to be fear. For the Romans, the nearness of Sicily to Italy meant that any domination there by Carthage would place the whole of Italy at the mercy of either invasion or quick naval descents upon its lengthy coastline. Geographical proximity, not different gods or languages, was the cause of the wars. Rome's mortal struggle in the early years of the Republic with the Etruscan city of Veii, just twelve miles distant, was not caused by underlying racial or cultural differences, but by an uncomfortable closeness, centering on the bids of the two cities to dominate the Tiber River's salt pans.[9] The proximity of states is often enough to explain why war occurred between them. Competition for land, trade, and dominion over groups of lesser states was enough to start many conflicts.

A worthy counterargument is that Carthage had maintained an extensive presence in Sicily for centuries, and it had not bothered the Romans before. Carthage maintained in Sicily what was in effect a colonial empire that comprised approximately the western two-thirds of the island.[10] What had changed, however, was that Rome had not then been the master of Italy, and the overlord of many subject Italian states with Sicily lying close by to them. Rome was no longer fighting Samnite hillmen or Etruscans within just a few days' march of its walls. By the third century BC, Its horizons had extended to encompass all of Italy. Expansion had made the Italian south part of Rome's dominion. The outside world was already encroaching. Pyrrhus of Epirus had engaged the Romans in several bloody battles in just the two decades prior to the First Punic War. One day there might be other interlopers interested in seizing the riches of Italy for themselves. When looking at the Mediterranean from this wider vantage point, a foreign power in control of Sicily was a threat, and Roman interests were bound to collide with those of Carthage.

Simple avarice also played a role. Polybius writes that in 264, Rome's consuls used the lure of the 'great gains' in the form of war spoils that might be had as a result of intervention in Sicily to persuade the citizens to approve military action against the Carthaginian menace.[11] At this time, Rome and central Italy were still materially less-developed than the wealthy Greek cities of the south of the peninsula or Sicily. Rome's conquest of such cities in the south almost certainly excited her cupidity for more booty. The Sicilian Greek cities no doubt offered the same attractions at what must have seemed to be a minimal price. When the opportunity arose to fight in Sicily, on the pretext of relieving a mercenary garrison at Messana, the prospect for plunder must have seemed fairly good.

Neither Rome nor Carthage could have guessed in 264 that they were about to embark upon a war of such astonishing length. The vicissitudes of this conflict, and the see-saw nature of the struggle, beggar belief. A major reason for the length of the war, twenty-three years, was that both sides were evenly matched. Each had different strengths and weaknesses, but overall there was a parity of power between the two. Polybius writes that they were both still vigorous, undecadent peoples when the war came. 'Corrupt ways had yet to mar the two states at that time; they were no more than moderately prosperous, and their armies were evenly matched.'[13] The spirits of the two had not been sapped by luxurious living or the vices that afflicted more refined peoples elsewhere.

Chapter One

Sources

Without doubt the main source that we possess for the First Punic War is the Greek historian Polybius. It is fair to say that a comprehensive account of the war would be impossible without him. In comparison, other ancient historians supply only particulars, and it is not always certain if they are reliable on those few matters. Polybius, the son of the Achaean statesman Lycortas, was born in Greece around 200 BC. As a young man he took part in the politics of Achaean League, which had been an ally of Rome during the Second Macedonian War. In the Third Macedonian War he found himself on the other side, fighting against the Romans as a cavalry officer. That war did not turn out well for the Achaeans. Polybius was brought to Rome after it ended in 167 as a hostage, one of a thousand, to ensure the good behaviour of his countrymen.

While in Rome he had the good fortune to become friendly with Publius Cornelius Scipio Aemilianus, a prominent Roman general of the middle decades of the second century. Aemilianus was the biological son of the consul Lucius Aemilius Paullus and the adoptive grandson of the famed general Publius Cornelius Scipio Africanus. As part of this 'Scipionic circle', Polybius gained access to some of the actors of the Second Punic War and obtained firsthand accounts from them of many of its events.[1] He began writing his *Histories* during the middle of the second century BC, and a reasonable case can be made for him starting upon it in the 140s.

Polybius' foremost characteristic as a historian was his careful approach to his research, whether it was his critical examination of his sources or his willingness to go and see for himself the physical remnants of the past. He would question eyewitnesses when he could, and he also made his own way north to trace for himself the Alpine route taken by Hannibal when he marched into Italy.[2] Polybius also tells us that he 'accepted all the hazards of travelling in Libya, Iberia [Spain], and Gaul, and sailing the sea that washes the outer coastlines of these places; [and] wanted to correct the mistaken notions of my predecessors, and give the Greeks reliable information about these parts of the world too.'[3] He sought to write a history that would instruct the reader, on the basis of accurate information, and did not want to produce a sensationalized tale.[4] 'An animal is completely useless,' Polybius wrote, 'if it loses its eyesight, and in the same way history without truth has as little educational value as a yarn.'[5]

The story of the First Punic War within his larger history (which Polybius called his *Histories*, but for the sake of convenience I will refer to it in the singular) was meant to be a prelude to the Second, or Hannibalic, War.[6] While he was able to meet and speak with some who had taken part in the Second Punic War, which was not excessively distant in time from when he wrote, the people of the First Punic War were long gone. For the details of that conflict, he had to rely upon written histories, passed-down tales, and other types of evidence, not the direct testimony of those who were eyewitnesses to the events he describes. This inability to obtain firsthand or reliable information may be why Polybius at times will introduce and dismiss First Punic War battles of great importance in just a handful of words. Additionally, Polybius was not writing a military history in the modern sense of the term. Though he of course shows a deep interest in military matters, his principal purpose was not to set forth the specifics of battles and campaigns.

This manifests itself at times in a lack of attention to the many fundamental aspects of military actions. Polybius writes a broad overview of the First Punic War, giving extensive reports of the war in some instances but only tantalizing glimpses in many others. His chief goal in writing his history was to explain the rise of Rome and the nature of the Roman people to a Greek audience.[7] He therefore wished to keep short his narrative of the First Punic War, which he saw more as an introduction to his history, with his primary focus on later events.

In some points his narrative does come off seeming a little hasty. What we are promised by Polybius at the start of his record and what we receive from him seem to differ. At the outset he declares that he intends 'to give a somewhat less cursory account of the first war between the Romans and the Carthaginians, the one they fought for possession of Sicily'.[8] This account is meant to be 'less cursory' in comparison with the mercenary uprising against Carthage that followed the First Punic War and the activities of Carthaginian generals Hamilcar and Hasdrubal in Spain during the interwar years. Polybius' narrative has a tension built into it at its inception. It is not intended to be his main story, but he does not want to pass over it with the same brevity as the other introductory portions of his narrative. Polybius will on occasion dwell on certain parts of this great war while passing over major events, or choose to emphasize certain incidents while virtually ignoring others. His own description of the conflict is at odds with his uneven treatment of it. 'It would be hard to think of a war that lasted longer, or for which the contestants were more thoroughly prepared, or in which events followed one another in quicker succession, or which included more battles, or which involved more terrible catastrophes for both sides,' he says, and justifies devoting more attention to it because the war 'affords a better point of comparison between the two states than any of those that occurred later'.⁹ In effect, Polybius is telling his reader that this portion of his history has been written to outline the natures of the combatants in preparation for his main task of telling the story of Rome's war against Hannibal. Polybius' First Punic War narrative thus comes to settle somewhere in the space between an encyclopedia entry and a full treatment of the struggle. His own admission concerning its length and importance calls for a much more extensive and meticulous study than the one that he delivers.

Polybius also cites his dissatisfaction with the histories of Philinus, a pro-Carthaginian Sicilian Greek from Agrigentum, and of the Roman Quintus Fabius Pictor, who was partial to his own countrymen. Polybius complains that both of their now-lost works are biased (almost certainly the case) saying that 'Philinus always has the Carthaginians acting sensibly, honourably, and courageously, and the Romans doing the opposite, while Fabius does the same the other way around.'[10] Despite his unhappiness with their products, Polybius nonetheless relied heavily on their works for the bulk of his own material for the First Punic War. It seems most likely that Polybius sought to balance and synthesize the two accounts, which may be presumed to have been near-polar opposites. He also used other sources to flesh out his story and come to what he deemed an accurate account. Polybius probably saw himself as well-suited to produce a neutral and objective history of the First Punic War superior to the partisan accounts of either Philinus or Pictor.[11] It may be presumed that Polybius' history was less patriotic in tone than that of Pictor, and less anti-Carthaginian too. But because Carthage was destroyed, and also because Polybius himself was resident in Rome for much of his life and a close friend of one of her leading aristocrats and generals, his history of the First Punic War is told mainly from the Roman perspective. He is nonetheless the most reliable of our sources as well as the most complete. It is usually best to give to Polybius the benefit of the doubt when it comes to matters that he describes. A fair judgment of him may best be described in the words that Polybius himself used to assess Fabius Pictor. '[R]eaders can safely assume that Fabius [Polybius] is reliable more often than not, but they should not regard what he says as gospel, rather, they should base their conclusions on the facts themselves.'[12]

It must be remembered that Polybius' goal was larger still, in that he was writing to tell the history of all the wars between Rome and Carthage, not just the first. The first five of the forty books of his history are complete but the others exist only in fragmentary form. It has been asserted that the medieval Byzantine tendency towards excerpting and anthologizing older authors contributed to the ultimate loss of much of Polybius. Polybius' work may well have been complete as of the tenth century AD, but as it came to exist predominantly over time only in excerpted form, the older, complete copies of his history were lost forever. That the first five books alone have come down to us intact is likely due to the interest that the Byzantines had in the story of the rise of the Roman Empire, a story that is more or less finished by the end of Polybius' fifth book.[13]

We can rely upon Polybius for the First Punic War, the interwar period, and the opening of the Second Punic War down to the Battle of Cannae in 216. For a coherent narrative of the subsequent events of the Second Punic War, our main source is Titus Livius, known commonly as Livy. Livy wrote in an artful style and his dramatic recounting of the war, especially of the dark times that followed the disaster at Cannae, is a marvel of literary composition. His history, *Ab Urbe Condita*, tells the story of Rome from its founding by the legendary Trojan Prince Aeneas to Livy's own era. Not all of the books of this history have survived, but the ones detailing the war with Hannibal have. Livy relied heavily upon Polybius for much of his own work, though he only makes mention of him by name once.[14] He included much information that Polybius did not, especially material concerning internal Roman politics, troop dispositions, and command appointments for each year. He also mentions in several places the differing accounts provided by other historians whom he used, providing a fascinating glimpse into how he composed *Ab Urbe Condita*.

Livy's narrative of the Second Punic War was probably preferred by later generations to Polybius' dryer history, and this helps to explain why the portion of Livy's work covering the war against Hannibal has survived complete whereas Polybius' has not. It may simply have been more popular, and thus more widely read. This would have caused it to be copied more often to meet demand for the texts, while Polybius' books covering the later years of the Hannibalic War languished, and were not recopied. Some of Polybius' books may have disappeared over the centuries through neglect as aged copies decayed or were heedlessly discarded. Others may have perished in the various disasters that beset Europe after the end of the ancient world.

Livy lived much later in time than did Polybius, in the transitional period from Republic to Empire of the Augustan age at the end of the first century BC. He was of course not able to meet or speak with any of the participants of the Second Punic War as Polybius had. He did utilize what was available to him, which, in addition to Polybius, included histories now lost, such as those of Fabius Pictor and Lucius Coelius Antipater. He was also a diligent archival historian, and made use of official records still preserved in his day.

There are other historians who shed light on the Punic Wars, but none to the extent of either Polybius or Livy. Diodorus Siculus, who wrote his *Library of History* in the first century BC, preserves some material not set forth by Polybius. Sadly, the portions relevant to the First Punic War, Books XXIII and XXIV, now survive only in fragments. Plutarch (first to second centuries AD), author of the *Parallel Lives*, a series of biographical studies of influential Greeks and Romans, provides some minor insights. Appian, a Greek of Alexandria, wrote the *Historia Romana*, in the second century AD. He is the chief source that we possess for the third and final war between Rome and Carthage and appears to have used Polybius heavily in composing his history.

The Byzantine John Zonaras was a twelfth century AD epitomator of the third century AD Roman senator-historian Cassius Dio. Dio's original work, written in Greek, survives today only in fragments, but Zonaras' *Epitome Historiarum*, a summary of other, previously written histories, relied heavily on Dio for this period. Zonaras has several things of interest to say about the naval aspects of the latter years of the First Punic War that Polybius does not touch.

Chapter Two

The Contestants

The Romans

The feature of greatest importance for understanding Rome's history is that her people were, first and foremost, farmers. The agrarian underpinnings of the Roman state are beyond dispute. Agriculture was the basis of the economy. The Romans were not merchant traders, like the Carthaginians, and they were not a horse-oriented feudal culture, like the Persians. The primacy of farming had the effect of creating robust peasants, who would prove to be excellent fighting material for the legions. The Roman army at the time of the Punic Wars was amply supplied with such men. They were free farmers, self-reliant, and inured to toil. The hard-working Italian peasantry had not yet been driven from the land by wealthy magnates, though this process would be accelerated by the devastation wrought by Hannibal on the Italian countryside.[1]

At some time in the late second millennium BC, the linguistic ancestors of the Romans, the Italic language speakers, began their push into the peninsula, either via the Alps or by making the short voyage across the Adriatic from the Balkans. The Italic peoples were part of the massive irradiation of Indo-European language speaking peoples who would carry their related tongues to such widely dispersed lands as India and Ireland. By the first millennium BC, Celtic Indo-Europeans dominated western and Central Europe, Germanic Indo-Europeans the north, and the Greeks and Italics the south. In the case of Italy, the Italics were by no means the genetic ancestors of all the Italian peoples, but they did predominate linguistically. One group of them, the Latins, would go on to produce the most powerful of Italy's communities, and all other Italic languages would ultimately become extinct.

The foundation of the city of Rome on the Tiber River has been dated by tradition to 753 BC. Actual habitation of the site long preceded that date, and true urbanization had to wait until sometime later. The history of Rome's early years, as handed down to posterity, is a haphazard mixture of patriotic mythology and uncertain legends.[2] The Romans could name only seven kings who were said to have ruled in the monarchical period of about two-and-a-half centuries, and thus had to give each ruler an almost impossibly long reign. A period of Etruscan domination arrived in the sixth century BC, if not earlier. The Etruscans, who lived to the north in what is now Tuscany, were not Latins (they spoke a wholly unrelated, non-Indo-European language) and were culturally more advanced than the Romans. Contact with the Etruscans and especially the Greeks in southern Italy accelerated the cultural development of the Roman people. This was apparent in many areas, not least of which was religion. Greek myths were taken over whole by the Romans with little more than the names of the gods changed. The Romans identified the major Greek deities with Italic ones with similar areas of concern. The Greek Zeus was the Roman Jupiter; Hera was Juno; Athena was Minerva; Ares was Mars, and so on.

Greek influence could also be found in the military sphere. The early Roman army was originally arrayed as a phalanx in battle. But the outcome of the Battle of the Allia River, which has been variously dated to 390, 387, or even 386 BC, however, changed Roman tactical organization forever. The phalanx was discarded, never to return. It was too unwieldy and could not adapt to unforeseen changes in situation. An unbroken wall of spearmen had proven ineffective in contending with the wild Gauls who swarmed the solid but immobile phalanx. The result was a total disaster which then led to the sack of Rome itself, an event that shamed the Romans forever. In time the Romans would adopt a much more flexible formation in battle, in which smaller units of soldiers organized into maniples ('handfuls') had the ability to react to opportunities or reverses in ways that were impossible for the old style phalanx. This was the origin of the Roman legion in its classic form. Though it would itself undergo significant development over the following centuries, this formation, possessing greater internal articulation and flexibility, would enable Rome to conquer an empire.

The Soldiers of Rome

The Roman army of the Republic was a citizen militia, wherein the rank and file legionaries were drawn from the body of citizens owning property. It may seem inaccurate to call the Roman army a militia, bearing as that word does a connotation of an untrained and unenthusiastic levy. Modern readers will most likely associate that term with erratic amateur soldiers whose performance may be at times commendable and at many other times leave much to be desired. The Romans were a different breed. They consistently fought hard, and even victories over them were grinding affairs that left the winner bloodied and thinking about eventual defeat. It was Pyrrhus, grimly contemplating the victorious outcome of the Battle of Asculum in 279 who exclaimed, 'One more victory like that over the Romans will destroy us completely!'[3]

Though the Roman soldier was typically a farmer, and is at times labelled a peasant, he was not at all like the medieval serf who was called up to fight for his lord with little training and poor equipment. The assembled legion was not a peasant rabble to be easily dispersed by a knightly cavalry charge. The legionaries had real training, and they became better fighters as they gained experience. The Romans did not go as far as did the Spartans with their rigorous and brutal *agoge* training, but there was no need. The Roman was a naturally fine fighting man who knew what was expected of him and did it. Even more importantly, he was aggressive too, a quality that could not be taught. Roman tactics were very simple, just a rush straight at the enemy for the most part. For such tactics to work the Roman had to be willing to get to grips with the enemy and carve him to pieces. He had to be ready to stand his ground and slug it out with a phalanx of Macedonian pikemen or naked Gauls armed with longswords and not much else. The killing power of the Roman soldier was such that his individual excellence, when combined with those of his fellows, could make up for the unimaginative tactics of his general.

He was a hard worker too. Much of Rome's successes in war can be attributed not only to the fighting abilities of the legionary, but to his skill with a shovel and pickaxe. The Romans were keen on improving their tactical positions by the use of field fortifications, which might be as simple as a log palisade or a ditch. A willingness to do physical work also made sieges of strong places more likely to succeed. The famous sieges of Syracuse, Numantia, and Alesia were only a handful of the fortified places taken mainly by the sweat of Rome's legionaries.

Rome's superiority in land battle can be attributed mainly to the high quality of her infantrymen. He was also critical to Roman naval hopes because the soldiers fighting aboard their galleys, commonly known as marines, were really legionaries at sea. His arms and armour were well suited to the close quarters fighting of shipboard combat. His tall shield, the *scutum*, was of plywood construction, and protected most of his body. The grip of the scutum, unlike that of the round hoplite shield, was set horizontal to the ground, so that the legionaries' knuckles pointed down when they held it. The single-hand grip made it possible to punch with the shield, and use it in an offensive manner. Polybius unhesitatingly credited these men with gaining Rome's victories at sea. Even though the Romans were 'much less skilled in the handling of their naval forces, they nevertheless prove successful in the end, because of the gallantry of their men; for although skill in seamanship is of great importance in naval battles, it is the courage of the marines which proves the decisive factor in winning a victory'.[5]

The primary weapon of the legionary was the sword known as the *gladius*. It is unclear whether the Romans had adopted the famous *gladius hispaniensis*, or

Spanish sword, by this time. The most likely scenario has the Romans learning of the impressive weapon either during the First Punic War, when Carthage's Spanish mercenaries used it, or later during the campaigns in Spain itself in the Second Punic War.[6] But the Romans would have employed similar short, stabbing swords of some kind before the wars with Carthage, and they were an effective combination together with the big shield.

Roman Expansionism

At the time of the Punic Wars, the Roman population was growing. This surge made the territorial expansion of Rome possible, enabling it to establish many colonies around Italy with its excess population on the confiscated lands of former enemies. This increase would last until the end of the third century BC.[7] A burgeoning population gave Rome the necessary manpower to take on the many enemies that surrounded it while also letting Rome sustain very heavy losses without compelling it to admit defeat. Several events during the wars with Carthage resulted in Roman losses on a horrifying scale, with many tens of thousands of men perishing in a single disaster. The Romans dourly replaced them, raising legion after legion, in the end wearing down their enemy by weight of numbers and an obstinate refusal to quit.

A comparatively generous policy towards defeated enemies enhanced Rome's staying power. The Romans did not often seek the total destruction of their Italian enemies. To be sure, Roman warmaking was far from gentle, and losing to Rome certainly felt like a defeat. The Romans' treatment of the defeated differed substantially to that of the Greeks, who regularly visited annihilation on defeated foes. The Romans would typically avoid wholesale slaughter and enslavement, and instead sought to incorporate beaten states into their own coalition as allies. They took away large amounts of land, on which they would then plant colonies, but left some of it in the hands of the vanquished. Local politics also played a role in building Rome's effective manpower pool. Many weaker Italian cities preferred Rome's distant dominion to that of closer rivals, making them willing allies.[8]

It became the duty of these states to supply Rome with fighting men to swell the ranks of the forces that she marshalled every year. Rome was always fighting somebody, somewhere, and it made good sense to add the strength of others to her own native legions. Indeed, though our sources tend to overlook the activities of Rome's Italian allies during the Punic Wars, it can be estimated that about half of any 'Roman' army was actually composed of allied troops. It is difficult to say much about these allied soldiers with any certainty, apart from that they were present. They may have fought in much the same manner as the Romans themselves, but that is open to question. Later we will see that Rome was capable of absorbing massive casualties in the wars against the Carthaginians, sometimes losing over 50,000 men in a single day. The Romans' resilience was made possible by their reliance upon allied states for additional manpower and to make up for any losses.

Rome was also very generous with the distribution of its citizenship. It is safe to say that one of the Romans' great strengths was their willingness to bring non-Romans into the fold. This openness to outsiders was something that the Greeks could never stomach, least of all the extremely military-minded Spartans. Though that city produced fantastic soldiers, its citizenship was so jealously guarded that the numbers of full citizen Spartans slowly dwindled over time to the point of military insignificance. The Romans increased their numbers instead. Though the Romans could be shortsighted and stingy in the treatment of their allies, on the whole their expansion was aided by a willingness to admit others into the Roman 'club'. Rome also wisely ensured that the elites of the cities brought into its confederation were contented, and this feeling of solidarity as a 'class' helped bind these Italian cities ever more tightly to it. It was also prudent that Rome neither demanded tribute nor exacted regular taxes from the cities.[9] Rome thereby succeeded in making many friends out of the ruling classes of these peoples, and most became loyal partners. This powerful sense of belonging engendered by these Roman policies would stand them in good stead when the Italian confederation of which she was the hegemon was subjected to enormous wartime stress under Punic attack, but did not crack.

Roman statecraft also benefited from having a steady hand to steer the ship of state. This was provided in the main by the deliberative body known as the Senate. It was originally only an advisory body to the kings, but over time had come to acquire jurisdiction over the conduct of foreign affairs and financial matters. There was no explicit foundation in the law for this, but the Senate's possession of such power had nevertheless gained the force of law by long tradition and precedent. This made the Senate central to Roman decision-making. Membership was circumscribed, and the senators were typically very wealthy. The Roman system of government was a resolutely aristocratic oligarchy. Rome was by no means a democracy, and the Senate was not a democratically representative body. However, its presence at the heart of Roman governance during the difficult years of the Punic Wars had the positive effect of giving Roman policy a much-needed coherence over time. Over the course of her early history the aristocrats had made certain accommodations with the lesser classes. This did not come easily. Civil strife was a real threat to Roman survival in the first centuries of the Republic, but by the time of the Punic Wars these difficulties had either been resolved, or at least kept manageable, giving Rome social stability during the sequence of wars that would begin in 264.

The Senate was the fixture in Roman government that persisted despite the vicissitudes of war, and it acquitted itself well during the hard years when Rome appeared to be in danger of failing. Not least among the services of the Senate was that it channelled and restrained the competition of its members, who were drawn from the leading families of Rome. The energies of the nobles were thereby used for the benefit of the Republic. The *cursus honorum*, or course of offices, was a sequential order of public posts which the men of Rome (this was a man's world) could compete for and hold. The hunger for glory and prestige was so great, the desire for honour before one's peers so overwhelming, that Roman aristocrats would go to extreme lengths to obtain these posts, with the greatest of all being that of the consulship. The Romans who entered into the *cursus honorum* were ambitious to a fault. The Roman system of government engendered a ferocious competition for prestige and honours among its citizens that was so powerful that it produced a people so aggressive, so driven, that they would ultimately conquer all those peoples with whom they came into conflict.[10]

Two consuls were elected annually to lead the state and the armies, and these men might be either good or bad. Usually they were mediocre. Apart from the consulship, there was one honour that could be bestowed on a Roman general that trumped all others: the triumph. Though in modern English 'triumph' is a mere synonym for victory, in Rome the *triumphus* was a staged and ritualized spectacle of dazzling proportions. The *triumphator* marched his victorious army along the streets of Rome to the Temple of Jupiter Capitolinus atop the Capitoline Hill. With his troops were paraded prisoners taken from among the vanquished enemy and spoils of war. All this was done before the eyes of throngs of cheering Roman people.[11] The triumph was a declaration, made in the most public manner possible, of the achievement of a successful general. In the endless competition for prestige among the major families of the city, there was little that could compare to it. Such was the regard in which those who had been awarded a triumph were held that their names were recorded and set out for public display in the Forum in lists known as the *fasti triumphales*.

Roman Naval Forces

It may, at first glance, seem odd that the Romans, an established military power on a peninsula set amidst the Mediterranean, should lean so heavily upon their allies for the provision of shipboard transport. This practice was nevertheless in keeping with their reliance upon other peoples to supplement the Roman military, and reflected an understanding that the allies often possessed troops with skills that they lacked, and could provide more effectively. The most obvious example was in the realm of cavalry. The army, extending from the era of the great wars with Carthage well into the time of the emperors, recruited horsemen from non-Roman peoples. Numidians, Gauls, Germans, Sarmatians, and more, would in due course be brought into the army because their skill at mounted combat was especially high. The Romans were used to fighting on foot, as heavy infantry, and that is where their talent lay. It was a simpler move to induct foreigners as cavalry than to try to raise a native Roman element which might not prove as useful.[12]

So too it was with ships. The Romans were a settled, agriculturally-minded people, and lacked the extensive nautical traditions of the Greek cities of the south. On the eve of the first war with Carthage, Rome had just made the transition from being a mere city state, powerful though it may have been in comparison with many others, into a superstate that thoroughly dominated the Italian peninsula. Rome had not yet become an empire of multiple nations. That would come later, and primarily as a result of the conflicts with Carthage, but it was no mere local power either, and the confederacy of Italian cities at which it stood at the head was a concentration of impressive military might.

The Roman preference for making war on land as opposed to fighting at sea was a longstanding one; it was their strength, after all, and their ultimate mastery of naval warfare would not change this predisposition very much. Prior to the wars, the Romans crewed their small fleet with rejects from the army, a sure sign that the navy was considered to be the junior service by a wide margin.[13] The imperial period historian Plutarch preserves a short conversation between Mark Antony and one of his centurions aboard Antony's flagship on the eve of the Battle of Actium in 31 BC. This heavily scarred veteran, none too thrilled by the prospect of a naval fight, approached his commander, and said, 'Imperator, why dost thou distrust these wounds and this sword and put thy hopes in miserable logs of wood? Let Egyptians and Phoenicians do their fighting at sea, but give us land, on which we are accustomed to stand and either conquer our enemies or die.'[14] A more Roman sentiment could not have been expressed.

The ultimate origins of this conservatism are hard to discern. The Roman preference was for land combat, and their naval force was not well developed until they found a pressing need for one, in which case they called upon their allies. A bit of chauvinism may have been a factor too. Naval warfare may have struck them as just not being truly Roman because of the need to rely so heavily for day-to-day operations on non-Romans.[15] That the Romans were themselves inhabitants of a city sited not very far from the sea, makes this reluctance all the more challenging to explain. Then again, the vagaries of history can result in oddities that are nonetheless the logical products of historical forces. The

United States, a nation with an extensive nautical tradition dating to the start of its peopling by European colonists, passed the final decades of the nineteenth century with a comparatively tiny fleet not at all commensurate with its population or its position straddling two oceans. This is comparable to Rome's own lack of a navy, but it may be explained by the inward focus of the Americans on the settlement and development of the nation, instead of making war against other nations overseas. Further, the Royal Navy was easily the strongest in the world during the long peace between Trafalgar and the First World War, and the security that it provided in the Atlantic made the maintenance of a large American fleet in the years after the Civil War (a war in which the US Navy had come to comprise an impressive 671 warships) unnecessary.[16]

The Roman Mind

The nearby presence of the Gauls was especially important in the development of Rome as an expansionist, and ultimately imperial, power. The Romans never forgot that it was a group of Gauls that had sacked their city in the wake of the disastrous Battle of the Allia. While the Romans were certainly influenced heavily by their Etruscan neighbours to the north and the Greek states to the south, it was the presence of the Gauls on the northern frontier of Italy that turned Rome into a battle hardened nation that would come to dominate Europe and the Mediterranean for centuries. Polybius would write that the Romans became 'true athletes of warfare' in part as a result of their wars against the Gauls.[17] Fear of these alien, barbarian peoples (the Gauls were not a single people but a collection of tribes) remained a constant fixture in the Roman psyche. Their determination to fight the Gauls, to prevent another sack, to secure Italy from their ravages, was so great that when they had only just finished their long and immensely costly war with Hannibal, the Romans without pause set about driving the Gauls out of the north of the Italian peninsula, an area which had become known as Cisalpine Gaul because of the presence of so many Gallic peoples living there. They did not relent until this operation was completed in 190. The crushing psychological blow of the sack of Rome had the positive effect (for the Romans) of making them a more cohesive and warlike people. They had a mortal enemy on the frontier that had to be resisted at all costs.[18]

Rome's struggles with Pyrrhus, just recently ended when the war over Sicily began in 264, almost certainly gave the Romans great confidence in their military abilities relative to non-Italian powers. The Romans had only narrowly lost two battles to Pyrrhus at Heraclea in 280 and Asculum in 279, and they had defeated Pyrrhus outright at Beneventum in 275.[19] This was a victory obtained over one of the great captains of antiquity, who fought in the combined arms style of

Alexander with an army trained and equipped on the model of the Hellenistic Greek armies of the east.

The experience of war with a sophisticated enemy does not seem to have induced the Romans to improve their tactics to any significant degree. The fine performance of Roman legionaries in combat with Pyrrhus' soldiers likely confirmed their belief that the critical qualities in battle were the killing power and endurance of their men, not fancy tactics. The standard Roman battle tactic, in essence a straight-ahead infantry rush at the enemy, could be turned against them by a canny enemy general, as Hannibal would do most spectacularly at Cannae in 216. Over the course of the long and drawn out wars with Carthage, Roman superiority in land battle would be blunted only at times, albeit dramatically, by the tactical prowess of Carthage's best commanders.

The Carthaginians

We learn of the Carthaginians what their foes or less than friendly sources have written about them. It is hardly fair to make any definitive assessment on the basis of such testimony. It is clear that they were neither all heroes nor all monsters, but real people, with good qualities and bad ones too.

The territory of Carthage proper and its hinterlands lay in what is now modern Tunisia. This consisted of a relatively small plot of about 600 square miles of arable land.[20] The city exerted suzerainty over the mainly Phoenician heritage cities of Libya to the east, and to the west over Numidia, roughly modern Algeria. Carthage's dominion was not always welcome. The nearby city of Utica and Gades in Iberia (Spain) were sovereign allies of Carthage, yet most other communities, even those of North Africa, were subject states, with lesser political rights. Carthage allowed these places to govern themselves, but demanded that tribute be paid as well as harbour fees.[21] In comparison to the Romans, the Carthaginians were very reluctant to extend citizenship to aliens. Who counted as an 'other' seems to have included even peoples of shared Phoenician ancestry. To be a Carthaginian meant being *from* Carthage. The city did not build the kind of wider cultural community with peoples of a similar origin as the Romans did with the Latins, and subsequently with other Italians.[22] This would have severe consequences for Carthage as the strain of war frayed, and in some cases severed, the ties between it and the other peoples of North Africa, who should have been solidly pro-Carthaginian. Carthage was unable to draw upon the manpower of North Africa to the same extent that Rome did on Italy's.[23] A terrible insurrection would break out among the disaffected non-Carthaginian inhabitants of Libya in the latter stages of the First Punic War, and though the Carthaginians would put it down, the severity of the war against them highlights Carthage's inability and unwillingness to incorporate outsiders into what could have been and should have been a larger and more powerful confederation. There was certainly a sufficient population base in Africa to build upon. A modern estimate gives a total of approximately 3,000,000 North Africans. When the inhabitants of her colonies in western Sicily and Sardinia are included, the total population of her empire would have been between four and five million.[24]

The Carthaginian dominion was emphatically a maritime empire. Seaborne trade was the lifeblood of the great edifice that Carthage had built in the central and western Mediterranean. Hard figures can't be had, but a modern estimate of the annual income of Carthage has been set at around 12,000 talents of silver.[25] Carthage stood at the apex of a trading system based upon a monopoly of the cargo-carrying trade in the western Mediterranean, which was something of a Carthaginian lake once she had stifled Greek expansionary moves into the seas west of Sardinia and Corsica. Her superior position owed much to the far earlier colonization efforts of her Phoenician forebears. Phoenicia, with its great trading cities such as Tyre, Sidon, and Byblos, had been an important maritime centre since the Bronze Age. A new world of wealth beckoned to the west, far beyond the eastern waters of the Mediterranean. Many of Phoenicia's colonizing moves were made as part of the hunt for metal, both base and precious. Her merchants ranged past the Pillars of Hercules (Straits of Gibraltar), the traditional boundary dividing the Mediterranean Sea from the outer ocean, as far as Britain in their search for tin, a primary ingredient in making bronze. The Phoenicians' navy was strong enough, and her hold on the area so secure, that she could bar passage out of the Mediterranean through the Straits into the Atlantic.[26] Spain was the source of large quantities of silver and gold, and Phoenician trading posts came to dot the coast there, as well as the northern shore of Africa. These were trading stations in their own right as well as waypoints where Phoenician merchants could stop, trade, take on and offload cargoes, repair their ships, and hire new sailors. Carthage was one of them.

Tradition holds that Carthage was founded in 814 BC by a royal woman of Tyre named Elissa.[27] She was a refugee from the bloody politics of her home city, and led a group of other exiles to found Qart Hadasht (Phoenician for 'New City') in Tunisia.[28] Though the historicity of Elissa's story can't be proved, Carthage was a reality, and developed rapidly into a prosperous trading state. Carthage never forgot her ancient links to her mother city of Tyre, and a delegation of thirty Carthaginians could be found there offering their annual tithe to the city's prime deity, Melqart, while Alexander the Great besieged it in 332.[29] Some Tyrian women and children were even sent to the daughter city for safety while the Macedonians laid siege.[30] When Tyre at last fell, the Carthaginian delegates still resident within it were granted a pardon by Alexander and allowed to go free.[31] These thirty went home with their ears stinging from Alexander's formal declaration of war against Carthage. Though Alexander could not as yet make good on his threat, he planned to conquer it one day.[32]

The capture of Tyre by Alexander was not the first time that it specifically, or Phoenicia more broadly, had been brought under the control of an alien (non-Phoenician) empire. Phoenicia had long since been a dependency of Persia, and had supplied the Great King with excellent sailors and ships for many years before Alexander entered the land. Prior to that she had been dominated by Babylonia.[33] With the political independence of Phoenicia gone, Carthage assumed the predominant position among the Phoenician colonial foundations and other posts that stretched from Libya all the way to Spain.

Carthage made its money via the lucrative carrying trade, and did everything that she could to keep Greek interlopers, who started appearing in the eighth century, out of the seas of the western Mediterranean.[34] Though moving cargo may not have been glamorous, it was and still is a reliable means to turn a profit. The movement of goods by sea was less expensive and faster than if done by land, and the geography of the Mediterranean allowed maritime merchants comparatively cheap and efficient access to multiple ports where their wares might find willing buyers. Carthage was no different from any other city, and did not remain static. Her growing wealth and population allowed her to expand her territorial holdings. One of the themes that runs through Carthage's prosecution of the struggle with Rome is that by the time the First Punic War opened, Carthage was not only the centre of a mighty seaborne trading empire but also that of an enormous and growing land empire in Africa. There was a strong faction among the Carthaginian aristocracy that saw the future as one lying in Africa, and was not as concerned with the Mediterranean-focused commercial ambitions of the mercantile class. This faction would not evince much interest in the war for Sicily, the primary theatre of the First Punic War. The difference in outlook would create a divergence, perhaps even confusion, over how to determine Carthage's war aims. African expansion even appears to have been ongoing while the war still went on in Sicily. This strategic disagreement would in the end bring Carthage much distress when her resources could not match the requirements of both holding Sicily and enlarging her dominion in Africa.

Carthaginian government was broadly similar in outward form to that of Rome. The monarchy was long gone and great matters of state were debated before the 'senate'.[35] Drawn from this body of 300 was a more select group, the Council of Thirty Elders, which acted as an advisory body.[36] The highest state officials were two annually elected magistrates called *suffetes*.[37] The *suffetes* are usually likened to the consuls that Rome also elected on a yearly basis. There was a major difference between them, which says much about the respective characters of the people under study. Whereas among the Romans the holding of political posts and military commands were combined in the persons of the two annual consuls, the Carthaginians preferred to keep them separate. Generals (who also served as admirals when required) were appointed by a body of 104 men, which Aristotle referred to in his *Politics* as 'the hundred'.[38] These men were drawn from the Carthaginian senate. It was their role to examine the decisions of a general when he was called to give an account of his conduct and determine whether he had been justified in making them.

A Carthaginian commander had to have good reasons for doing what he had done. It helped to be a winner. The penalty for defeat was harsh in the extreme: crucifixion in the public square of Carthage itself. Defeated generals were routinely crucified, and the ultimate punishment would be applied to defeated naval commanders during the First Punic War too. Crucifixion could also be inflicted by the soldiers themselves, without reference to the mother city. It would be interesting to know just who among the troops decided upon this sanction. Unfortunately it is not clear from the sources. Most of Carthage's warriors were hired men, and for them to kill a general on their own initiative would have been a hazardous course of action no matter how poorly their commander had performed. It therefore stands to reason that crucifixions 'in the field' were carried out by the Carthaginian officers themselves, and only when they believed that they could completely justify such an extreme deed to their own superiors.

This gruesome practice had no analogue among the Romans, who were more forgiving by far of unsuccessful generals. It was a forbidding system in which to be a commanding officer. It does seem for the most part to have produced generals who were focused and resourceful and not prone to making amateurish blunders of the sort that Roman consuls made on occasion. The imposition of such a draconian system may be explained in part by the different constraints under which Carthage fought its wars. The Carthaginians were always few in number, and had to rely upon paid soldiers to fill out the rank and file of their armies. Second-rate or half-hearted commanders were not welcome. The dire punishment meted out to failed captains also served to protect the Carthaginian 'system' from doubt, even in the wake of defeat. By crucifying a defeated general, the state was able to shift any fault for a loss away from itself and onto a single man, thereby maintaining in its soldiers and its people faith in the rightness and wisdom of Carthage itself.

Carthage's citizen body was very small, and could not supply the numbers of men needed for its armies. It had to find mercenaries or levies from subject or allied states to fill the ranks.[39] The Carthaginians were traders, craftsmen, and the like, and were not, in the main, a warlike people. Their preference was to engage in profitable economic activity, and use the proceeds to pay others to fight for them. Carthaginian recruiting officers could be found all across the Mediterranean world inducing foreign fighting men to join their forces. Others would have served because of ties of alliance or because they were in a subject relationship with Carthage. The subject peoples of Libya provided the most disciplined soldiers.[40] Spanish warriors were noted for their bravery and skill, and provided infantry and cavalry. The Numidians of North Africa were renowned for their fantastic light cavalry. Ferocious warriors from Gaul also served in large numbers. From the Balearic Islands came talented slingers. Leading all of these soldiers speaking many languages and coming from very different lands, was the Carthaginian officer corps. These men were all Carthaginian citizens. Apart from officering the armies, a picked group of Carthaginian citizens had once formed the 2,500-strong Sacred Band, but this regiment had been destroyed long before the Roman-Carthaginian wars, and did not take part in them.[41]

From the perspective of shipboard combat, which was to become a hugely important facet of naval warfare in the First Punic War, it is impossible to know how these various types of soldiers fought as marines. We can presume that slingers and javelineers were aboard every ship ready to harass enemy troops as they tried to board. Some other men must have been prepared to fight as heavy infantry in boarding actions. From the record of their encounters with the Romans the Carthaginians were much inferior in this sphere. During the First Punic War the Carthaginian navy would find itself challenged by a Roman fleet outmatched in shiphandling skill but long on the courage of its marines. With a handful of exceptions, the numbers of enemy vessels captured in battle as a result of boarding greatly favoured the Romans.

Carthage's naval installations were impressive. The remnant of a circular naval harbour has been discovered at Carthage which was large enough to berth and service some 170 war galleys. This force was paid for by the tribute of the empire's subject peoples. In exchange the navy provided maritime security for them.[42] Though the Carthaginians were clearly recognized as the better seamen in the Punic Wars, they would have great difficulty translating their superior shiphandling skills into victories against the Romans. The contest between the two rival fleets was to be one of manoeuvring and rowing skill pitted against a direct, brute force approach that sought to win via boarding actions where the Roman edge in heavy infantry could be brought to bear. Carthage would lose major naval battles far more often than not. For them, their greater experience in maneuvering could typically only be displayed and used to the full in actions in which smaller numbers of ships took part, and not in large battles of hundreds of galleys where these numbers made their technical virtuosity less employable.[43]

One other Carthaginian matter deserves mention. The Carthaginians seem to have used the same few names over and over, at least for their menfolk. The history of the Punic Wars is a nearly endless parade of Hasdrubals, Hannibals, Hamilcars, and Hannos. This seems to have been done for the express purpose of confounding future generations of historians. As much as possible, I attempt to make some kind of distinction between individuals who bear identical names. Sometimes the precise identities are not clear. On occasion I will use nicknames (such as Barca, as in Hannibal Barca) or the names of fathers (such as Gisgo, as in Hasdrubal Gisgo) as substitute surnames to help distinguish between Carthaginians having the same personal name, even though these were not family names as we would understand them in modern times.

Chapter Three

Sicily: Theatre of War, History of Blood

The island of Sicily was a rich and attractive prize for many would-be conquerors. 'Sicily is the noblest of all islands', wrote Diodorus Siculus, 'for it can contribute greatly to the growth of an empire.'[1] It was large and strategically located, sitting astride sea routes leading from the eastern Mediterranean to the lesser developed lands in the west. In its earliest days it was neither Greek, nor Carthaginian, nor Roman. The original inhabitants were unknown peoples who had occupied the islands from far back into prehistory. They were joined over the millennia by Sicels, Sicans, Elymians, and latterly the Greeks, Carthaginians, Romans, and a host of other peoples from places near and distant.[2] Sicily was involved in the wider doings of the Mediterranean world since the Late Bronze Age. The Shekelesh warriors who troubled Egypt at the end of the second millennium BC have been plausibly linked to the Sicels who crossed to Sicily from Italy and gave the island the name by which it has been known to history.[3] Sicily was transformed by the planting of Greek colonies there beginning in the late seventh century BC, with the first being made at Naxos, followed just a year later by the foundation of Syracuse. The important city of Gela would be founded in 688. Every newly planted colony had a mother city from whence the colonial enterprise was launched.[4] Slowly but surely the eastern portion of the island became thoroughly Hellenized and integrated into the wider Greek world.

Relations between the natives and the newcomer Greeks could vary. In some areas of Sicily, they were more hostile than elsewhere on the island, but the long-term trend was toward the Hellenic acculturation of Greek settled areas.[5] Soon the island was the home of some of the largest and wealthiest cities of the Greek world, and the rulers of several, such as Dionysius I, Gelon, Agathocles, and Hiero would be as well known as any in mainland Greece. Syracuse was the most prominent of the Sicilian Greek cities, and it is a testament to its size and power that its aid was sought in the defence of Greece against the Persian invasion of Xerxes in the early fifth century BC. In 481 an embassy came to the Greek new world of the west to seek help for the old. Xerxes' Persians were intent on completing the job of conquest left unfinished by his father Darius. Gelon, the tyrant of Syracuse, pledged to provide enough wheat to feed the entire Greek army, along with 200 war galleys, 20,000 hoplites, 2,000 cavalry,

2,000 archers, and 2,000 slingers. In return, Gelon demanded that he be made the overall commander of the Hellenic army gathering to resist the Persian onslaught.[6] Gelon's offer was turned down – he had asked for just a bit too much – but the contribution that he was prepared to make is indicative of the extraordinary power and wealth of Syracuse in the fifth century, just one Greek city among many in the island.

Syracuse would soon be embroiled in a war with another colonizing nation in Sicily: Carthage. The Greeks of Phocaea had fought her naval forces before for control of the western Mediterranean at the Battle of Alalia (Aleria) off Corsica in about 535.[7] A Phocaean fleet had met and defeated a combined Carthaginian-Etruscan naval force, but their plans for further expansion in the west were thereafter stymied by Carthage's growing power. In 480 a huge Carthaginian invasion army landed at first in the west of the island at Panormus, and then moved by land and sea to Himera. Gelon showed that the offer of military aid that he had made to the Greeks had not been just talk but could be backed up by actual might. His army fell upon the Carthaginians, crushing them utterly and slaying their general, Hamilcar. The Greeks burned the Punic warships while they were laid up on the beach.[8]

Sicily would again play an outsized role in the history of the Greek world during the Peloponnesian War (431–404 BC). In 415 Athens mounted an invasion of the island. The focal point of the war became the city of Syracuse, where Athenian land and naval forces became bogged down for two years. Support from other Sicilian cities that disliked Syracuse failed to materialize, as they liked the Athenian outsiders even less. Athens ultimately concentrated its efforts on a siege of the city, which included a circumvallating siege wall, a struggle for the Epipolae Heights above the city, and several ferocious naval battles inside Syracuse's Great Harbour. Everything that could go wrong did go wrong for the Athenians, and the 'Sicilian Expedition', as it is known to history, has become a byword for ill-considered military adventure. It all ended very badly for Athens, in complete failure. Even the retreat from the city became a rout, with all of the Athenian survivors being either killed or captured.[9]

A few years later, in 409, Carthage again intervened in Sicilian affairs when it answered the plea of the city of Segesta for help against the city of Selinus, which had attacked it. Selinus was destroyed and its people slaughtered. A Syracusan force that had come to fight the Carthaginians was mauled.[10] A period of wrangling followed until 406 when Carthage landed a new and enormous army of 120,000 on the island.[11] Though figures for ancient armies are notoriously unreliable, the size of the expeditionary force must have been remarkable. It also demonstrated the seriousness with which Carthage sought to prosecute the war in Sicily. The great majority of her troops would have been mercenaries, and their hiring would have cost her treasury a tremendous sum of money, not something she would have parted with if she had been half-hearted in her desire to achieve success in battle. The Carthaginian assault was highly effective, with the cities of Agrigentum and Gela falling to its troops despite stubborn Syracusan resistance. The Carthaginian commander, Hamilcar, is alleged to have killed 3,000 prisoners of war on the same spot at Himera where his grandfather Hamilcar had fallen.[12]

An outbreak of plague spared Syracuse itself from further Punic attention.[13] A peace treaty was made, after Carthage's field army had lost half its number.[14] In 405 the Carthaginians packed up and departed for North Africa, but their military successes had secured their Sicilian possessions. The treaty recognized Carthage's territorial dominion in the west of the island, and several cities agreed to pay an annual tribute to her.[15] For the better part of the next two centuries, Carthage would be a major player in Sicilian affairs. Within a few years she would found Lilybaeum (modern Marsala) and turn it into her premier naval base in Sicily.[16]

The struggle for Sicily continued in the fourth century BC. A major battle was fought between the Syracusans and the Carthaginians at the Krimisos River in 341 BC. The Syracusans were wildly outnumbered, at least as Diodorus reports the matter, but they were aided by driving rain and hail which struck the Punic soldiers full in the face. The Carthaginian's elite Sacred Band infantry regiment was annihilated and the rest of the army was routed.[17]

The Syracusans and Carthaginians clashed again during the reign of Agathocles. Agathocles was an adventurer of a type common in the Hellenistic world. He was long on military ability but short on political legitimacy, and had made himself tyrant of Syracuse by gruesome means.[18] The war had gone against Syracuse, and the Carthaginians were superior on land and also at sea. The island was more or less under their control with the exception of Syracuse itself, which was under siege. Agathocles decided upon a bold stroke. In 310, during his war with Carthage he landed an army in Africa, determined to take the city. He thought that the Carthaginians proper were soft civilians, and would collapse if and when he appeared outside their city with his veteran troops. He led a naval expedition to Africa, and landed at Cape Bon, where he burned his ships.[19]

In a panic, the Carthaginian government placed Bomilcar and Hanno in command of the army. They did this in the belief that these two men, who had a history of bad blood, would thus not themselves use their power to conspire against the state. If this logic does not seem to make much sense with a hostile army marauding just outside the gates of Carthage, then it must be understood that Carthage was frightened that its own over-mighty generals might seize power for themselves. There was an underlying tension between the Carthaginian government, which feared its own generals with their military power, and the generals who feared being crucified if they either failed or simply became too threatening to Carthage's political establishment. This was one of the great and longstanding flaws in the Carthaginian military system. Though the use (on occasion) of horrific punishment discouraged amateurs and eliminated ineffective commanders, it also sometimes scared them into doing things that were not to the benefit of Carthage's overall security. Diodorus observed that Carthaginian generals in time of war were expected to 'be first to brave danger for the whole state; but when they gain peace, they plague these same men with suits, bring false charges against them through envy, and load them down with penalties'.[20] They would either desert their commands, or try to become tyrants, 'fearing the trials of the courts'.[21] Carthaginian generals were compelled to spend too much time worrying about what their own side might do them.

Bomilcar, writes Diodorus, had 'long had his heart set on tyranny but had lacked authority and a proper occasion for his attempt'.[22] He had one now. Agathocles defeated the Carthaginian army in battle, and Hanno was slain. He next placed Carthage under siege. (This was a historical oddity in that two warring powers were besieging each other's capitals simultaneously.) In 308, with his home city under dire threat, Bomilcar took the opportunity that his military command had granted him to seize power, declare himself tyrant, and murder his political opponents. His coup quickly failed, and luck favoured Carthage in that Agathocles was unaware of the upheaval inside the city.[23] Agathocles went back to Syracuse to deal with several subject cities that had rebelled against him. Carthage, bloodied but unbowed, defeated the Syracusan forces left behind in Africa. Agathocles returned to Africa but could do nothing to restore his fortunes there. He now abandoned his army, knowing that he would be unable to make an escape with it.[24] The Carthaginians shrewdly accepted the surrender of the stranded Syracusan troops. Most either entered Carthaginian service or settled in the Carthaginian controlled city of Solus in Sicily.[25] Peace was made in 306, and so ended another great war for the island. Despite terrible injuries, Carthage had retained its hold on its territory there.

The last of the Greek warlords that Carthage faced in Sicily was Pyrrhus, King of Epirus. Pyrrhus was schooled in the same advanced military tactics that Alexander had used to conquer the Persian Empire a generation before. He had won two victories in 280 and 279 against the Romans, but only at great cost in each battle, and had been forced to retire to his base at Tarentum in southern Italy. Syracuse offered him a command against the Carthaginians in Sicily. He crossed over in 278 and captured Carthaginian strongholds one after another.

In the end only Lilybaeum was holding out. Lilybaeum was very well fortified, and Pyrrhus was unable to take it. He began to think about an invasion of Africa, just as Agathocles had done decades earlier, but his arrogance and demands had soured his Sicilian allies on him. In 276, he was invited back to Italy by the south Italian Greeks who were still struggling against Rome. He took the opportunity to pack up and leave Sicily to try his luck against the Romans once more, and was defeated by them at the Battle of Beneventum in 275.

There can be no doubt that Carthaginians' centuries-long experience of war on the island taught them the value of perseverance, and that holding on, even by their fingernails, was a viable strategy. This strategic outlook would have a major impact on the course of the First Punic War in Sicily when Rome and Carthage at last came to blows over it. In the Greeks, Carthage had faced opponents who would seek an end to war when circumstances had turned against them. They knew when to quit. The Romans would show themselves to be very different.

Chapter Four

War at Sea in the Age of the War Galley

The main warship of the ancient Mediterranean world was the war galley. This was a slender ship that could be rowed or sailed as conditions required. In battle, rowing was much preferred as a galley could be manoeuvred without regard for the wind. The design of the galley reached a high level of development with the advent of the trireme. 'Trireme' means 'three oars,' and modern reconstructions have shown that the vessel was rowed with three banks, or levels, of oars to a side, with each rower pulling a single oar. The trireme is often compared to a racing shell used in modern competitive rowing. While this analogy should not be taken too far, as the trireme was far larger, the basic principles behind the oar-based propulsion of both types of craft are the same. Men rowed facing opposite to the direction in which the ship moved. Sails were typically reserved for travel when battle was not expected. Before battle the masts could be either lowered or removed, and the sails taken down and even placed ashore. Sails were more of an impediment to the vessel in battle when quick manoeuvring was critical.[1] The trireme galley, like the racing boat, was built chiefly with light weight and speed in mind. Rowing at fifty strokes per minute, a trireme could achieve burst speeds of up to ten knots per hour.[2]

The speed of a trireme can be roughly ascertained by reference to ancient sources that record the travel times of ships on voyages between points that can be accurately measured today.[3] The speed may also be inferred from the performance of the *Olympias*, a full-scale replica of an ancient Athenian trireme built by Greece in the 1980s. The *Olympias* is an incomparable asset, being a working example of a ship type that had disappeared centuries ago. It may not be exact down to every detail, but the modern trireme grants a special window into how ancient galleys were rowed and how they handled in battle.

While rowing and sailing the galley at the same time was possible, it was not found to be useful except under very limited conditions. With a following wind pushing the trireme at speeds of up to four knots, adding the power of the rowers to the sails, known as power sailing, could add about one or two knots worth of speed without demanding too much of the oarsmen. However, as soon as the galley began to lean just a little to one side, perhaps by as few as four degrees, rowing efficiency was compromised because the short and fast stroke on that side allowed scant recovery time to the rowers. Trying to keep this up was very hard on the oarsmen, and tired them. Trials with the *Olympias* demonstrated that with a following wind, power sailing could achieve between five or six knots. If the wind were too strong, rowing would not be of much, if any, benefit to the overall speed of the galley.[4] It must also be noted that we do not have any evidence that power sailing was ever used in ancient times.[5]

A trireme's speed could be lessened by several things. An inexperienced crew would not be able to produce the sustained rowing performance that a more highly trained crew would. Ships would also be slowed by becoming waterlogged and by the presence of marine growths on their hulls. The timbers of ancient galleys became waterlogged as a matter of course because the woods used, such as pine and fir, absorbed water greedily, despite being coated with pitch. A waterlogged galley was naturally heavier than a 'dry' one, and its performance was noticeably poorer. The absorption of water could not be avoided, and so ships were beached often to let them dry out. This was done each evening if possible. The requirement that ships be dried ashore also made them vulnerable to attack by a fleet already at sea. The Battle of Tyndaris, fought in 257, saw a Roman fleet have difficulty getting itself into battle because at least some of its ships were still embarking their crews when a Carthaginian fleet appeared.[6] Beaching also allowed water that had accumulated in the bilges to flow out. Once the trireme had dried, the hull could be cleansed of marine growths and repitched.[7] Pitch was obtained from coniferous trees such as pine and fir. It was applied as a coating across the entirety of the hull, and is the reason why Homer called such vessels 'black ships'.[8]

Ancient ships were susceptible to other things besides water. Various species of shipworms thrived in the Mediterranean. The *teredo* (borer) was a mollusc that was an endemic pest in those waters. It spawned in the summer, releasing its shipworm larvae. These sought out wood to eat. Any kind of wood would do. An expensively built trireme was just as much a feast as driftwood. The *teredo* attached itself to a ship and bored a hole into its hull planks. Once lodged within, its mouth faced out to the sea to draw in seawater while its shell drove ever more deeply into the ship's timber. After a month of such occupation, the *teredo* spawned a new generation of larvae, which then went in search of a new meal.[9]

Countermeasures could be taken to limit the damage. Careful attention had to be paid to the vessel before any problems became too bad. The galley had to be hauled out of the water regularly, checked for unwelcome shipworms, infested planks removed, and hulls repitched. If done properly, a trireme could be kept in battleworthy condition for up to twenty-five years. The alternative to this diligence was unattractive. If the *teredo*'s activity was left to progress unchecked the hull's integrity would be compromised, possibly fatally, and a ship could break apart while underway without warning.[10] Such were the perils that mariners faced when sailing the Mediterranean in a ship made of organic materials.

Foul weather could sink a ship as readily as an enemy vessel. Sea transport in the Mediterranean was typically confined to the period between 10 March and 11 November, but such travel was judged only truly safe between 27 May and 14 September.[11] Our information on naval battles is usually too sketchy to give a reliable date to when major actions occurred. Only in exceptional circumstances can we assign a relatively firm date to an event. For the most part it is reasonable to assume naval warfare took place in these putatively calmer months. This security could be illusory. One of the worst storms to hit the Romans struck in July, during the period when sea travel was estimated to be less dangerous, and the Romans would lose hundreds of ships to storms during the First Punic War.

In modern historical writing, the trireme is very often called the 'ship of the line' of the classical period, as are its later and larger derivatives such as the quadrireme and the quinquereme. If this term can be limited to meaning that it was the mainstay warship of ancient navies, then it is a fitting term as far as that. In actuality, it was not at all like the ships of the line of the Age of Sail. Those were enormous and bulky gun carriers built to bring large numbers of heavy weapons to bear, firing broadside at the enemy. Their ability to be stable platforms for these guns was far more important than their sailing qualities. Galleys were built to be weapons themselves, as the presence of bronze rams at their prows demonstrates. Even when ramming was not practised, the galley deployed not artillery but infantry to defeat enemy warships.

Broadly speaking there were two methods of fighting at sea with a galley. These were ramming and boarding. In a ramming attack, the ship was propelled by the rowers to a speed sufficient to break the oars or pierce the hull of an enemy ship. Rams were not delivered at an especially high speed. A trireme could achieve a rowed top speed of about ten knots per hour for short bursts. The quinqueremes used by both Carthage and Rome would have been heavier and a bit slower. The ramming attack relied more on the great inertia of the moving galley at impact than its speed to do its damage to the target vessel. Once the ram had been accomplished, the attacking vessel would then attempt to extricate itself, by backing water, from the stricken enemy craft. At the prow of the galley was set a bronze ram to enhance the power of a ramming strike and protect the attacking ship's hull from the collision. The other fighting tactic was boarding. Boarding actions were not for the faint of heart. This required soldiers aboard the attacking ship to cross over to an enemy galley and take possession of it. Such an endeavour was in reality a skirmish on land transferred to the heaving deck of a ship. A successful boarding action brought with it the benefit of a 'prize' ship, though it is not clear from ancient sources whether enemy vessels were ordinarily put to use after being captured.

Too much is sometimes made of the dichotomy between ramming and boarding tactics in ancient galley warfare. To be sure, skilled practitioners of naval manoeuvring as the Athenians preferred ramming attacks, in which the ship itself was the weapon, as opposed to boarding, in which the soldiers embarked on the ship were the means of defeating the enemy. In this marked preference, the Athenians were very much like their fellow Greeks, the Phocaeans and the Rhodians, as well as the Carthaginians, all of whom honed their rowing skills to enable them to manoeuvre their ships, whether triremes or quinqueremes, better than their opponents. This was necessary if they were to be able to ram and back water to extricate themselves once they had done so. These superior skills were used to achieve naval mastery, and the reputations of these peoples for being fine mariners, at various times and places, shows that they actually did develop nautical skills to a greater extent than did most others in ancient times. The list of nations that displayed such high ability is not a long one. Genuine rowing skill of a magnitude to make more than a marginal difference in battle was not easy to cultivate.

Ramming and boarding would have been carried out as the opportunities presented themselves. One tactic was not necessarily used to the exclusion of the other. A navy that had faster ships and more highly trained crews had the advantage in ramming, at least in the initial phase of an engagement. Boarding would have been more readily accomplished as the battle progressed, with slowed or damaged ships now vulnerable to boarding attempts by marines on enemy galleys.[12] With the vagaries of naval combat, however, no ship captain could be certain that he would not have to fight a boarding action.

The ram itself was a marvel of engineering. Whereas most wood from a ship dating back to the ancient world has long since decayed, outside of exceptional circumstances, bronze rams have been found in well preserved condition. The most famous of these is the Athlit Ram, discovered in 1980 near Athlit, Israel. Though no other pieces of the ship to which the ram had once been attached have ever been found, an estimation of the size of the war galley that bore the Athlit Ram can nevertheless be made. After his victory at the Battle of Actium in 31 B.C., Octavian, later Augustus, erected at Nicopolis in ancient Epirus the Actian Naval Monument, also known as Octavian's Campsite Memorial. This was a celebratory victory monument into which were set the bronze rams of enemy war galleys captured by Octavian's forces at Actium. From a comparison of the sizes of the various rams that would have once been mounted there (the rams themselves are gone but the mounting sockets remain) the size of the Athlit ship can be extrapolated. It would have been on the smaller side for ships of the era, most likely a quadrireme. The ram was hollow, being approximately 7–10mm in thickness. It weighed 476kg, or about 1,047lbs. The length of the ram was 2.26m (roughly 7.4ft). Many rams on larger ships would have been substantially bigger and heavier. The Athlit device was made out of a high-grade bronze alloy cast in just a single pour. From marks found upon the ram, it has been surmised that it was cast in Cyprus and mounted aboard the Cyprian fleet of the Egyptian Ptolemies in the late third or early second centuries.[13]

Battles at sea were fought as adjuncts to campaigns on land. Even in modern times, it has been rare for a naval battle to occur without relation to a concurrent ground operation, whether it be Midway, in which an assault was projected on Midway Island itself, Leyte Gulf (the invasion of the Philippines), or the more recent Falklands War, wherein a major assault force withstood air and sea attack before deploying troops to retake the islands. The famous battles of Salamis and the Great Harbour of Syracuse were conducted alongside land operations. Though it may seem needless to say so, the object of naval warfare is to secure some sort of benefit to those who live on land. In ancient wars this was usually the possession of territory, especially cities. With regard to the First Punic War, several naval battles were fought in and around heavily defended Carthaginian-held port cities in Sicily or in relation to the movements of Roman invasion fleets. It is impossible to discuss the naval war around Sicily without reference to what was happening on the island. The same held true for Rome's subsequent conflict with Carthage, the Second Punic War. Events on land often dictated the naval policies of each combatant.

Fleets were difficult to direct. Travelling ships could become separated as a result of weather, poor handling, or darkness. Once engaged in combat individual warships were most often on their own. A fleet whose ships could come to the aid of friendly vessels under pressure had a great advantage over an opponent. The transmission of orders between ships in a fleet was accomplished by hoisted signal flags.[14] Orders were also relayed by smaller ships of various types. Polybius calls them *lemboi*, in Greek. These lighter craft played a role in the battlefleet analogous to the frigates of the Napoleonic era, scouting ahead for the main fleet, picking up survivors, and slaying enemy sailors dumped into the sea during a battle. They did not usually participate in the battle proper, being too small for this, but they were invaluable for their speed and manoeuvrability for these other tasks. They are rarely mentioned in the histories, but when they are there is no sense that their presence was in any way unusual, and so they must have accompanied a fleet as a matter of course. In what numbers they did this or how they were positioned is unknown. We can reasonably infer that they ranged ahead of the main fleet by several miles to reconnoitre, and that once an enemy fleet was spotted they would signal back to the larger warships about the presence of the enemy. In spite of their use there were occasions on which both Roman and Carthaginian fleets seem to have been surprised to their detriment by the approach of the enemy. There are many mysteries concerning the operation of navies of the ancient world, and the deployment, numbers, and usage of these smaller ship types are among them.

The operational range of a war galley was extremely limited. Endurance, the ability to operate for long periods of time away from port, was minimal. Long-range runs were not typically feasible. On the basis of recorded movements surviving from the ancient world, such a ship could travel for about five days at most before it was required to put into a port or beach itself, but a voyage of this length should be considered as exceptional. Frequent, nightly stops to pull the ships out of the water for the night were much more the norm. Most fleet commanders would beach their ships for the evening so that their men could rest and take their meals on land.

A galley required a crew that was very large for its size because of the limited power that any one oarsman could contribute, which was about one-eighth of a horsepower. To propel a galley to its maximum speed required a large complement of oarsmen, and each oarsman also had to propel his own weight. So there was a diminishing return on speed when the crews were expanded beyond a certain point. Further, there was no place aboard ship for the men to sleep.[15] The ship would also become a filthy, reeking place in short order once the hundreds of men packed into it had urinated, defecated, and vomited all over it. It was also unable to obtain supplies for its crew from the surrounding land, as an army could.[16] A restricted range was the fundamental limiting factor for the galley in this and all subsequent centuries.

The war galley has been compared to the steam powered warship of the nineteenth century on account of its ability to travel by rowing in any direction regardless of the wind. This was something that sailing ships could not do. Such a capability made sharp manoeuvres possible that could not be readily achieved by sailing ships. To make use of this required a high level of skill among the rowers to achieve maximum efficiency. Rowing was not as simple as pulling an oar. A trained crew could execute more complicated manoeuvres than an unskilled one. A well handled galley could attack and then back away to attack again faster than a poorly handled ship.

In the sphere of ship manoeuvres, the Greeks knew two simple types. The first was the *diekplous*, or breakthrough, in which an attacking ship forced its way into the line of opposing warships and either struck them in the sides or passed through to strike at their sterns. The other was the *periplous*, in which an attacking vessel would row around the flank of an enemy formation to hit at the sides or sterns of those ships. They were not complicated manoeuvres in theory.

In practice, such things were made arduous by the difficulty in synchronizing the rowing movements of the oarsmen. It required a crew with long experience to execute such manoeuvres in battle with any facility. The Athenians, who devoted themselves to seapower, could employ them. So could the Carthaginians. Newcomers to naval warfare found them challenging to master. A simpler tactic was preferred when combat against a more skilled opponent was looming.

The importance of head-on ramming collisions as a standard tactic distinct from the *diekplous* or *periplous* increased in the years after the Peloponnesian War. It is probably not a coincidence that the invention of the heavier quinquereme ('five oars') war galley in 399 can be attributed to Dionysius I of Syracuse. Less than a generation before, his city had defeated a combined land and sea attack by Athens. The Syracusans had done this by employing the blunt tactic of frontal collisions to defeat the Mediterranean's finest navy in the city's Great Harbour. Not only had such a tactic been proven to be effective, it did not require an extensive investment of time or training for the rowers to accomplish it. It did require a skilled steersman to guide the ship properly in this dangerous attack, but even that requirement declined in importance as the technology of casting durable bronze rams, as exemplified by the Athlit Ram, improved. Such rams enabled galleys to absorb the extreme shock of a frontal collision with reduced risk to the ship's integrity.[17]

Ships became larger in the decades following Alexander the Great's death. In part this increase in size was driven by the wars of the Macedonian successor states for dominance. The sea was just one more arena in which their bloody rivalry played out. One theory holds that it was not for simple sea battles that ships of the Hellenistic era grew larger, but instead for their use in the naval sieges of coastal cities in the eastern Mediterranean.[18] A galley larger than a trireme, such as a quadrireme ('four oars') or a quinquereme was heavier and had a more robust structure. It could withstand the enormous impact of a head-on collision more readily than could a lighter vessel. Such ships would have been better suited to the defence of important harbours than more lightly built triremes. Quinqueremes especially rose higher above the water than triremes, and were superior platforms for the casting of missiles.[19] With their higher decks, they would also have made superior platforms for boarding actions too.

Galleys larger than a trireme are usually lumped together under the umbrella term of 'polyreme'. This is a neologism meaning 'many oars' and was not used in ancient times. A salient feature of the Hellenistic era naval warfare was the stunning growth in size of these polyremes. The exact architecture of the various polyremes is not known today, but there are attestations in multiple sources of sixes, sevens, nines, tens, sixteens, twenties, thirties, and even a gargantuan forty which was likely so large as to be a catamaran-style fusion of two lesser hulls.[20] It is important to note that the larger of these superships were used as linebreakers to force their way through the harbour defences of an enemy city. The 'smaller' quadriremes and quinqueremes were present in the besieging fleet mainly to provide protection for the bigger units from attack while they carried out their siege-related tasks.[21] Significantly, neither the Carthaginians nor the Romans would follow the same path towards ever larger galleys as did their Hellenistic Greek peers in the eastern Mediterranean. Both settled on the quinquereme as the primary warship of their navies.

Maritime nations such as Athens, Carthage, and Rhodes placed big bets on the ability of their superior mariners to give them the edge in naval fighting over less skilled opponents. They were very often rewarded with remarkable victories. Problems could occur when peoples not as talented in sea warfare took dedicated steps to blunt theur advantage in naval combat. This involved boarding enemy ships and fighting it out on the decks for possession of the vessels. Though this method was not as sophisticated as manoeuvring, it could be successful when employed assiduously. Herodotus tells us of the Battle of Artemisium in 480 between the Greek and Persian fleets that the day's fighting was inconclusive. He goes on to mention that the Egyptians in Xerxes' fleet performed several great feats that day, including the capture of five Greek triremes along with their crews.[22] Artemisium was not a battle of manoeuvre, and in no way a showcase for the abilities of a trireme. If room to manoeuvre could be reduced or denied altogether, rowing skill was of no account, and brute force was the arbiter of victory.

In the heaving mass of war galleys, confusion reigned as the Persians were hindered by their own numbers. Several Persian ships smacked into other friendly vessels in the press and wrecked them. The fight turned into a brutal hand-to-hand combat between the marines of each ship. Boarding, not ramming, was the only sure tactic in the close confines once the galleys of the fleets had smashed into each other. Marines on the Greek ships were just fourteen in number, while the Persian triremes carried thirty. The Greek marines were in actuality hoplites, however, and their superior arms and armour evened the odds. Significantly, the Egyptians who managed the extraordinary feat of boarding and capturing five Greek triremes were themselves heavily equipped, carrying spears, axes, shields, and wearing armour. With the Egyptians employing a presumably greater numbers of marines, they overwhelmed these five underdefended triremes.[23] The Athenian galleys had been roughly handled, and it is worth noting that the Egyptians were able to perform so well against the Greek fleet with their inelegant but very effective boarding tactics.

For Rome, solving the problem of Carthage's highly skilled navy required the application of naval tactics that were much like the Romans themselves: blunt, and straightforward. Fortunately for the Romans, they had been tried before. The Egyptians had gone to Artemisium prepared to fight hand-to-hand, and had shown that naval manoeuvring was of limited value in the close press of a battle. Other peoples would show what could be achieved when their ships were designed to make boarding actions more feasible.

Chapter Five

Breaking Athens: A Case Study

Over the course of the fifth century BC the Athenians developed a remarkable fleet that relied upon skillful manoeuvring in battle to defeat their enemies. To a great extent, Athens turned its fleet into a professional force through constant training in the same way that Sparta had made its army a professional entity. They were not nearly so single-minded in their determination to do this, and did not reorganize the whole structure of their society to accomplish this goal, but they did make service in the fleet worthwhile. Each rower, and there were 170 such men per trireme, was paid one drachma per day, which was about the daily wage of a skilled craftsman of the era. The rise in importance of the navy also caused an increase of the political power of Athen's lower classes because they were needed to provide the rowers for the ships. Athenian democracy became correspondingly more 'democratic' as a result of the heavy demands now placed on Athenian manpower by the fleet.

The Athenian edge in shiphandling over her enemies was truly extraordinary, and was the basis of Athens' naval superiority in the early years of the Peloponnesian War. The Athenian fleet could at times literally row circles around an enemy force. Off Chalcis in 429, an Athenian flotilla of just twenty triremes under the command of the talented admiral Phormio encountered a Peloponnesian fleet of forty-seven. The Peloponnesians were not expecting the smaller Athenian fleet to attack, and had outfitted their ships more as transports for hoplites than as warships ready for a general action. As they sailed the Athenians struck them in the open sea. The Peloponnesians formed a *kyklos*, pointing the prows of their ships outward, a completely defensive formation. Instead of ramming immediately, however, the Athenians bided their time, rowing around the Peloponnesians again and again. The Peloponnesian circle became smaller each time that they pulled in when the Athenians feinted a ramming attack. Their triremes began to bunch together. Then a wind came up and the result was chaos. The Athenians chose this moment to strike, sinking or disabling several galleys and capturing twelve others.[1]

Phormio's fleet again showed what superior manoeuvring could achieve not much later near Naupactus when a Peloponnesian fleet of seventy-seven triremes arrived to take on his fleet of twenty. The Peloponnesians pursued the heavily outnumbered Athenians, who were sailing in single file along the coast, and worsted the nine in the rear of the line, several of which were forced to beach themselves. The eleven ships in the lead of the Athenian line managed to make good their escape to Naupactcus but for a single trireme, which was trailed by a lone Peloponnesian ship ranging far ahead of the rest of its fleet. As it approached Naupactus, the Athenian trireme came upon an anchored merchantman, circled around the vessel, and struck at her pursuer. She delivered a powerful ram, and the Peloponnesian ship sank, just as the rest of the Peloponnesian fleet arrived, already singing the *paean* of victory. The shock of seeing their trireme sent to the bottom caused them to panic. They had also failed to keep in formation, believing that the battle had been won. The Athenian sailors in Naupactus saw all of this happening, and heartened by the action of the lone trireme, immediately counterattacked. The Peloponnesians were in no state to resist, and fled. The Athenians captured six enemy triremes, and reclaimed those of their stragglers that had been forced ashore earlier in the day. The adept rowing performance of just a single trireme had reversed completely what had been a disastrous encounter for the Athenians.[2]

The Athenians favoured the use of hit-and-run manoeuvres to ram an enemy ship with a trireme, hole it with a heavy bronze ram attached to the prow, and then back water to extricate itself. This would leave the enemy trireme, heavy with water and listing, and unable to enact such an attack itself. The freed Athenian galley would then find another target and repeat the process. The Athenians understood boarding tactics very well, of course, but they felt that the best use of their greater skills was in utilizing ramming tactics as opposed to boarding. Thucydides writes that the need to strike prow-to-prow against an enemy ship was considered to be indicative of lesser skill on the part of a trireme's steersman.[3] The preferred move for an Athenian trireme was to manoeuvre around to ram the sides or stern of an enemy galley. This required much more skill in rowing to accomplish, but the Athenians had enough practice to make it work.

The great difficulty arose for the Athenians when they could not make the tactic work. Athenian triremes were handled like light cavalry on land. They were not to get stuck in lengthy combats with enemy ships but to strike speedily and then get away so that they could strike again. They built their triremes to be light and swift. Just as heavy cavalry could not catch light cavalry, an enemy trireme that carried less skilled oarsmen or was a heavy ship itself would be at a disadvantage in a battle of manoeuvres with an Athenian trireme.

An enemy contemplating combat with the Athenians had two options. It could either try to fight the Athenian fleet with the same tactics, which would almost certainly place itself at a disadvantage relative to the experienced Athenians with their fast triremes, or it could seek to negate the Athenian advantage in naval manoeuvring altogether. The usual step taken, be it on land or sea, by a force that was trying to contain a faster, speedier, or more numerous opponent was to choose a narrowed battlefield where space and thus freedom to manoeuvre would be limited. The Greek coalition achieved this at Salamis. At Agincourt, a small English army placed itself in a narrow field and let the French knights break upon its shortened line. An Athenian fleet would either have to be somehow held in position or trapped in a confined area if its advantage in ramming were to be reduced.

The Limitations of Naval Manoeuvre Tactics

The Corinthians developed an effective counter to Athenian tactics, and this was the very essence of simplicity. At the Battle of Erineus in 413 they decided to row straight at the Athenians, and hit them head-on. Fancy manoeuvring would not be attempted at all. It was not a big battle. There were just thirty-three triremes in the Athenian fleet and a slightly smaller number in the Corinthian force. It was a brutish fight, and the result was not in favour of either party. The Corinthians lost three triremes, but more significantly, the Athenians had seven of their own triremes rammed prow-to-prow by the enemy, and these were put out of action. The Corinthians had reinforced the catheads at the prows of their ships and made them wider, and attached outwardly projecting planks to the sides of the prow. Once a collision had occurred, a Corinthian ram would slide past an Athenian ram and strike the weaker sides of its prow. These strengthened prows now crashed through the lighter bows of the Athenian triremes. It was enough for the Corinthians that they had not lost the battle outright that they deemed it a victory, while the Athenians, expecting victory, considered the drawn result to be instead a loss.[4] The Corinthians had shown the way to counter the more skilled Athenian fleet. The answer was to go straight at the enemy's galleys and hit their lighter prows. Though the tactic did not sink any Athenian triremes, it did cripple several Athenian ships by ripping away their oars.[5]

The Athenians could also be their own worst enemy by adopting positions that negated their fleet's ability to make use of its considerable skill in manoeuvring triremes. The Sicilian Expedition in 415 BC arose out of the decision of Athens to intervene in an internal Sicilian conflict between the city of Selinus and Segesta. Segesta appealed to Athens for aid, and it sent a military force to Sicily. This brought war with the powerful Greek city of Syracuse which lay on the eastern side of the island and was an ally of Selinus. The Athenians assented to the request, but Thucydides claimed that the true reason for the decision to launch the expedition was greed. The Athenians wanted to subjugate the entire island of Sicily, and the provision of aid to their allies was a suitable pretext for the expedition of conquest.[6]

A large fleet of sixty triremes and forty troop transports conveying thousands of hoplites was sent to attack Syracuse, but the Athenians, overconfident in the extreme, unwisely placed the fleet within the large but still cramped confines of the Great Harbour. The siege of Syracuse was enacted by land and sea, but in neither realm did the Athenians establish dominance for long. They were as much the besieged behind the siege walls that they built around Syracuse as were the Syracusans themselves. In 413 a series of battles was fought within the harbour by the fleets of Athens and Syracuse which resulted in severe losses to Athens. Even though it was acknowledged by all involved that the Athenians were the finer seamen, the Syracusans rapidly adopted the innovations and tactical methods of strengthened prows and head-on collisions that the Corinthians had displayed at Erineus as a means of countering the Athenian edge in rowing.

The Athenians had no room to enact their favoured *diekplous* or *periplous* manoeuvres in a harbour clogged with triremes, both theirs and the enemy's.[7] They even lacked the space to back water, which was critical to extricating a trireme once it had rammed a Syracusan ship. Athenian galleys also suffered a marked deterioration in their performance as a result of the need to keep them in the water for long periods to maintain the blockade.[8] These triremes became waterlogged and heavy, whereas the Syracusans could beach their ships more often to let them dry out. The results of the clashes within the Great Harbour were much like that of the Battle of Erineus. The stronger prows of the Syracusan triremes smashed in the weaker prows of the Athenian ships. Syracuse's fleet had no intention of employing complex manoeuvres, and so made heavy use of embarked javelineers whose presence aboard the triremes would otherwise have upset their stability. These men injured Athenian oarsmen with their missiles, thereby hampering the rowing efficiency of the Athenian triremes. Their actions were supplemented by other javelineers in small boats that boldly rushed in amongst the larger ships. The expedition began to teeter on the brink of destruction.

A force of seventy-three triremes came to reinforce the Athenian ships in the Great Harbour, and a battle quickly followed in which the Syracusans, with just seventy-six ships, were victorious over an expanded Athenian fleet of eighty-six.[9] Even with an edge in numbers, the Athenian navy was no longer a match for that of Syracuse. This was when the Athenians turned all of their thought and energy to escape. There was no chance of victory left. The only thing that might be salvaged was the physical survival of what was left of the once grand expeditionary force.

For the Syracusans, now that they were assured that their city would not fall, the goal was to crush the Athenians completely. They decided to try to block the mouth of the Great Harbour and trap the Athenian fleet within it. The Athenians at last tried to alter their tactics and embraced boarding actions as their primary means of fighting. Instead of worrying about overweighting their triremes and making them hard to handle, they placed large numbers of hoplites, archers, and javelineers aboard. Once contact had been made with an enemy trireme, the Athenians would not try to back water to get free as they usually did but instead would hurl grappling hooks about the Syracusan ships to keep them stuck in place.

The final battle in the Great Harbour took place amidst an atmosphere of apocalyptic doom. The Athenians desperately wanted to escape, but the Syracusans wanted to annihilate the Athenians, and they had them surrounded, with ships stationed inside and outside of the harbour entrance. Nearly 200 triremes fought inside the harbour, and because of the extremely limited space, the ships both rammed and were rammed in quick succession.[10] It rapidly became a land battle at sea, as the ships of both sides became packed together. While this was not the kind of naval battle that Athens would have wanted, as their rowing skill now counted for nothing, it was at least what they had planned for when they increased the complement of hoplites and missile troops aboard their triremes.

Their new tactics and strenuous efforts would not be enough. The Syracusans defeated them decisively, and those Athenian triremes that were not captured were forced to flee ashore inside the harbour. Though they still outnumbered the Syracusan fleet by roughly sixty ships to less than fifty, the Athenians were completely dejected, and there was no fight left in them for another attempt to force the passage at the harbour mouth. The sailors would not even man their ships.[11] An attempt to escape by land was a catastrophe, and what was left of the proud Athenian expeditionary force was destroyed in the Sicilian countryside.[12]

The expedition was over. It was a total disaster for Athens by every measure, and had brought nothing of value in return. Athens was far from defeated in the great war that it was still fighting against Sparta, but the end was nearing, and failure at sea would be crucial to Athens' loss in that conflict. The Athenians were themselves at fault for limiting their room to manoeuvre by bringing their fleet inside the Great Harbour. The Athenians trapped themselves inside a confined area in which they could not make full use of their hard-earned proficiency in handling their triremes for potent ramming attacks.

The Athenian failure at Syracuse had deeper roots though than simply a poor tactical choice. The decision to favour manoeuvre tactics over straight ahead ramming or boarding tactics had more to do with the Athenian defeat. Athens had a large population base upon which to draw for its manpower. A large fleet was not out of its capacity to man. It was also very rich. At the outset of the Peloponnesian War, the yearly income of Athens was about 1,000 talents and one talent could fund the entire crew of a trireme for one month. In addition to this income, Athens also had a treasury packed with precious metals. There were 6,000 talents' worth of silver coins, 500 of uncoined gold and silver, and forty talents of gold plate that covered the statue of Athena on the Acropolis which could be melted down for emergency usage.[13] Much of this vast store of wealth was spent on the fleet. At the beginning of the war, Athens had as many as 300 triremes ready for service, and when the vessels of its allies were counted, the combined naval force at its disposal was 400 ships. Though Athens was outnumbered in numbers of hoplites, together with its allies, it had an advantage of about four-to-one in warships, and had much better crews.[14]

Two questions must now be asked. Did Athens do the correct thing by maintaining such a large fleet? If the answer is yes, did it build the kind of fleet that would have served it best? As to the first question, the answer can only be yes. Athens was a maritime power that relied upon the sea to bring in food and tribute from long distances. A navy was necessary to protect that trade. Once Athens had built its Long Walls connecting it to its harbour at Piraeus, it was well-nigh invulnerable as long as it controlled the sea.

Where Athens made its mistake was in placing so much emphasis on sophisticated manoeuvring as a means of doing battle with its triremes. Not only did this approach require a very high level of competence, it did not necessarily bring an adequate return on the investment made in Athenian crews. In ideal or near-ideal conditions, the Athenians could use their rowing skills to outmanoeuvre enemy triremes and affect their devastating *diekplous* or *periplous* attacks. In certain conditions, however, such tactics could not be employed properly, if at all, and the Athenians were at a steep disadvantage against opponents who were ready for an approach to naval combat that relied upon frontal collisions, as the Corinthians and Syracusans did, or on infantry-led boarding tactics. That the Athenians recognized that there was a flaw in their naval doctrine is shown by their belated decision to put large numbers of hoplites on their ships towards the end of the series of fights in the Great Harbour. By then it was too late to save the situation, and Athens' fleet was mauled badly by a force inferior in numbers.

Athens, with its large population of about 300,000, and its vast wealth, could have instead adopted frontal collisions as its primary tactic. It was certainly not beyond the mental abilities of its naval architects to conceive of the idea to strengthen the prows of its triremes just as Corinth's seamen would do to theirs. If Athenian triremes also carried large numbers of marines then these soldiers could have been the primary means of winning battles at sea. It would not have been an elegant mode of naval warfare, perhaps, but there is no reason why it would not have brought victory too. Further, it would have been workable in those situations in which *diekplous* or *periplous* ramming were not. Being unable to back water would not have been such a great disadvantage, as it was in the Great Harbour of Syracuse, if the Athenian fleet had been prepared from the outset to wage a different kind of naval war.

The prejudice against simpler but more widely applicable tactics is observable in Thucydides, who was himself an Athenian. When recounting a naval battle between the Corinthians and Corcyraeans at Sybota in 433, he describes the engagement as being of 'a somewhat old-fashioned kind since they were still behind in naval matters'.[15] What was the sign of this old-fashioned approach to naval warfare? Both fleets, Thucydides wrote, had 'numbers of hoplites aboard their ships, together with archers and javelin throwers'. The combat was 'hard enough', he admits, 'in spite of the lack of skill shown'. The encounter was 'more like a battle on land than a naval engagement'. Thucydides' negative assessment of the conduct of each fleet was predicated upon his belief that 'it was a battle where courage and sheer strength played a greater part than scientific methods'. Instead of trying to manoeuvre, 'both sides relied more for victory on their hoplites, who were on the decks and who fought a regular pitched battle'.[16] If Thucydides, who was himself an Athenian general as well as a historian who wrote extensively about the great failure of the Athenian fleet at Syracuse, could not grasp the flaws in Athens' naval doctrine, or that Corinthian style fighting was a worthwhile alternative, then perhaps we should not be surprised that it remained in effect for as long as it did without revision.

Part II

The First Punic War

Chapter Six

Trouble at the Toe of Italy

Two cities lay across from each other at the Straits of Messina between the toe of Italy and the island of Sicily. These were Rhegium, on the peninsula, and Messana, now Messina, on the island. The actions of two bands of mercenaries were to have profound effects on the future of Roman power, and bring about a war between the two greatest states in the western Mediterranean. From these small affairs would spring events that would alter civilization in the Western world forever.

The Mamertines were Italian mercenaries from Campania who had originally taken service with Agathocles, the tyrant of Syracuse. These men, dazzled by the riches of Messana, seized power there at some point in the 280s, murdered many, expelled others, and helped themselves to the helpless citizens' wives and property. In Rhegium, the threat posed by Pyrrhus or a naval attack by Carthage caused the citizens to ask Rome to install a garrison for their protection. A force of 4,000 was duly sent by the Romans under Decius, who was himself a Campanian.

Over time, however, the lure of the great wealth of Rhegium proved irresistible. As had happened at Messana, the garrison troops in Rhegium killed or threw out the citizens, and seized control, giving as their excuse, claims Appian, the fiction that the Messanans were set to turn the garrison over to Pyrrhus. The Romans could not intervene immediately because they were themselves preoccupied by the contest with Pyrrhus. Eventually, though, the Romans stirred to action, and they captured Rhegium in 270. Most of the former garrison died in the assault; those that did not were taken to Rome and publicly flogged and then executed in the Forum.[1]

The fall of Rhegium was a poor turn for the Mamertines still ensconced in Messana. It seems that they had cooperated well with the Rhegium mercenaries and benefited from their presence there. While the Roman-Campanian garrison had been in power in Rhegium, the Mamertines had raided the Syracusans and Carthaginians, as well as imposing tribute on other parts of Sicily. They were likely already under pressure from a revivified Syracuse under its new king, Hiero.[2]

Hiero was a fine combination of benevolence and ruthlessness. He was noted for his probity in the administration of Syracuse, but when he recognized the dangers posed by the veteran mercenaries in his own army, had he moved ruthlessly to crush them. He led his army out to do battle with the Mamertines at the Cyamosorus River, and deployed his force in two lines, with his own mercenaries in the lead, and the native Syracusan troops to the rear. Hiero gave the mercenaries the order to advance, he purposely failed to support them, and they were duly destroyed by the Mamertines.[3] Having disposed of the mercenaries, Hiero went back to Syracuse, and enlisted new mercenaries that he himself selected.

Hiero then set his citizen troops upon an intensive training programme to improve their military skills. He inflicted a sharp defeat on the Mamertines at the Longanus River in 264. The mercenaries' ambitions had been checked, but they still held Messana, albeit less securely than before, as Hiero placed the city under siege at this time.[4] It was then that they made their fateful bid for support from outside of Sicily.

One can imagine the nerve that the Mamertines possessed to send their delegates to request aid from the Romans. Now that they were trapped in a city that they had stolen from its citizens, they were asking the Romans to help them out of a tight spot. They pleaded that they would willingly hand Messana over to Rome in exchange for rescue. If the perfidy of the Mamertines was in any doubt, it should be known that some others of that group were at the same time making a similar pitch for aid to Carthage too, which seems to have agreed. A force of Carthaginian soldiers arrived and took control of the city's citadel.[5]

The Romans for their part were in a morally difficult position. The Mamertines were scarcely different from the soldiers who had seized power in Rhegium, soldiers that the Romans had only recently separated from their heads right in the Forum. To give succour to the Mamertines would expose the Romans to the charge of hypocrisy, and the Romans were extremely finicky about presenting themselves as being in the right when they went to war. The Mamertines had the foul odour of betrayers clinging to them. A decision was long in coming.

Strategic needs outweighed whatever moralistic qualms the Romans might have had. Carthage was already well established in Spain and Sardinia. If Sicily were to be added to its expansive maritime empire the Romans would be presented with a potential enemy just a few days' sail from Rome itself, with much of Italy lying closer still. Sicily would be the ultimate forward base for Carthaginian attacks against Italy, a land with a long and hard-to-defend coastline vulnerable to quick descents by hostile ships. The Romans feared that the fall of Messana would presage the creation of a Carthaginian stepping stone for a future invasion of the Italian peninsula.[6] Many of the cities in Italy, especially those of the south, had only recently been joined to Rome by treaty, and their detachment by a powerful foe operating out of Sicily would have been a genuine threat. To foreclose on the possibility of any such dismemberment, the Romans decided on war and an army would cross the Straits.

Crossing to Sicily

Polybius' account of the Roman crossing is brief. He says only that Appius Claudius Caudex made a 'hazardous, night-time crossing' of the Straits.[7] There arises the matter of the crossing from the Carthaginian perspective. Why did Carthage's fleet, which had mastery of the sea during the early years of the war, fail to prevent the crossing?

Actually preventing a crossing was far more difficult than merely positioning ships to wait on the Romans to board their ships and set sail. The initiative lay with the Romans. The Carthaginians certainly seem to have made an effort to stop them. Polybius reports that the Carthaginians lost one of their quinquereme war galleys in their attack on the lumbering Roman transports as they made the move to Messana. This ship, which would attain great importance later on in the war, went too close to shore and ran aground, and the Romans captured it. So the Carthaginians were far from negligent in guarding the Straits. It can be inferred, though Polybius does not say so explicitly, that the deciding factor in making the Roman crossing a success was that the Romans could protect their own ships from attack. This protection came courtesy of their Greek *socii navales*, or naval allies, of southern Italy. The Romans were able to achieve enough security in a limited area for their vulnerable troop and horse transports to get across without disaster.

Diodorus' account of the crossing is far more involved than that of Polybius. In this account, the consul sent envoys to both the Carthaginians and to Hiero of Syracuse. Caudex wanted them to raise the siege of Messana, but Hiero scoffed at the request. The Romans, he told them, would do well to stop their phony talk about how they needed to come to the aid of their Mamertine allies out of a concern for keeping good faith with them. Their real motive for going to help the mercenaries was utterly transparent and ignoble. The Mamertines had despoiled the cities of Camarina and Gela, and were assassins who had stolen Messana right out from under its citizens. The siege had been commenced with all justice, Hiero insisted, and the Romans should stop trying to protect the wretches who had only 'the greatest contempt for good faith' and were 'utterly godless'.[8] If the Romans were to come to the aid of the Messanans, it would be clear to all that what they really wanted was to capture Sicily.

Diodorus says that the Romans and the Carthaginians thereafter fought some kind of naval engagement. This appears to have been the first attempt by the Romans to cross the Straits, and it may be the occasion on which the Carthaginians lost their quinquereme. Now it was the turn of the Carthaginians to send envoys to the consul. It seems that the Carthaginians were doing their best to prevent the outbreak of a full-scale war with Rome over Messana. It is probable that the Carthaginians had severe doubts about how to react. They chose to believe that a full-scale war was not possible, though it should have been apparent that the Romans, by the size of the force that they were planning on bringing to Sicily, had larger aims than taking Messana. Such a force could only have been meant to be used in an extended campaign in Sicily that would necessarily interfere with Carthaginian interests there. A collision with Rome was not something that Carthage could avoid. It was already happening, but Carthage pulled its punches.

Carthage's best move at this juncture would have been a determined effort to prevent a Roman crossing. That they did try to intervene is clear, but from the limited reference made to it the attempt was not especially effective. For Polybius the effort serves mainly to explain how the Romans came upon their captured Carthaginian quinquereme. The Carthaginians were not wholly at fault in allowing the Romans to cross, as they were still restricted in what a blockade could accomplish in preventing a crossing by the limited capabilities of the galley itself. The ship had little in the way of endurance, and could not enforce a blockade for long because its large crew would have run out of food and water. Poor weather would also have endangered these ships, and further reduced their effectiveness.[9]

The Romans may also have been able to delude the Carthaginians into letting down their guard somewhat. A story preserved by the Roman historian Sextus Julius Frontinus has Appius Claudius Caudex deliberately putting about rumours that he was not about to conduct a war without the authorization of Rome, and made as if he intended to sail back there. The Carthaginians swallowed the deception and dispersed their fleet, thereby allowing Caudex to cross.[10] Zonaras puts forth a supporting story in which he claims that Caudex resorted to spreading rumours knowing that Carthaginian traders in Rhegium would bring these rumours back to their own forces. The implication is that they relaxed their guard.[11] Perhaps the Carthaginians were in fact lulled into believing that the Romans would not attempt to cross, at least not yet. They certainly seem to have wanted to believe that the Romans would not come over.

The unwillingness to risk an outright war with Rome, which in any case was already underway, was to prove detrimental to Carthaginian fortunes in Sicily. Had Carthage utilized its fleet more aggressively, the Roman invasion might have been thwarted. What if the Carthaginians had not waited for the Roman crossing at all, but instead had struck at Roman forces currently massing in

Italy? Such a move would have had the advantage of surprise, and even if the endeavour had failed to kill many enemy soldiers, it might well have succeeded in destroying some ships that were needed to ferry the legions to Sicily. The invasion might have been either aborted or at least delayed for a year while the Romans reorganized. In the interim the Carthaginians could have improved their defences. The Carthaginians had only recently installed their own garrison in Messana, and this could have been strengthened too. Further, if Carthage had shown itself to be strong by defeating the Roman incursion, Hiero of Syracuse might have been induced to side more strongly with Carthage if the Romans could be made to seem vulnerable.

The Carthaginians instead held themselves back. They told the consul that they thought it was incredible that the Romans would try to cross while the Carthaginians had control of Sicilian waters. If the Romans persisted in their foolishness, they warned, their previously good relations would be finished and the Romans 'would not dare even to wash their hands in the sea'.[12] The Romans then responded by saying that the Carthaginians should not make them learn naval warfare. The Romans made apt pupils, they said, and the Carthaginians 'would soon see that the pupils had become superior to their teachers'.[13] The Romans in Diodorus' telling then somehow made it across even in the face of a hostile Carthaginian enemy fleet.

There is a tradition that claims that a first Roman crossing fared very badly, and the Romans had to retire to Rhegium. The Carthaginian commander in Sicily, Hanno, then returned the ships that he had captured and would have been willing to return the prisoners he had taken too if it meant an end to Rome's hostile action against Messana. If it can be trusted, and in the broadest outlines it probably can be, then the Carthaginians were doing whatever they could to avoid a war with Rome. These gestures of goodwill came to nothing, as Caudex managed to get across the Straits on his second attempt.[14]

The Romans were relieved of the problem of ejecting the Carthaginian garrison of the citadel in Messana by means of trickery. The Mamertines, not especially effective in battle, were at least masters of subterfuge, and by means of 'threats' and 'false information' convinced Hanno, commander of the Carthaginian force inside the citadel, to abandon his otherwise secure position. This was a terrible error on Hanno's part, and we can only speculate as to what would have convinced him to leave the safety of the citadel. From within Messana he could have resisted Roman attempts to control the city for as long as his food and water would have held out. Unfortunately, it seems that his nerve failed, and he departed with his soldiers. He may have saved the lives of his soldiers by leaving, but his own life was forfeited. The Carthaginians crucified him for his mistake.[15]

Following the initial foray at Messana in 264, the Romans sent an army of about 40,000 (a very large number for the time: Polybius says it was the *whole* of the Roman army) to Sicily in 263 BC under the consuls Manius Otacilius Crassus and Manius Valerius Maximus. The appearance of such a large body of troops on the island had the effect of detaching various cities from Carthage and Syracuse, which then went over to the Romans. Diodorus reports that they placed Echetla under siege, but that operation was not successful. They had more luck at Hadranum, which was taken by storm. A total of sixty-seven Sicilian cities came over to the Roman side as the offensive gained momentum.[16]

Hiero himself saw that the situation favoured the Romans, and he too sought their friendship. The consuls were glad to have the king as their friend, as they were worried about their supply situation. The Carthaginian navy was in control of the sea and the continued flow of supplies from outside the island was questionable. Hiero could provide the sustenance needed to maintain the Roman army. The Romans and the Syracusans made a treaty under which Hiero returned Roman prisoners and paid an indemnity of 100 talents of silver.[17] Hiero, in return, became a friend and ally of the Roman people. He also kept control of Syracuse and its subject cities, which were Acrae, Leontini, Megara, Helorum, Neetum, and Tauromenium.[18] Hiero's enviable position in his mini-empire in the east was thus secured by his timely switch of allegiance. A Carthaginian fleet under the command of Hannibal arrived at Xiphonia at about this time to lend assistance to Hiero against the Romans, unaware that their ally had just struck a treaty with Rome. They quickly left.[19]

Now that Syracuse was an ally, the Romans felt confident enough that they could reduce their forces in Sicily and withdrew all but two legions back to Italy. The Carthaginians, meanwhile, calculated that the strategic picture in Sicily had turned against them, and sent more troops there, including Spanish and Celtic mercenaries. The main Carthaginian stronghold would be Agrigentum, lying just across from Carthage on the southern coast of Sicily.

The consuls for the year 262 BC were Lucius Postumius Megellus and Quintus Mamilius Vitulus, who went to Sicily with their legions (including, most probably, allied legions that were commonly part of the total Roman force).[20] Upon learning that the Carthaginians were turning Agrigentum into a fortress city, and concentrating their men and supplies there, the consuls decided to attack it at once. Every other operation was brought to a halt, and the entirety of their combined forces was brought to besiege Agrigentum. Polybius relates that the Roman camp was set up at a distance of one mile from the city, and because the grain crop was now ripe, the legionaries began to harvest it themselves. A quick sortie by the defenders put the scattered Romans to flight, and the Carthaginians continued their attack with an attempt on the camp. The legionaries stood their ground and prevented the enemy from storming it, and inflicted heavy losses on the Carthaginians, who raced back to Agrigentum.

The sharp reverse suffered by the Carthaginians made them more circumspect in attacking their besiegers, and the Romans learned to forage more cautiously. With the enemy unwilling to close with them, the Romans felt confident enough to establish two camps around Agrigentum. Each camp received an inner trench, facing toward the city to prevent a sortie from the garrison, as well as an outer one to stop attacks from without. From the description provided by Polybius, the trenches, strongpoints, and pickets must have been extensive enough to also foil outsiders from gaining access to Agrigentum to bring in supplies. Aided by the Sicilian cities that had joined them, the Roman supply situation was good, with a major depot established at the nearby city of Herbesus.

Five months of siege followed with the expected result that the Carthaginians, in a city of 50,000 inhabitants, became hungry first. However, since they still had access to the sea, as Agrigentum was a port, their commander, Hannibal, was able to send word of their predicament to Carthage. Reinforcements were sent to Sicily under another Hanno, who made his base of operations at Heraclea Minoa about twenty miles to the north-west of Agrigentum on the southern coast.[21]

Hanno sensed the vulnerability of the Roman supply centre of Herbesus to a swift assault, and captured it. The stunned Romans were now at risk of starvation. Their thought was to lift the siege of Agrigentum, but King Hiero stepped in and supplied them with enough to maintain the city's investment. An epidemic had struck the Roman army, in the meantime, and Hanno judged, with the Romans weak from the illness, that it was a good time to do battle. With fifty elephants and a contingent of Numidian cavalry, Hanno advanced on Agrigentum. The Numidians drew the Roman cavalry into a trap, and savaged them. Hanno set up his own camp not far from the Romans. For two more months the Romans and Carthaginians stared at each other, all the while Hannibal in Agrigentum sent smoke signals to Hanno reminding him of the starving people of the besieged city.

In 261, Hanno was moved to seek battle, and the Romans, themselves hungry, were glad to provide it. After a tough encounter, Carthage's mercenaries and elephants were routed, and most, Polybius says, were slain on the field. The Romans were so tired from their exertions that they failed to mount a proper guard that night, and Hannibal escaped from Agrigentum with his troops across the trenches before the Romans could stop them.[22] The Romans contented themselves with sacking the defenceless city.

With the victory at Agrigentum came celebrations in Rome, along with overconfidence. The defeat of the Carthaginians had occasioned an enormous haul of booty, and the Romans could have declared victory and sought a negotiated peace. Instead, the Senate set its sights on driving the Carthaginians entirely out of the island. In 261, the land war there under the new consuls Lucius Valerius Flaccus and Titus Otacilius Crassus was proceeding well, with one nettlesome problem that prevented total victory. Carthage had a powerful navy, while Rome did not.

After the fall of Agrigentum many inland Sicilian cities had come over to the Romans, but several coastal cities broke away and allied themselves with Carthage because of their fear of the Carthaginian navy. The Italian coastline was also repeatedly raided by Carthaginian ships, no doubt throwing Roman impotence into stark relief before its allies. The Greek states of Italy would have been right to question Rome's commitment as their protector if nothing was done to stop the raids, and perhaps even switch their allegiances to Carthage to safeguard their lucrative trade with Sicily.[23] The Romans could make little headway in Sicily because of the ability of the Carthaginians to appear anywhere along the Sicilian coast, and the war degenerated into a stalemate.

Rome Builds a Great Navy

The Carthaginians were frightening coastal Sicilian cities into their camp through the power of their fleet, and the Romans recognized also that their armies were incapable of preventing either these detachments or the bothersome raids. In 260, the Romans therefore decided to build their own fleet, practically from scratch. Polybius saw this as so important that he even wrote that one of his purposes in telling the story of the war was to explain the origin of Roman seapower. His readers should not be ignorant, Polybius explained, of 'how and when and for what reasons the Romans first ventured upon the sea'.[24]

The Romans had some help of a kind from the Carthaginians themselves. A Carthaginian war galley had grounded itself on the coast back in 264 when it had tried to oppose the Roman crossing to Messana. The Romans captured the galley, of a type known as a quinquereme, intact, and used it as the model for their own ships, which were part of an initial building programme of 100 quinqueremes and 20 lighter triremes. In modern parlance, the Romans reverse-engineered the Carthaginian craft, and produced their own versions of it.

The ships themselves would be ready for action relatively soon, albeit they would not be of the highest quality. We find repeated, negative comments about Roman ships in the sources, and we can trust that they were crudely constructed compared to the finer ships of the Carthaginians or the Greeks. The crudeness of the copies would not have slowed down the process of constructing them. Since the Romans were making their galleys according to the quinquereme model that they had obtained from Carthage, they could put them together using quasi-industrial methods in which many identical parts could be prefabricated and then fitted together.

Some scepticism has been expressed about a claim by Pliny that Rome built these ships in just sixty days. There is no compelling reason to doubt this achievement, or to believe that some of the ships were acquired from other builders. Roman inexperience with ship construction would not have prevented them from building so many so speedily. There was no requirement for sophisticated shipyards. The vessels could well have been constructed right on the beach in improvised facilities. The image of a highly developed yard comparable to one maintained by the Royal Navy in the eighteenth century is likely inaccurate. A galley had to be light enough so that it could be dragged out of the water by its crew and onto a beach to dry out. It follows that it could have just as easily been launched in the same manner with equivalent manpower, or perhaps the aid of mechanical devices such as a rope and pulley system to achieve the same result.

The tradition that the Romans copied every last detail of the captured Carthaginian model suggests that they also mass-produced the parts that went into each identical quinquereme. The scale of the project must have meant that the Romans made each part in large numbers and held them ready for assembly as each vessel took shape. Stocks of completed parts were probably stored close to the ships and there would have been no delay in funnelling them to galleys that were ready to receive them.

Galleys could be produced rapidly by using this kit-building method. That such a speedy method of mass production was genuinely used is shown by the 1969 find of the wooden remains of a Carthaginian galley in the waters near Lilybaeum, the modern Marsala, one of Carthage's foremost ports during the First Punic War.[25] These timbers are adorned with numerous shipwright markings. The presence of these marks indicates that these pieces were made in large quantities with an eye toward quick assembly. It stands to reason that the Romans, themselves practical to an extreme, would have adopted such a no-nonsense production method themselves. It would be welcome to have more substantive information about the building of these war galleys. Hard information on this point is sadly lacking. But the galley production of Mediterranean shipyards in various times and places, at least, have been recorded. The Roman figure of 120, while prodigious, is not different enough to defy belief. It was also not the only production prodigy that Rome would claim. In 254 she would build 220 quinqueremes in only three months to restore the fleet to fighting strength after it had been badly depleted by weather-related losses.[26]

In the sixteenth century, Venice's famous Arsenal had the ability, with all of the needed pieces already at hand, to build and ready for service thirty galleys in just ten days. The Venetians were capable of even more astonishing feats when desired. In 1574, one of their galleys was put together and launched in just two hours.[27] The parts of the Venetian ships were already cut to the precise size, and stored for use at the Arsenal, and so only had to be placed together by the craftsmen. This industrial building method accounts for the rapidity of construction of the vessels, and the adoption of a similar system is likely why the Romans could produce an 'instant navy' of their own. That being established, it was likely also the case, as will be seen later, that haste almost certainly meant a sacrifice in quality.

Crews

The supply of trained oarsmen would necessarily be a limiting factor in how many ships the Romans could actually employ, as opposed to how many hulls it could produce. These were recruited from the fifth and poorest class of citizens at least as far as the strictly Roman population went.[28] The historian Suetonius preserves a snide remark made in 246 by the sister of a later consul, Publius Claudius Pulcher. In 249, this Pulcher had lost a naval battle, badly, and with it a large number of crewmen, on the order of tens of thousands of men. Pulcher's sister is reported to have snorted, after haughtily surveying the teeming populace in the streets as she rode by in her carriage: 'If only my brother were alive to lose another fleet! That would thin out the population a little!'[29] It stands to reason that she was referring to the proletarians of the great city. The Romans would somehow have to overcome their own deficits in ships and rowers if they hoped to defeat Carthage's navy.

In earlier times the Romans had gotten by with employing the ships and crews of their naval allies in Italy, in particular the Greek city states of the Italian south, such as the Neapolitans and the Tarentines. Now the Romans, aware of the scale of the endeavour into which they were plunging, would have to produce their own crews to man the large numbers of ships they intended to construct.

Skilled rowers could not be willed into existence. They had to be trained. The soon-to-be oarsmen were schooled on benches on land (there being no ships yet to train on) in the same seating arrangement that they would occupy when aboard a real galley. This is not at all far-fetched. The entire fleet was being made from scratch. Given the short period of time in which the ships were made available for combat, there is no reason not to believe that the Romans would have wasted time and not begun training on land for their shipboard assignments. This is not to say that rowing an oar on land is the same as doing so from a bench aboard a moving quinquereme, but the basic mechanics of the rowing stroke would have been learned, as well as how to row in unison with the other oarsmen aboard, a critical aptitude if the ship was going to have any useful motive power or manoeuvreability.

The quinquereme, or five, was first developed by Dionysius I of Syracuse at the beginning of the fourth century BC.[34] Thus, at the time of the First Punic War, the quinquereme as a design was not new. A quinquereme was used by Alexander as part of his amphibious siege of the Phoenician city of Tyre in 332.[35] As currently reconstructed, the quinquereme had three banks, or levels, of oars per side, with five men rowing every group of three oars. There would be ninety oars per side, with two men rowing together one of sixty of those oars, while another thirty oars would have a single oarsman attached to it. This tallies as 150 rowers per side, or 300 rowers all told, which matches the figure given by Polybius for the Roman ships at the Battle of Ecnomus later in the war.[36]

There is the possibility that the Romans adopted a variant of the quinquereme that used a simplified oar system. In place of the one described above, this utilized a single bank of oars with five men per oar.[37] In this view, the Romans would have found it desirable to utilize the fewest number of oars per boat while still retaining the muscle power that five men could provide. Being so new to the naval game, they would have seen the advantage in the single-oared five because it would have reduced significantly the number of experienced rowers required for successful movement of the ship. Only the rower at the innermost end of the oar would need to have had any competence. While he guided the oar, the other four men would only have had to pull hard.

The five-man-sweep theory has less likelihood of being correct than the more complicated version. While such a system would perhaps have been easier to row, it also directly contradicts Polybius' emphatic statement that the Carthaginian quinquereme was used as a model for all of Rome's ships, with the Roman galleys being built 'according to its specifications'.[38] There is no reason to believe that the Carthaginians themselves used such a system, and so the Romans themselves almost certainly did not either. Further, the continuing references to the Romans' difficulties in manoeuvring their quinqueremes seem to indicate that they had indeed chosen to go with a tough-to-master oaring system.

The typical quinquereme was about 120ft in length, with a beam measured at the hull of 14ft, and 17ft at the outrigger.[39] The Lilybaeum find offers some evidence of what woods were used in galley construction. The planks were made from pine, the keel from maple, and the reinforcing ribs were of oak. The hull planks of the ship were attached to one another first using the mortise and tenon method. A notch half as deep as the tenon was long was cut into the planks, and into each was inserted a wooden tenon. Once inserted, the tenon still projected halfway out of the plank, and this end was itself fitted into a mortise in another plank. Each tenon was secured inside the planks by means of wooden dowels. The hull was then caulked and covered with sheets of lead.[40] The ship's ribs were now included as a means to enhance the vessel's structural rigidity.

The Lilybaeum wreck stands apart from other such ancient wrecks because it was a warship, not a round-hulled, cargo-carrying merchantman which is the more usual find. A connection between the wreck and the final battle of the First Punic War, that of the Aegates Islands in 241 BC, has been advanced. In this theory, after the close of that battle, the Punic ship sought to flee back to Carthage. An abrupt change in the winds forced it to instead seek the shelter of the nearby friendly haven, which was Lilybaeum, where it met its end.[41] That this vessel was on a military mission is supported by the presence of materials recovered from the wreck that indicate that it carried only enough supplies as required for operational duty. Animal bones found at the site indicate that the Carthaginian sailors were eating meat, and also chewing *Cannabis sativa*.[42] This may have been done to make the strain of rowing easier to bear.

Chapter Seven

Opening Moves

In 260, the Romans' first fleet commander was consul Gnaeus Cornelius Scipio. With seventeen ships he sailed on a mission to Messana to obtain naval stores for the rest of the fleet, which was still under construction. While there, Scipio must have received word that the town of Lipara, on the island of Lipari in the Aeolian group, was vulnerable. Capturing these islands would have been a great benefit to Rome, since their position between Sicily and Italy made them excellent forward bases from which Carthage's warships could strike at the Italian coast.[1] Polybius says that he had the chance to capture it by 'treachery'.[2] Perhaps a faction inside the city friendly to the Romans had sent him word that the place could be seized if he struck quickly. He should have been more cautious. The Carthaginians, based at Panormus (Palermo), were aware of his movements, and after he had stationed his squadron in Lipara's harbour, an enemy fleet of twenty vessels under the command of Boödes, a member of the Carthaginian Council of Elders, arrived during the night.[3] The Romans were trapped.

There was to be no epic first clash of the Roman navy at Lipara. At daybreak, the green Roman crews lost their heads completely, and abandoned their ships while Scipio was forced by circumstance to surrender. For his foolish error the Roman people gave him the *agnomen* Asina, which means 'she-ass'. Scipio Asina later would be released from Carthaginian captivity at some unknown date, but it was before 254, when he held the consulship for a second time.[4] During this subsequent term he would again be given a major naval command alongside his co-consul.[5] He was fortunate that the Romans were more forgiving of failure than were the Carthaginians, as he did not end up nailed to a cross like Hanno. The whole Lipara affair was an inauspicious beginning to Rome's quest for naval mastery. The psychological preparation of the Romans for battle at sea left much to be desired.

Just a few days after the debacle at Lipara the rest of the Roman fleet sailed south. Before he had departed from Rome, Scipio ordered his remaining captains to set out as soon as their ships were ready. This fleet met a Carthaginian force near the Cape of Italy (close to the toe of the peninsula) a few days after the debacle at Lipara. The Carthaginian fleet comprised fifty ships under the command of Hannibal, the general who had been besieged in Agrigentum and daringly escaped from it when it fell. The Roman fleet appeared and the Carthaginians had no warning of its approach. The Romans were already in formation, while the surprised Carthaginians were likely still travelling in line. The Carthaginians lost more than half of their ships, according to Polybius, which would put their losses at twenty-six or more, and Hannibal, again showing a talent for fleeing, managed to escape with the remnant of his fleet.

The other consul for the year was Gaius Duilius. While Scipio had been entrusted with the fleet, Duilius was leading Roman land operations in Sicily. The news that he received was awful. Scipio's entire squadron had been captured and the consul taken captive. He left the land forces and took command of the fleet that had just soundly defeated Hannibal's ships. The Carthaginians were busying themselves raiding the lands around Mylae, the modern Milazzo, a city about twenty-five miles west of the north-eastern tip of Sicily. Duilius would have to stop them.

The Corvus Boarding-bridge and its Origins

The Roman fleet in the meantime waited for Duilius to arrive, presumably at Messana. Polybius writes that they then hit upon the idea of employing the corvus boarding-bridge on the decks of their ships.[6] Practical experience, it is asserted by Polybius, had made them aware of the limitations of their own ships, which were hard to manoeuvre and badly fitted-out. Polybius says very little about the origins of the corvus. He writes that its use was suggested to the Romans by a person who is never explicitly identified. The context indicates that it is meant to be a person not originally with the fleet, perhaps a Sicilian Greek who had an idea to make the boarding of enemy galleys easier.

Some historians have even suggested that it was the brainchild of the young Archimedes, who was living in Syracuse at this time, but there is no hard evidence to support this theory. Polybius never states specifically where the Roman fleet put in before it decided to incorporate the corvus. Since Messana was closer, and in Roman hands, that city makes the most sense as its destination. The fleet may have instead gone on further, to Syracuse, which had a much richer nautical history than Rome, though that in itself was not a mark of much distinction. It is possible that while there, in Syracuse, the Romans received recommendations about how to make their ships more effective in battle. Given their perceived limitations, the Romans may have taken to the suggestion that they mount the corvus boarding-bridge as a means of grappling a Carthaginian ship and holding it in place. Syracuse had been an enthusiastic practitioner of Corinthian-style battle tactics in which its ships collided prow-first with enemy vessels as long ago as the Great Harbour battles of 413. The corvus boarding-bridge would have been a technical development very much in line with that mode of naval warfare. Even if the Roman fleet did not travel as far as that city, Syracusans may well have been in the same port as the Romans dispensing advice to them.

There are nonetheless serious problems with this version of the origins of the corvus. Given the apparently short period between the battle at the Cape in which they had so soundly defeated the Carthaginians, and the assumption of the fleet's command by Duilius, which does not seem to have been of long duration, it is difficult to completely accept Polybius' account of the adoption of the corvus. The overall impression given by the Polybian account is that the Carthaginian fleet was still operating in the area while the Romans were in port in Sicily, and that the Romans made haste to mount the corvus on their ships during this time. But the corvus was a cumbersome device that had to be carefully installed on the deck of a quinquereme. It also had large moving parts, and the marines also had to have been given some modicum of training to use it effectively. Further, it seems reasonable that such a major addition to their ships could not have been contemplated and carried out without the consul's approval, and never so hastily.[7] The story as related by Polybius lacks any details as to precisely whose idea it was to use the corvus, where the work was done to put it on the ships, or how long it took to do so. Such a silence is not out of the ordinary for Polybius' history, as he does not give much information on how the ships themselves were constructed either. It does seem odd, nonetheless, that this important device should appear all of a sudden with no mention made as to its provenance.

Polybius' account is likely a confused tradition, and his chronology may in fact be backward. It is far more reasonable to presume that the Romans were already fully knowledgeable about the defects of their ships, as well as of their crews, and had from the beginning planned to make use of their legionaries in the role of marines as their main naval weapon. That the Romans had intended upon using their ships as delivery platforms for their infantry is shown by the large complement of marines placed aboard. When battle was expected each ship carried 120 of them, with most, perhaps as many as 80, drawn from the legions.[8] When the Romans decided upon a fleet, it is a reasonable assumption that they thought carefully about how to stack the odds in their favour. Anything that would improve their chances of a successful boarding of an enemy ship would have been welcome.

The corvus was likely an adaptation of some other boarding device then in use, perhaps as simple as a plank, that had been used on war galleys beforehand. With their deep-rooted infantryman's mentality, it is possible that the corvus was derived from a siege engine's boarding system used to surmount city walls. The boarding-bridge atop a siege tower was not a new combination. Gangways had also been deployed by Alexander's Macedonians from the decks of their galleys against Tyre's walls during the same siege.[10] The use of a large boarding plank to cross from a ship to something else thus had a long history behind it. Dropping an object onto the deck of an enemy ship was also not a new concept either. The Athenians had erected beams aboard several of their merchant ships from which were hung 'dolphins' when they occupied the Great Harbour in Syracuse in 413. These devices are not described well by Thucydides, but presumably they were heavy metal objects that were dropped from a height sufficient to result in severe damage to two Syracusan triremes that, as Thucydides said, 'went too near' to the Athenian merchant vessels bearing down on them. Their impact was severe enough to sink one trireme outright and completely incapacitate a second, leading to its capture.[11]

The essence of Roman tactical thinking as embodied by the corvus may be discerned from the placement of the device at the fore of the ship. Polybius writes that if the galleys had come together side-by-side, the Romans could have used traditional means to board, but if the contact came prow-to-prow, the corvus would be deployed. The marines would then cross two abreast, with those in the lead holding their shields in front of them, while those that followed after would hold their shields to the sides for all-around defence.[12] With the corvus at the bow of their quinqueremes, the Romans avoided as much as possible the need for hard-to-execute manoeuvres to attack the sides or rear of a Carthaginian ship, which were still beyond the abilities of their inexperienced and untried rowers. They could instead go straight at the bows of the approaching enemy and drop the corvus on their decks. If the Carthaginians attempted to turn to avoid the device, they would expose their sides and rear to attack, against which the corvus (or the ram) would work equally well. The prior presence and possible use of the corvus may also help explain the lopsided Roman victory at the Cape of Italy, which Polybius leaves almost completely undescribed apart from the assertion that the Carthaginians lost most of their vessels in the encounter.[13] Why the Romans would be so disappointed in their ships' performance after a clear-cut victory that they would then embark upon a radical redesign of their quinqueremes is not considered by Polybius.

The Corvus in Operation

The corvus, which means 'raven', in Latin slang, is described by Polybius as an approximately 24ft tall pole of about 10" diameter. This was situated near to the prow of the quinquereme. A pulley was attached to the top of the pole, and this was connected to a gangplank that was 36ft long and 4ft in width, with railings on each side.¹⁴ An oblong slot was cut 12ft from one of the ends of the gangplank, and the pole was erected within this opening. The dimensions of this slot are not given. The gangplank could be turned about in an arc to the fore, port and starboard sides of the galley.¹⁵ At the other end of the gangplank was a downward thrusting iron spike with a ring on the unpointed end. Through this ring was run a rope, and this rope was connected to the pulley on the top of the pole. By pulling on the attached rope, the gangplank could be raised and lowered. By some means, not explicitly described, it could also be swung about. When lifted high in the air, it could be dropped down on the deck of an enemy ship with sufficient impact to lodge the spike in it.

Polybius relates only a bare-bones description of the corvus. A deeper inquiry would seem to have been required at this stage of his narrative. While it was not quite a wonder weapon in and of itself, as it needed Roman soldiers to rush across it to do the actual fighting, by Polybius' own estimation the corvus did allow the Romans to equalize the odds in naval combat and defeat the Carthaginians. Surely such a device deserved a more thorough examination of its construction and function than the meagre one that it received. It is plain the Polybius was not very interested in the mechanical workings of this mysterious appliance. We can only ponder why not, and use our own imagination to determine more about its usage.

A cottage industry of sorts developed in modern times around the reconstruction of the corvus.¹⁶ Significant portions of such writing on the subject seem to consist of lengthy examinations of other historians' ideas and the rejection of same on various grounds. Modern attempts to reconstruct the device often add unattested parts to it, such as guy ropes on the sides, or hinges, that Polybius does not mention and that need not have been included in the device for it to function. These are typically added so as to justify a historian's particular explanation as to how the corvus functioned. The corvus, however, was probably much simpler in form than the modern mind might suspect. The gangplank was raised and lowered by pulling or releasing the single rope spoken of by Polybius. The gangplank, he writes, could be turned about so that the gangplank could then be dropped on the deck of an enemy ship, but he does not specifically state that it was swivelled by means of the rope, or by any other implement. The simplest means of turning the boarding plank around the bow of the ship would have been by using the muscle power of the marines themselves. The oblong slot into which the pole was inserted probably would have had enough space in it so that the plank at its base could have been manhandled by the marines to point the spiked end in the direction of a Carthaginian target. Nothing else would have been necessary to raise the device and then turn it in a semicircular arc.

The crucial moment came when the boarding plank was dropped on the deck of an enemy galley. Polybius said that it had an iron spike affixed to the bottom of the far end of the plank. He compared its action to that of a pestle used to pound grain. The most important thing would be to ensure that the spike descended with sufficient force so that it could penetrate the deck of the target ship deeply enough so that it would remain lodged within it. The amount of force and the chance of actually sticking in the deck would have been contingent on several factors, including the height from which the gangplank was dropped, which presumably would have been raised near to the uppermost limit, which should have been close to 36ft; the weight of the end of the plank and its spike; and the thickness and sturdiness of the deck timbers into which the spike was being driven.

From the descriptions of the combat use of the corvus, which are very limited, it seems that the corvus did not have much trouble in lodging itself in Carthaginian ships. The standard Polybian narrative is that the corvus was dropped and the Carthaginian ships were stuck fast. Boarding then followed, and the Romans were victorious. Why were the Carthaginians unable to free themselves from the grasp of what was just a single spike with a gangplank attached? The size of the spike is not given by Polybius, but it cannot have been impossible to remove, especially when considering that the Romans themselves would have to be able to do so to free their own ships from their captures during and after the battle.

The bobbing and jostling of ships that had just collided violently must also have made the corvus vulnerable to dislodgment. The purchase provided by the business end of the corvus hardly seems to have been able to provide the unshakable grip that Polybius implies. The deck timbers could easily have split or the hole created by the spike widened just enough to make the attachment of the corvus to the deck insecure. Several armed and armoured men traversing it at once would also have added to the stresses placed upon it by the combined motion of the now-connected ships.

There is also the matter of the other end of the corvus, the pole and how it was attached to the boarding-bridge. This point of attachment had to be strong enough to resist the stresses placed upon it by the motion of ships while connected together by the bridge as well as the weight of several men rushing across it for an assault. Polybius does not tell us how the corvus pole was secured to the deck of the Roman ship that carried it. Common sense informs us that it must have been by a very stout bond to prevent the corvus from being ripped off the deck of the attacking Roman galley. Presumably the pole was inserted in a similar fashion to that of a mast, with a portion of it extending well below the deck. Had it been attached in a more flimsy manner, the corvus might have come loose on the Roman end of the device, and it is impossible to see how a Carthaginian galley would have remained fastened by it for any length of time. If the pole did not descend for some length below the deck then it would also have been vulnerable to snapping right off where the pole met the surface of the deck.

It is possible that the corvus pole was inspired by the boat mast, which was a shorter mast situated towards the bow of the quinquereme forward of the larger mainmast that sat approximately amidships. The boat mast was likely raked, that is, it leaned forward, but it could also have been set upright as was the corvus. Could the corvus pole have simply been the boat mast set in an upright position to which a boarding-bridge had been affixed? Polybius' description says nothing about that. On the other hand, he provides so few details as to not foreclose on the possibility either.

But Polybius is insistent that Carthaginian ships were held tightly by means of the corvus. The link created by the corvus with the enemy ship must therefore have been durable. This must have been due in part to a lengthy spike on the far end of the gangplank that would embed itself well enough in the Carthaginian ship's deck to endure the expected bobbing of the ships as well as a strongly set pole on the Roman ship. How long such a bond could be maintained under actual battle conditions is an open question. A reasonable solution is that Polybius' description of the corvus and its use is not so much flawed as it is not quite the whole story of a Roman boarding action from start to finish. A clue may be found in Polybius' description of how the corvus was employed. The corvus seems to have been used primarily as a means to board after prow-to-prow collisions. If the two ships had instead come alongside each other, the Romans could have boarded all along the length of the galleys without need of the corvus. The corvus, by implication, was a means of achieving a successful boarding primarily when ships had met at their bows. The single spike is unlikely to have been so robust as to prevent any and all means of dislodging it. There would certainly have been instances where the spike did not implant itself as firmly as the Romans would have wished. The attachment could only be considered temporary. It would have been of absolute importance for the Roman marines to rush across the boarding-bridge as soon as it had thumped down into the Carthaginian deck. There was no time to lose. Polybius writes that 'as soon as the [corvus] was embedded in the planks of the deck and fastened the ships together, the soldiers would leap into the enemy vessel'.[17]

Once the Romans had crossed via the boarding-bridge, and established themselves on the deck of the enemy craft, there is no doubt that other means of securing the ships together, such as grappling hooks, would have been used. Whatever limitations the corvus might have had in making a secure connection between ships was of little importance once it had allowed the Romans to board initially. The corvus, was not perfect, but it did grant speed to a Roman assault that allowed them to get onto the deck of an enemy ship quickly, and in sufficient numbers to overwhelm all opposition.

The Romans had clearly understood that to fight the Carthaginians in a battle of manoeuvre would be folly. There is no compelling reason to fight an enemy in the manner he prefers, and to try to match the rowing prowess of the Carthaginians would have been to neglect Rome's own greatest strength, its infantrymen. These were legionaries with years of experience in close combat. The confined space of a ship's deck would have been a suitable arena in which to make use of their skills.

As mentioned above, there exists the strong possibility that the Romans conceived of the implementation of the corvus at the same time that they decided to build their fleet. Repeated references to the heavier construction or poorer build quality of Roman ships compared to their Carthaginian counterparts highlights the edge that the enemy possessed in overall ship quality. This negative assessment of Roman shipwrightry would persist long after the First Punic War. As late as 191, when the Romans were fighting Antiochus III for control of the Aegean, there was the dim appraisal that Roman quinqueremes were 'unskillfully constructed and unwieldy'.[18]

That such a statement might be made over seventy years after Rome had built and deployed its first quinqueremes is startling. The Romans were noted for making quality items, especially things meant for battle. That its ships were perceived as being of a lower quality compared to those of the Carthaginians or the Hellenistic Greeks does not accord well with our picture of a Roman people who were mechanically talented and resourceful. The mystery is deepened further when one considers the tradition that Rome based the design of its quinqueremes on a captured Carthaginian example.

The reasonable expectation is that practice makes perfect, and that, whatever the defects in fit or finish might be found in the first copies to take to sea, Roman shipbuilders would at least have gotten the hang of things after the initial batch of quinqueremes had been completed. That they seem not to have made ships that were equal in build quality to those of their enemies is nevertheless alleged on a number of occasions, and does seem surprising. The superiority of individual enemy ships was readily acknowledged. Not long before the Battle of Drepana, for example, there was a Carthaginian captain named Hannibal who had acquired the moniker 'the Rhodian', probably as a result of his fine seamanship. The Romans captured his vessel, a quinquereme, which, upon examination, was commonly agreed to be of extremely good construction. By this judgment it is to be understood that it was deemed better than anything they themselves had, even after eleven years of sea war. The Romans were still the students in the field of naval architecture and construction.

The evidence suggests that the Romans may have preferred to build for quantity rather than quality. There is no sense that any other kind of Roman war material was similarly substandard. It should be remembered too that Rome's 'inferior' ships were not abysmal performers; they merely did not match up to Carthaginian equivalents.

Since there is no reason to doubt that the Roman ships were modelled on a Carthaginian craft, the differences between the original and the Roman copies can only be guessed at. Upon their arrival in Sicily Roman ships were noted as being poorly equipped and challenging to manoeuvre.[19] Given the speed with which the Romans brought their new fleet's ships into being in 260, they may have had to skimp on the materials used by selecting less than ideal woods for all or part of their construction. The weight of Roman ships may have been increased for this reason, and was perhaps also exacerbated by cruder, but presumably quicker, methods of joinery. The level of craftsmanship was probably not as high as that found in the typical Carthaginian ship. The ships may also have rotted sooner because of their presumed use of green wood, which decays more rapidly than seasoned wood.[20]

There is also the logical and very possible solution that the Romans meant for their ships to be heavier than Carthaginian quinqueremes all along, and that they successfully achieved this desired result. The excellence of the 'Rhodian' ship may have been due partly to its being built for speed and handling, not prow-to-prow collisions. That Polybius does not realize this may have been because he was himself a Greek, and was thereby more cognizant of all the qualities that made a war galley a useful weapon intended for ramming, the tactic that was considered more sophisticated in Greek naval war. The tradition that the Roman quinqueremes were copies of a Carthaginian ship is likely correct, but only up to a point. They were clearly not identical in all respects.[21] Roman quinqueremes were perhaps more ruggedly built (and thus heavier) so that they could better survive the expected shock of a bow-first collision with a Carthaginian ship, and then drop a corvus down upon it. The Roman quinquereme was probably 'designed' to carry the corvus, and the corvus was meant to be placed aboard a quinquereme optimized for the use of boarding tactics. It defies reason to argue that the Romans, aware of the inferior handling characteristics of their galleys, would have decided long after the completion of their construction to make them even *less* handy by emplacing tall poles and long boarding-bridges aboard them.

Once in battle, the Romans were labouring under the disadvantage of a heavier vessel that was also being propelled by inexperienced rowers, with their problems exacerbated by the towering and ungainly corvus at the prows of their ships. Some of this extra weight was also probably due to the more numerous complement of marines aboard the ship. At this early stage of the war, the Romans almost certainly were carrying more marines per ship than the Carthaginians were. If the marines aboard were at full strength, they alone would have added a minimum of several tons to the overall weight that the oarsmen needed to move over and above the weight of the ship and its rowing crew. A Carthaginian galley with fewer marines aboard would not have experienced this drawback to the same degree.

The Roman penchant for carrying large numbers of infantry aboard their galleys would also explain why their ships were considered to be clumsier in operation long after the fleet had apparently dispensed with the corvus and should have learned how to make ships equal in quality to all comers. They may have given up on the corvus, but not on boarding tactics. Their marines would have been a hindrance to manoeuvre with a corvus present or without one, but a heavier, stouter ship would have still conferred many of the same advantages when attempting to board an enemy vessel. Taken altogether, it is a small wonder that the Roman captains should complain of the demands of directing such a craft at sea. Also, improbable as it may seem, the very historicity of the corvus has been dismissed as fiction on the grounds that the device would have rendered any ship carrying one completely unstable.[22] Given the paucity of the source materials at hand, which tell us very little about the origin of the corvus, it shall simply have to be stipulated that a corvus was sitting on the decks of Rome's quinqueremes in time for the Battle of Mylae in 260.

Chapter Eight

Mylae, 260 BC: Rome's Fleet Sails in Harm's Way

Now that Duilius was in charge of the fleet, he cannot have been entirely happy with what he found waiting for him at Messana. Though the good showing of the fleet off the Cape of Italy would have been the cause of a measure of optimism, other concerns must have weighed on the consul's mind. Scipio's ill-considered mission to Lipara and the loss of his squadron there had reduced Rome's own total fleet size by seventeen without costing the enemy a single ship in return. The fleet's captains were themselves unhappy with the performance of their ships and crews in the battle at the Cape, and felt that they had allowed the Carthaginians to escape because of their slow and bulky galleys. Roman crews were green and could not handle their ships well. The quinqueremes were big and slow, unlike the more nimble Carthaginian ships. Then there was the matter of the corvus. Duilius had arrived after the work to install them had started and let it continue. He was far more comfortable with war on land. What did he really know about fighting at sea? That was supposed to have been left to his colleague Scipio to deal with, but he was now languishing in Carthaginian captivity. Duilius would certainly have preferred to continue the fight against Carthage's army in Sicily rather than its navy. Right now, he had no choice in the matter. The corvus was a dubious looking contraption. It was ungainly, and resembled nothing so much as a boarding-bridge that would have been placed atop a siege tower. If it made boarding faster and easier, and Duilius must have hoped that it would, then he would give it a try. Anything that got his seasick marines onto the decks of enemy ships quickly deserved a chance.

Duilius gave orders that his ships would sail to intercept the Carthaginians who were despoiling the coasts around Mylae. The Carthaginians, under the command of Hannibal, once again, saw his fleet approach and quickly boarded their own ships. They were ready to get to grips with Roman seamen that they knew were not their equals in sea warfare. They outnumbered the Romans, with 130 ships to the enemy's 103. Polybius says that 'they all sailed straight for the enemy, like predators after easy prey'.[1] There can be no doubt that the Carthaginians had every right to expect victory. The Romans were new to the game, while the Carthaginians as a people had centuries-long heritage on naval mastery. What could go wrong?

As it turned out, many things could and did go wrong. The Carthaginian captains of the leading group of thirty quinqueremes made no pretence of arraying their ships in a proper battle formation. They were too confident for their own good. In attacking the Romans before they were formed up, they sacrificed all the advantage that a formation would bring. Ships travelling in close proximity could immediately lend support to one another. The presence of friendly ships besides them would protect them from attacks on their sides. A stricken ship could be rescued by a friendly one before it was either overwhelmed or sank. Instead the Carthaginians attacked without the mass that their larger fleet should have provided.

The Carthaginians bravely bore down on the Romans, and their quinqueremes crashed together in a mass of shattering timbers. The difference in this encounter was the corvus. Once these ravens had dropped down on the decks of their ships, the Romans held them fast. There was no escape. The Roman marines clambered aboard the bridge. Rushing across it, their tall shields held high on every side, they threw their pila to drive the enemy away. Once on an enemy deck, the Roman soldiers were at an advantage. They were better hand-to-hand fighters. They were better protected. They probably outnumbered the Carthaginian marines by a substantial margin too. Holding his shield out in front of him, a Roman marine would punch with his shield and then stab with his sword. His shield would also limit his vulnerability to Carthaginians' missiles, such as the deadly bullets launched by mercenary slingers from the Balearic Islands. His training was good too. He knew enough not to become separated from his comrades. With them at his side, a Roman soldier's flanks were defended. He could not be taken down from behind. It was a bloody but methodical business.

His enemy was also not as highly motivated as he was. Carthage's reliance on mercenaries or the contributed troops of allied and vassal states was necessary, as she did not have the population base to sustain large armies composed entirely of her own native citizens.[2] It also placed her fleet at a disadvantage when Rome made the battle turn on several small infantry battles on the decks of Carthaginian ships. A close-in fight required aggression and discipline, and in these areas Carthage's marines were overmatched.

The Carthaginians were shocked by these new tactics. The corvus was an innovation, true, but boarding was not an unknown tactic by any means. Their surprise must have arisen from the sheer speed with which the Romans assaulted their ships with such large numbers of men. In situations where the corvus was not used, it is most probable that the Carthaginians relied on their skill at the oars to extricate their ships from contact with an opposing vessel before the fight could be transformed into a hand-to-hand action. The corvus foreclosed any such possibility. The Carthaginian galley was going nowhere fast with a big spike driven deep into its deck. With the advantage of time, the Romans were able to overrun the enemy ship, and make the fight into what they had always desired: an infantry battle at sea.

The first thirty ships to engage the Romans were all captured through the use of the corvus. Hannibal's spectacular flagship, a massive septireme, or 'seven', that had itself once been the pride of Pyrrhus' fleet, was taken. Hannibal was forced to flee ignominiously in a small boat that the seven carried.[3] Now the rest of the fleet arrived. Polybius says that the first ships to make contact with the Romans had not known what the ravens were, but the following ships were now wary of them, after seeing how their brethren had been boarded and taken. So they manoeuvred, trying to stay out of reach of the corvus and attempt a ram on the sides and rear of the Roman ships. The corvus could be deployed in an arc to the fore and sides of the prow, but not much further aft. As described by Polybius, the flank and rear attacks failed. The Romans turned the corvi this way and that and grabbed hold of the faster Carthaginian ships. Since the corvus itself was exclusively mounted at the bow of a quinquereme, it cannot be that it negated an attack on the sides or rear of an individual ship. Instead, it must have been the case that the battle had become a disorganized melee in which Roman ships were entangled with previously-captured Carthaginian galleys. The later-coming Carthaginian ships were almost certainly struck by Roman ships other than the ones that they had tried to attack, which could deploy their corvus in support of a threatened friendly vessel. There was no counter to the corvus. The Carthaginians had approached expecting a very different type of battle from the one that they experienced. By its end, they had lost fifty quinqueremes.[4] Roman losses are not given by Polybius.

Rome had won a resounding victory at sea. The corvus was the key to making up all of the deficits in nautical skill and ship construction that existed between the Roman and Carthaginian fleets. It also enabled them to make up a shortfall in ship numbers. Polybius does not give the total size of the Roman force at Mylae, but there is scant reason to believe that it was any different in size from the fleet that sailed south and fought in the earlier battle at the toe of Italy. Of the initial production run of 100 quinqueremes and 20 triremes, it is most probable that the Romans would have had 103 ships at sea for Mylae, when taking into account the loss of the 17 ships at Lipara. The Roman fleet may also have been augmented by the incorporation of captures from the earlier fight at the toe of Italy or by ships from their Italian Greek naval allies, but this is not certain.[5] Nowhere is there mention of a reinforcement of any size of the original fleet that had sailed to Sicily, which was likely just 103 in number, being the remainder of the 260 building programme.

Duilus was the man of the hour back in Rome, where he was given the first-ever triumph in honour of a naval victory. He hung several bronze rams taken from the prows of the captured Carthaginian galleys on the speaker's platform in the Forum. From this came the practice of calling such a platform the *rostrum*, or beak, which is what they called the prow of the ship. Musicians went wherever he did as he walked the streets of Rome in the wake of his victory. He also set up the *columna rostrata* inscription to mark his great exploit against the Carthaginian navy, along with several bronze rams taken from captured Punic warships.

Hannibal, on the other hand, was no one's hero. He wisely stayed away from Carthage after the battle. Diodorus reports that his fear of punishment by the Carthaginian senate was so great that he sent a friend of his to the mother city to ask the senators whether Hannibal should give battle if he, when in possession of a fleet of 200 ships, should come across a Roman fleet of just 120. The senators loudly agreed that in that case, yes, Hannibal should certainly engage the Romans. 'Very well', Hannibal's friend replied to their enthusiastic affirmation, 'that is just why Hannibal did fight, and we have been beaten. But since you commanded it, he is relieved of the blame.'[6] Had Hannibal just half the instinct for naval tactics that he had for shrewd politics the outcome of the war might have been very different.

The Problem of the Corvus at Mylae

The corvus was a rare thing in ancient warfare. It was a truly original means of attacking an enemy ship. It completely dominated the action from the moment of its first use. Like the Byzantine 'Greek Fire' of the Middle Ages, it gave the possessor an almost insuperable advantage in battle. The surprise employment of the boarding device was such that the Carthaginian seamen were left dumbfounded by the rapidity of the Roman marine assaults on their ships and their inability to escape once they had been grappled by the corvus. The lopsided outcome also vindicated the Roman approach to naval warfare in another way. By seeking out prow-to-prow collisions, the Romans did away with the need for fancy, Athenian-style manoeuvring which required a high degree of training to effect. The Athenians had been the past masters of the ramming attack, but they too had found the opportunity to use their skill at the oar circumscribed when they fought in Syracuse's packed Great Harbour in 413.[7] The Syracusans consciously decided to use Corinthian-style head-on tactics to make up for their disadvantage in crew training and skill. They had gone so far as to equip their triremes with reinforced bows to better absorb the shock of impact, just as the Corinthians had at Erineus, which succeeded in knocking several Athenian triremes out of action.[8] Though the battle's result was a draw, brute force had definitely trumped sophisticated Athenian manoeuvring in the tight confines of the harbour, as it did also at Mylae.

The Romans did not have the benefit of a geographically-narrowed battlespace, but the corvus provided something that closely approximated it. The Romans turned their sea fights into replicas of the clashes inside Syracuse's Great Harbour by dropping the corvus onto enemy ships. Every naval battle then became a boarding fight.[9] It may be presumed that the Romans kept their ships relatively close together when seeking to engage in prow-to-prow ramming. Since the goal was to force a collision with the bow of an enemy vessel, a close-order battle formation would prevent opposing ships from slipping between approaching Roman galleys. The need of these ships for room to manoeuvre was minimal apart from that necessary for the unimpeded use of their oars. There was no reason for the Romans to try to ram the sides or stern of a Carthaginian vessel if a straight-on ram would do the trick. The enemy galley would not sink this way, but it would be open to capture once Rome's marines had boarded. The corvus made getting away very hard. This 'shock' approach to naval combat also had the virtue of limiting the vulnerability of Roman quinqueremes to attacks on their sides and sterns. Rome's quinqueremes were staying close together, like heavy cavalry, while the Carthaginians were prevented by the corvus from employing their faster and swarming light cavalry-style tactics.

While the Carthaginians are claimed to have had 130 galleys at Mylae, and thus outnumbered the Romans, they sent their ships into combat piecemeal, and did not make effective use of their numbers. The first thirty were quickly overcome, and then these were followed by an unknown number of other ships which met a similar fate. It is possible that the full Carthaginian fleet did not even engage in the battle. The Romans, in this view, defeated the 'vanguard' of the Carthaginian fleet, and then dealt with the limited number that arrived in the second wave. With discretion being the better part of valour, the remaining Carthaginian galleys may have turned and made their escape. The Romans thereby may have met and defeated only a portion of the Carthaginian force present. Nevertheless, the victory was total.

The context of the battle raises an intriguing question. Why did Hannibal and the Carthaginians approach the Romans with such confidence when they had so recently suffered a serious defeat at the Cape of Italy? From Polybius, it would seem that little time had elapsed between the first engagement and that of Mylae. 'Their spirits were high', writes Polybius, and they 'eagerly put to sea' as soon as the Roman fleet was spotted.[10] This does not sound like the reaction of a force that had just been defeated by the same Roman fleet. One would have expected a more careful approach to the Roman ships than the one that occurred. Instead the Carthaginians displayed an arrogance that bordered on foolhardiness. Hannibal, an already defeated admiral, inexplicably seems to have led the charge against the Romans. Surely the best seafarers in the Mediterranean would have utilized better tactics than what was on offer at Mylae.

There is a theory that Polybius misinterpreted the sources at hand and did not realize that the battle at the Cape of Italy and Mylae were one and the same. In this view, the Cape engagement was actually Mylae as described by Polybius' pro-Carthaginian source, Philinus. Polybius' account of Mylae was the same battle as derived from a pro-Roman source. Without doubt, there are similarities to both battles. The Carthaginians were not in proper formation for battle when the engagements began. Could their disorganized entries into each fight have been describing the very same haphazard movements to contact? In each case, the Romans are the ones in good formation, while the Carthaginians are not. In both battles, the Carthaginians either have no foreknowledge of the location of the Roman fleet (the Cape) or manned their ships only after becoming aware of the Roman presence nearby (Mylae). Also, both fights end with Hannibal escaping with his surviving ships. Doing away with the first encounter would help explain why the Carthaginians were so full of confidence that they rashly attacked the Romans at Mylae.

A certain answer is beyond reach. If the first fight at the Cape was the Carthaginian account of Mylae, then it lacks mention of the corvus, which was otherwise of immense importance at Mylae. The simplest answer on this point is to accept that Polybius was correct when he asserted that the corvus was fitted only after the fleet had reached Sicily. The reason why the corvus does not receive a mention in the Cape battle is because it was not yet present. Also, there is the matter of Polybius' quality as a historian. It is hard to accept that he would have been working with two separate accounts of the same battle and not recognized them for what they were. If he had an account from a Carthaginian source for the first fight at the Cape, he would certainly have then asked why it did not also mention Mylae.[11]

There is the possibility that the Romans could have had the corvi aboard their ships from the start but only put them into use at Mylae. Every galley had a main mast, as well as a smaller boat mast forward of the main mast, but these could either be lowered or removed when battle was expected. In combat it provided no benefit because the ship would rely exclusively in its rowers for propulsion, and a rigged mast would just have slowed the vessel. In some cases they were even left ashore. There does not seem to have been much fuss about lowering or extracting a mast from a warship, and this was done as a matter of course. Why should the corvus have been any more trouble to lower or to detach than a mast? It may have been a simpler matter altogether. It stands to reason that if a mast could be taken down when battle was anticipated, then it should have been possible to lower the corvus when battle was not expected and the Roman fleet was simply travelling, as it was at the time of the Cape encounter.

Once lowered or removed, both the pole and the boarding-bridge could have been laid down on the deck when not needed for immediate employment. This would solve the problem as to why the corvus is not mentioned in either the Lipara harbour encounter or in the engagement at the Cape of Italy. In both instances, the Romans were themselves not expecting to do battle with the enemy, and thus may not have had the corvus upright and ready for action. Then, upon arriving in Sicily, they erected the corvi on their decks and thereafter sought battle.

Polybius may have interpreted use of the corvus at Mylae as being the result of an idea that struck them just then, after reaching Sicily, but instead it may only have been the first occasion on which the Romans could deploy it. The Carthaginians would thus have been surprised by the appearance of the corvus as they would not have seen it in use in the putative earlier battle at the Cape. This particular supposition, which is all that it is, would at least accord with the broad outline of the account given by Polybius of the early battles of the Roman navy with that of Carthage while not raising any concerns as to the time it would have taken to construct and fit these new devices onto the decks of Roman ships in Sicily.

To add another wrinkle to the problem, it should be noted that the inscription left by Duilius on his *columna rostrata* made the assertion that he was the *first* Roman to secure a victory over a Carthaginian fleet.[12] What are we to make of this extraordinary claim? Should we simply accept it at face value? Surely there would have been many men who had participated in his triumph who also would have been present at the battle at the Cape of Italy before Duilius had arrived to take command of it. Would not every last one of them have said something about the victory that had preceded Mylae while Duilius was being celebrated as the great hero? This prior battle at the Cape had resulted in the loss of more than twenty-five ships by the Carthaginians, a not inconsiderable number. We can assume that Duilius was not an ignoble and glory-hungry fool who would go so far as to blithely ignore the earlier engagement when so many of his crews would have taken part in it. If our numbers are anywhere close to accurate then Duilius' Mylae fleet would have been in all essentials the same fleet of 103 that had departed Rome at some time after Scipio had sailed for Lipara.

If we take Polybius' figures of 300 oarsmen and 120 marines as standard, that gives 420 men per quinquereme, with a smaller number for each of the triremes. A conservative estimate is that there would have been approximately 40,000 men aboard the fleet of 103 galleys, quinqueremes and triremes, at the Cape engagement. Certainly they would have complained if their achievement there had been slighted by the consul and this would have been noted in the historical record in some form or another. The simplest explanation is that the historicity of the Cape battle is doubtful, or else Duilius, as boastful as he may have been in setting up the *columna rostrata*, would not have etched such an untruthful claim in stone. This oddity lends support to the idea that the Cape battle was just another version of the Battle of Mylae, and thus that Polybius' account of the origin of the corvus is also spurious. One possible explanation for Polybius' problematic account is that he was so tightly wedded to his own origin-story of the corvus, for reasons unknown, that he missed its inherent logical flaw, despite his quality as a historian.

Chapter Nine

After Mylae

There would be an ebb and flow to the naval war after Mylae. The Romans would tend toward big efforts in which they put large numbers of ships (and of course, men) to sea. Would it have been a superior strategy to have maintained a more constant pressure on Carthage at sea as opposed to these major pulses? Were there limitations on Roman strategy that are not immediately apparent in the historical record? It is possible that the Romans were pressing at the upper limit of their logistical capability. Their manpower may not have been sufficient to meet the enormous needs of both the fleet with its many ships and the legions at the same time. The sheer cost of manning and maintaining a fleet for an extended period was almost certainly prohibitive. Every quinquereme was carrying some eighty legionaries who were thereby not available for service with the legions on land. There may have been upwards of one-and-a-half legions' worth of *infantry* at sea at Mylae. Such a force had to be drawn from somewhere, and that was the army. The potency of any operations that it undertook must have declined, and perhaps were even put off until the soldiers could be returned. The naval allies also likely wished to be released from service. A large number of them were foreigners, i.e. non-Romans, whether Greek or Italian, and they could not have been enthusiastic about lengthy terms of service with the fleet. A mutiny in 259 of Samnites conscripted for naval service shows that dissension with Rome's naval campaigns was very real.[1] The Samnites also seem to have been in league with Carthaginian prisoners of war as well as some slaves for the conspiracy, so the threat of insurrection could not be dismissed.[2]

During the Napoleonic Wars, Britain maintained an enormous navy, but the size of its army deployed to the Continent was (usually) relatively small. Britain preferred to subsidize her European allies so that they could keep large armies in the field, thus enabling it to concentrate on outbuilding Napoleon's fleet. For Rome, the demands of war on both land and sea would have been even especially acute because it could not rely upon its allies to supply the large numbers of troops required to keep the Carthaginians occupied in Sicily while at the same time she asked them to man a fleet numbering in the hundreds of ships.

Reducing the number of Roman ships at sea may also have been related to concerns about the return of naval allies to their homes. Many of the crewmen would have been Italian Greeks, and in some respects they would have found the Romans to be just as foreign as the Carthaginian enemy. Most would have preferred to be home, to help with the harvest, and to provide for their families. There may have been a ceiling on what Rome could expect from its allies.

For the time being at least, the Romans had won control of the sea. The naval advantage that they now possessed made them more assured and this increased their resolve to continue the fight against Carthage. Duilius followed up his victory at Mylae by renewing pressure on the Carthaginians in Sicily. Duilius lifted the siege of Segesta, an inland city in the north-western corner of Sicily. On his return (probably to Messana), he took the city of Macella in a rapid assault. The Romans did not everywhere enjoy success. There was a seven month long siege of Myttistratum that failed.[3] Though the fortunes of war at sea now favoured Rome, this was not enough to bring about a collapse of the Carthaginian position on the island. Far from reeling, the Carthaginians were now holding on grimly as they had for centuries in the face of powerful opponents. It was critical that they keep at least one base for themselves on the island. If they could do this, they could eventually reinforce their position and then reverse their losses. A war of sieges also allowed the Carthaginians to lessen the great Roman advantage in open battle. Sieges were brutal affairs for all involved. While on the defence, at least, Carthage would not have to ask as much of its army of mercenaries and allied troops, and would need to secure the services of fewer of them than would be required for an offensive war.

Carthage's approach to warfare would prove to be an important difference between it and Rome. Sicily is a hilly island, and in ancient times most of the inhabitants lived in fortified towns. What ensued in the years after Mylae was grinding siege warfare. One investment followed upon another. There was no great advance to be made during this period. Rome's generals (the consuls) were elected to one year posts, and their control over their armies ended with the expiration of their time in office. This constant turnover in command was ill-suited to the slow pace of Sicilian warfare, which required the patient and relentless application of military pressure against Carthaginian strongholds to bring success. While the introduction of new consuls every year meant that more Roman aristocrats were able to attain the prestigious position of consul, and possibly win martial glory on the battlefield, the system hardly encouraged long-range planning. In distinction, the Carthaginians kept their victorious (they crucified the losers) generals in place for years at a time. They understood the nature of the war that they were fighting and were content to stand on the defensive and let the Romans batter themselves against the walls of their cities.[4] Over time, and at fantastic cost, the Romans would reduce the Carthaginian presence to just a handful of major fortress seaports, such as Lilybaeum and

Drepana. Much of the land and naval war would come to revolve around the sieges and blockades of these strong places.

Rome's strategy in the aftermath of Mylae has been questioned as to why it was not succeeded immediately by further naval operations against Carthage. It is probable that Rome recognized that while the Punic navy had been defeated, it had not been destroyed. Hannibal had retired from the Mylae battle with about eighty ships, and there must have been more in Carthage's possession elsewhere for his reinforcement.[5] The operational range of the galley fleets also placed limits on what Rome could hope to achieve right away. Carthaginian strength was centred on several strongly-fortified cities, including Panormus in the north-west, Lilybaeum in the west, and Heraclea Minoa on the southern coast. These cities were located to protect Carthage's lines of supply to its forces in Sicily. Rome could not hope to cut them because its own ships were based too far away to intercept those of Carthage.[6]

The Carthaginians did show some offensive spirit in the wake of these setbacks on land and sea. Their general, Hamilcar, at his base of Panormus (Palermo) received word that the Romans and their allies had begun squabbling over the award of battle honours, never a safe thing to do in the midst of a war, and perhaps a sign that overconfidence, the bane of many successful campaigns, had gotten the best of the Romans and her Italian allies to such an extent that they could descend into argument about awards and not worry too much about the enemy. Rome's allies had become so disaffected that they packed up their baggage and detached themselves from the Roman army completely, going so far as to set up a camp of their own in the area between Paropus and the hot springs of Himera. Hamilcar took advantage of the chaos in the Roman camp, assembled his army, and fell upon the allied troops as they marched from their former camp to their new one. The result was a slaughter of some 4,000 of the allied force.[7]

In Sicily, 259 saw little progress for the Romans and Polybius declines even to give details concerning the events of the year. Zonaras records a Roman naval expedition/raid on Corsica and Sardinia commanded by consul Lucius Cornelius Scipio, the brother of the unlucky Scipio Asina who was trapped at Lipara. He says that the Romans first took Aleria, Corsica's biggest city, and then subdued the rest of the island. The fleet then sailed on to Sardinia where a Carthaginian naval force was sighted. Scipio pursued but the faster Carthaginian ships escaped. He next came to the city of Olbia on the island's north-eastern coast. There he found an enemy garrison waiting, and the Carthaginian fleet had also appeared. He departed, Zonaras writes, because he had insufficient infantry with him.[8] Whether this lack of troops aboard caused him to decline to prosecute either a siege of Olbia or to fight a naval battle, for which Roman tactics would have required large numbers of marines, is not stated. It can be presumed that both reasons were equally valid.

The Romans again took the offensive in 258 under the new consuls, Aulus Atilius Caiatinus and Gaius Sulpicius Paterculus.[9] The consuls marched on the Carthaginian base at Panormus, hoping that the enemy would emerge to give battle. The Carthaginians instead decided to remain behind their walls, and so the Romans contented themselves with capturing several other cities, including Hippana, Myttistratum, Enna, and Camarina. The town of Lipara, in the Aeolian Islands, and the scene of the humiliation of Scipio Asina in 260, was blockaded.[10]

Hannibal, whom we had last seen escaping from the scene at Mylae, took the surviving portion of his fleet to Carthage where he remained for a short time to restore his ships. He again readied his fleet for action, taking with him some of the best captains in Carthage to Sardinia. Paterculus had earlier landed troops there and had taken much of the island. After Hannibal had put in to port, the consul departed and set sail for Africa. This seems to have been a stratagem of some sort to get Hannibal to come out to fight, as Zonaras claims that the Romans had made their intention of striking at Africa known to the Carthaginian commander via 'false deserters'.[11] If so, then the deception worked. Hannibal hurriedly weighed anchor and rowed out to follow the Romans ships. In the ensuing battle off Sulci, Paterculus sank most of Hannibal's vessels, aided by a mist that had come up and hid much of what was going on from the confused Carthaginians. Hannibal fled and made landfall at Sulci. He abandoned his surviving ships in the harbour, which he considered indefensible. Paterculus seized these ships as Hannibal retreated with his crews into the city. Hannibal's men were not grateful for the move, even though it was to the greater security of Sulci. They took matters into their own hands, arrested him, and in keeping with longstanding Carthaginian tradition, crucified the unlucky admiral.[12]

The year 257 saw a naval action take place off Cape Tyndaris (Tindari) on Sicily's northern coast. The commander of the Roman fleet, consul Gaius Atilius Regulus, learned that the Carthaginian fleet was sailing nearby but out of formation. While the consul's own squadron was already at sea, and hurriedly raised anchor, the rest of the Roman fleet was still readying itself, with their men either still getting aboard or just beginning to sail. Though left unsaid by Polybius, the fleet may have been engaging in one of the periodic drying-outs necessary for maintaining the ships in good fighting trim. The approach of the Carthaginian fleet caught them by surprise as they were returning their ships to the water. In this position, the Romans were extremely vulnerable. Those vessels that could make headway were probably seriously outnumbered by the

Carthaginians, and the ships ashore or not yet fully prepared were dangerously exposed to attack.[13]

Regulus elected to strike at the Carthaginians with the ten ships that he had at his immediate disposal, no doubt to protect the rest of his fleet as it struggled to get off the beach. The consul's squadron headed straight for the enemy, was surrounded, and sunk, with the exception of Regulus' own vessel, which Polybius tells us owed its escape to its having a full crew aboard.[14] After this initial, lopsided engagement, the rest of the Roman fleet arrived on the scene and formed a line of battle. The combination of Corinthian-style prow ramming tactics and the corvus proved decisive, with the Romans sinking eight Carthaginian galleys and capturing ten others. The Carthaginians turned and fled to their base in the Aeolian (Lipari) Islands.[15]

Polybius' account of the action off Cape Tyndaris is hardly satisfying. Numbers for neither side are given, a *sine qua non* of a worthwhile analysis of a battle. Of the course of the action we are told little besides the consul's early sortie against the cruising Carthaginian fleet. Roman losses are not mentioned except to say that nine of the ships in the consul's squadron were sunk. The reasonable assumption to make about the first phase of the battle was that the Romans were badly outnumbered, and that they were overwhelmed by Carthage's galleys. Ramming tactics could be very effective, but here the Carthaginians certainly benefited from a numerical advantage that negated that danger of the corvus to them. The corvus is left oddly unmentioned in the account, though there can be little doubt that the Romans had them aboard their galleys and that they used them to good effect just as they had at Mylae. This would explain the rapidity with which the Romans turned the tide of the battle once the bulk of their fleet joined the engagement. Given the available, if limited, evidence, the most suitable interpretation of the fight off Tyndaris is that the Romans possessed the more effective fleet at this stage of the war.

Chapter Ten

Ecnomus, 256 BC

The outcome of the Tyndaris fight convinced both the Romans and the Carthaginians that their naval forces were on a par with each other. This understanding caused both to increase their efforts at sea. Polybius writes that in this phase of the war 'the land-based armies did nothing worth recording, but occupied themselves with minor and incidental engagements'.[1] Though it might be easy to take Polybius to task for passing over these engagements without further comment, and wish that he had been more assiduous in detailing the events of the post-Tyndaris period in Sicily, his ignoring of the small actions does fit with the model of land and naval activity established in the wake of the Battle of Mylae. Rome and Carthage were so evenly matched in total military power that for one to concentrate heavy resources on either land or sea forces would mean weakening the other, perhaps dangerously. Such efforts could not be made every year, or sustained for very long. This was especially the case in the naval sphere, because the fleet required such large numbers of men to serve as both rowers and shipboard marines. For the Romans, these last would have to have been drawn from the Sicilian legions, and thus they would have depleted the land forces available for sieges and other operations on the island.

The Roman naval armament of 256 was staggering. The Romans launched a fleet, ready for action by the summer of that year, of 330 quinqueremes. This dwarfed the size of the first one that put to sea in 260, and is evidence of the scale of Roman ambition for the year's campaign. Such a naval force would have needed 99,000 rowers if each galley were to be crewed fully. This figure does not encompass each vessel's complement of marines nor its ancillary crewmen. If every ship carried its standard contingent of 120 marines, then another 39,600 men were also at sea with the fleet that sailed to Messana that summer. The total of 138,600 rowers and marines is nothing short of astonishing, and ought to elicit a sense of wonder at what a pre-industrial civilization such as Rome could achieve. From a logistical standpoint, the construction of so many ships, of which many must have been newly built, is remarkable. That nearly 140,000 men were mustered, trained, divided into ships' companies and their associated marine complements, was outstanding, and a testament to the Roman genius for organization.

Though Polybius spends little time on it, the preparation of the 256 expeditionary fleet must have been made possible only as a result of a maximum national effort. Rome itself could not have supplied all of the men for the ships. Later in his history, when discussing Roman preparations to defend against an invasion of Gauls in 225, Polybius gives a detailed overview of the numbers of infantry and cavalry available for service to Rome when including the contributions of her Italian allies. The total given by him is 770,000.[2] That figure, however, was the result of the willing support of other Italians, who felt themselves threatened by the Gallic invasion too. The prospect of naval service against Carthage would not have elicited such eager aid to Rome. To fully crew so many ships would thus have required contributions from her naval allies at a higher level than had been demanded in other years, and would not have been provided so willingly. This naval service can hardly have been popular, but it is probable that for most involved it was not meant to last for very long, as events will show. The naval campaign was likely envisioned as one of short duration, perhaps only for the summer, with the men from other Italian cities to be released as soon as the need for them was over, in time perhaps to return home to help out with the harvest.

With the Roman fleet at Messana, its next move was to sail south along the eastern coast of Sicily, round Cape Pachynus (Cape Passero), and then sail to Ecnomus (modern Poggio Di Sant'Angelo), where some of the Roman army was currently operating so that they could embark legionaries. The object of this tremendous armada was to bring the war to Africa, and make it 'the main theatre of the war instead of Sicily'.[3] Rome's strategy for 256 had some logic to it. By bringing the war to Africa, a war that in Sicily bore all of the hallmarks of a stalemate, the Romans must have hoped to either force Carthage to withdraw enough troops from Sicily to fatally weaken its position there or perhaps even to strike a fatal blow at Carthage itself. They had certainly embarked enough soldiers aboard their ships to make the conquest of Carthage a real possibility.

Yet does the Roman plan hold together upon examination? That can only be answered by determining what exactly Rome's war aims were. She had originally gone to war out of fear as to what a Carthaginian-dominated island might mean for the safety of Italy. In that case, an invasion of Africa was not the best move. The Romans would have been better served by getting the Carthaginians out of Sicily first. This was the reason for her intervention at Messana eight years previously. The Carthaginians had proven that they could recover lost territory in Sicily by retaining just a single fortified port from which to launch a reconquest. The Romans also knew from bitter experience just how formidable Carthaginian defences were. The fortress city of Lilybaeum was especially well defended. Only by conquering that and every other Carthaginian possession would the Romans be assured of mastery of Sicily. Until that time, their own holdings there would be vulnerable to attack by Carthaginian armies.

What about an attack on Carthage? Wouldn't this have succeeded in ejecting the Carthaginians from the island too? It is reasonable to assume so, but success would have required inflicting such a terrible defeat on Carthage that she would be willing to evacuate Sicily completely so as to ensure her own survival. The outright conquest of Carthage would also have probably provoked the fall of Carthaginian Sicily, as garrisons either surrendered or were overcome, bereft of further support. The premise of the African expedition seems not so much wrong as not the best use to which to put the vast fleet assembled at such great expense could have been put in 256. The proper target for that year should have been Lilybaeum and Carthage's other Sicilian possessions. Once these had been cut off from outside help by the fleet, the Roman army could have captured them. Then Rome would have had Sicily to itself and its allies; its use as a springboard for an invasion of Italy would have been removed; and the threat of a Carthaginian counterattack on the island would have been very much reduced. If Carthage proved recalcitrant and unwilling to make peace, it could have been dealt with the following year, if necessary, by an attack on Africa.

Given the successes that the Romans had enjoyed, especially those of 258, when it had taken numerous Carthaginian strongholds in Sicily, it could be asked why they decided to so radically alter their strategy and take the war to Africa. A (mostly) Sicily-only strategy had been paying dividends if the list of successes in 258 is to be believed. It may be that overall Roman military policy was subject to change as old consuls departed and new ones took up their commands, though the scale of Rome's endeavour in 256 would almost certainly have required the strong backing of the Senate. There seems to be no compelling reason why the Romans embarked on such a massive alteration in strategic focus away from Sicily. Polybius gives an insight into Roman thinking when he says that the Romans wanted the Carthaginians 'to feel that their very existence and their homeland were at risk'.[4] The Carthaginians, for their part, were anxious about such a possibility, considering Libya to be weak and incapable of resisting Romans' arms should the enemy come in force. To prevent this possibility, the Carthaginians were ready to assemble a fleet that could meet and defeat the Roman expeditionary fleet before it reached Africa.

The Roman fleet was prepared for a major sea action too. The cream of their legions was distributed among the ships of the fleet, which was itself divided into four squadrons. The First Legion was paired with the First Squadron, the Second Legion with the Second Squadron, and so on. The land-minded Romans even went so far as to retain the term *triarii*, as they named the third (and rearmost) line of their battleline on land, for legionaries that they paired with the Fourth Squadron. It is plain that the Romans wanted for nothing more than to fight a land battle at sea.[5]

We have seen that the Romans mustered an unprecedented number of men to serve with the fleet. The Carthaginians matched them with an outstanding effort of their own, though no doubt they resorted to their time-honoured expedient of hiring mercenaries of one sort or another. The Punic fleet of 256 numbered 350 ships, of which some would have been survivors of earlier campaigns and others newly constructed craft. Interestingly, Polybius writes that the Carthaginians 'equipped their ships almost exclusively for fighting at sea'.[6] This is an odd statement when one considers that fighting at sea is what warships did. It is comprehensible when it is understood that what Polybius meant by it was that the Carthaginians had organized their fleet solely for battle, a pure battlefleet, while that of the Romans was a composite invasion force including horse transports carrying mounts needed for fighting on land in Africa. The number of men that Polybius believes were embarked with the Carthaginian fleet is set at 150,000. Polybius' arithmetic is difficult to fathom, but it appears that he assumes that the Carthaginian quinqueremes at this date were carrying even more rowers and marines than a Roman warship did to allow him to arrive at the 150,000 figure. This was not impossible if the Carthaginians had decided, after having received several drubbings from the Romans in previous years, they had to be prepared for boarding actions themselves. Carthage may therefore have sought to blunt the tactical advantage that the Romans had enjoyed with their big complements of marines by taking aboard similarly large sea soldier contingents of their own.[7]

The Carthaginians were under no illusions about the importance of the coming battle. Before their crews embarked they warned them that victory meant that the war would be confined to Sicily, but if they were defeated the Romans would land in Africa and instead it would be their families and country at stake, which had the effect of focusing their minds on the struggle ahead of them. Thus, these seamen were 'in a mood of combined confidence and dread' as the Carthaginian fleet put to sea.[8] They would soon be engaging the Romans in what may have been, in terms of the number of men involved, the greatest sea battle of all time.

The Romans were afraid of the striking power of the Carthaginian fleet, knowing that they would have to cross a long stretch of open water to reach Africa. During this transit they would be vulnerable to the faster moving ships of the enemy, a telling worry if we are to take Polybius' numbers for the embarked crews of Carthaginian ships at face value. These quinqueremes would have had at least as many men aboard as their Roman equivalents, and any difference in speed can only be attributed to superior rowing, even if it was degraded by the extra weight of the additional men aboard. The Romans assumed that the Carthaginians would have the edge in manoeuvring, and were perhaps unaware of the measures that they had taken to bulk up the marine contingents aboard their galleys. So the Romans adopted a formation that would be especially hard to attack as they rowed. This took the form of a moving wedge, with their biggest ships, two hexaremes, or 'sixes' because they had two rowers to each oar, which were arrayed in three levels, at the apex. Aboard each six stood one of the consuls. Lucius Manlius Vulso, in command of First Squadron, was on the right, and Marcus Atilius Regulus, at the head of the Second Squadron, was on the left. Behind each consular hexareme came the ships of the First and Second Squadrons. These vessels were deployed in a staggered line, each ship extending a little outward and to the rear of the preceding galley in the formation, giving the formation the look of an arrowhead if viewed from above. At the base of this was stationed the Third Squadron, arranged on a line abreast, which was towing the horse transports for the invasion. Just a little behind them was the Fourth Squadron, or *triarii*, acting as a rearguard. It is evident from the Roman disposition that they had adopted this moving 'doughnut' arrangement to protect the horse transports, shielding them with their own ships from Carthaginian attack. The *triarii* of the Fourth Squadron were meant to defend the rear of the Roman fleet from the Carthaginian warships that they presumed would try to encircle them in a *periplous* manoeuvre.

The Romans sailed with the Sicilian coast to starboard. The Carthaginian fleet, approaching from the opposite direction, was under the command of Hamilcar, who had direct control of the left wing, closest to the coast, and Hanno, who had the right, extending out to sea. Upon learning of the formation that their enemy had adopted, they arranged their own ships so that three-quarters of their ships were in line abreast, just one ship deep, facing prow-to-prow with the Romans. These vessels were under the command of Hamilcar, who was stationed in the middle of the line. The right wing, the remaining quarter of Carthage's ships under Hanno, was oriented forward at an angle from the rest of the fleet.

The Romans saw that the Carthaginians had extended their line very thinly so as to have an extra-long battleline. They drove straight for this weakened centre and pushed through. This was all part of the Carthaginian plan, however, and Carthage's ships in the centre of the line had been under orders from Hamilcar to retreat in the face of the onrushing Romans to break up the Roman formation. The Carthaginians had long experience with the Romans and their unsubtle tactics. If they were presented with a suitably weak-seeming target, they would charge straight ahead, and open up their battle formation to attack as their leading elements raced away from the rest of their fleet. This ploy worked just as Hamilcar had intended. A gap yawned as the Roman quinqueremes chased their foes, leaving exposed the Third and Fourth squadrons who were at the base of the floating triangle. Once Hamilcar sensed that the time was right, he gave the signal to counterattack. The Carthaginian galleys that had been fleeing from their Roman pursuers just moments before suddenly turned about and fought.

Into the gap created between the First and Second Squadrons and the Third and Fourth plunged Hanno's lurking ships on the Carthaginian right wing. These galleys hit the rearmost Roman (the Fourth) squadron, the *triarii*, while the remainder of the Carthaginian fleet, those ships positioned closest to the shore on the other end of the line, turned to their starboard, and attacked the Roman Third Squadron which had been towing the horse transports. These were unceremoniously cut loose, and the Third Squadron's quinqueremes took up the fight against the Carthaginian left wing. The battle devolved into three distinct fights, with the consuls engaged against Hamilcar's ships in the centre; Hanno fighting the Roman *triarii* rearguard; and the Roman Third Squadron engaged with the Carthaginian left.

The battle with Hamilcar in the centre resolved itself first. These Carthaginian ships were forced to flee, and Vulso gathered the captured ships together while his colleague, Regulus, rowed back to the aid of the Third and Fourth Squadrons. Hanno's squadron, on the Carthaginian right, was caught between the ships of the Fourth Squadron and Regulus' reinforcements. These Carthaginians turned and rowed out to sea. On the other end of the line, the Third Squadron was being pinned against the Sicilian coastline by the Carthaginian left wing. The Carthaginians were only stopped from pressing their advantage and wiping the Romans out by fear of the corvi that were aboard the Roman ships. The Carthaginians dared not ram them for fear of becoming entangled and unable to manoeuvre. Meanwhile, Vulso and Regulus had both finished their business elsewhere, and now arrived to rescue the trapped Third Squadron ships. Fifty Carthaginian ships were captured in this segment of the battle alone.

The outcome of the battle was a clear Roman victory. The Romans sank thirty Carthaginian ships while losing twenty-four of their own. It was in the number of ships captured, however, where the result was most disparate. Sixty-four Punic warships and their crews were taken, whereas the Carthaginians did not manage to capture a single Roman vessel.[9] The greater part of the captures (fifty!) made by the Romans came at the end of the battle when both consular squadrons came to help the hard-pressed Third Squadron. From Polybius' description, it seems that the Carthaginian ships were caught between the hammer and anvil of the Third Squadron, which was heretofore pinned between the enemy and the Sicilian shore, and the late-arriving First and Second Squadrons under Vulso and Regulus. So while the final tally of ships lost stood greatly in favour of the Romans, the combats between the ships apart from the fight between the Carthaginian left wing and the Roman Third Squadron were much closer. The numbers of ships sunk on either side - over thirty Carthaginian ships downed as opposed to twenty-four Roman - hardly indicates that the Carthaginians were overmatched in any significant way. The ravens deployed aboard Rome's quinqueremes had been of great value in the fight, as fear of these boarding-bridges had kept the Carthaginian galleys of the left wing from pressing their attack against the hemmed-in Roman ships of the Third Squadron.

On the other hand, the corvus does not seem to have been quite the outright battle-winner that it had been earlier in the war. This is not to say that it had not been useful. Circumstances at Ecnomus were somewhat different from what had been seen at either Mylae or Tyndaris. At Mylae, the corvus had enabled the Romans to reduce Carthage's superiority in manoeuvring to such an extent that it could win the battle decisively. At Tyndaris, an engagement in which the Romans had been caught by surprise, it may be reasonably presumed that the corvus allowed the Romans to stave off defeat and win the day once sufficient numbers of their ships had arrived on the scene to aid the overwhelmed consular squadron.

At Ecnomus, however, the ratio of Carthaginian galleys sunk to Roman was just 5:4. That the Carthaginians had not developed an ingenious countermeasure to the corvus may be shown by their stark unwillingness to approach the cornered Roman galleys of the Third Squadron for fear of getting stuck by their boarding-bridges. The corvus was still a thing to be avoided. What then was the reason for Carthage's commendable performance? The simplest explanation is that it was Hamilcar's intelligent plan that allowed the Carthaginians to implement the superior manoeuvring tactics for which they were famous. It was taken for granted that the Carthaginian ships were speedier, and that they were better-handled too. The corvus had made the unimpeded use of such skills as the Carthaginian seamen possessed nearly impossible by holding their ships fast once they had been rammed. By luring the leading Roman squadrons out of formation, the Carthaginians did succeed in opening up enough space for them to fight the battle of manoeuvring and ramming for which they were best suited. For the few navies that had energetically pursued manoeuvring as their favoured naval tactic, their greatest difficulties arose when they were deprived of adequate space in which to perform those manoeuvres, as had happened to the Athenians in Syracuse's Great Harbour. Prior to Ecnomus the Carthaginians had never been able to fully employ their favoured ramming tactics, except perhaps briefly in the opening phase of the Tyndaris fight, because of the corvus. Even if they had successfully used ramming tactics at Tyndaris, and there is no reason to doubt that they did so, once the rest of the Roman fleet arrived their boarding-bridges gave the Romans the victory in the general action that ensued when numbers were more even.

Credit must be given to Hamilcar for recognizing the Roman penchant for frontal attacks and using this bullheadedness to his advantage. The Carthaginian centre squadron calmly drew the Romans further and further out of position as they retreated in a 'feigned flight', and then turned about once they had opened up a gap in the Roman formation large enough for the rest of the fleet to exploit. Once they had turned, they were able to use their rams to good effect against the exposed sides and sterns of the disorganized Roman ships chasing them. That this successful trick did not bring victory was due to the corvus and the inherent staying power of the Romans. It did at least make the battle close.

On To Africa

The route to Africa was open. Once they had fixed their damaged ships and resupplied, the Romans made the crossing, touching first at Cape Hermaeum and then making landfall at Aspis, where they pulled their ships ashore and erected a defensive trench and stockade. Aspis was placed under siege and soon fell.[10] Then a curious thing happened. While the Romans were contenting themselves with despoiling the African countryside, orders arrived from Rome. One consul was to stay in Africa, while the other was to return to Rome immediately. The reason for this command is not given by Polybius, who merely reports that Vulso went back to Rome with the bulk of the fleet and the Carthaginian prisoners while Regulus remained with 15,000 infantry, 500 cavalry, and 40 ships.[11] The reasoning behind this major redeployment is hard to fathom. The Romans must have known that though the Carthaginians had been defeated, they had not been annihilated. If we take Polybius' figures for Carthaginian manpower and ship numbers at face value, then the Carthaginians lost approximately 40,000 men at Ecnomus, either killed or captured. This was still just a fraction of the total Punic force at the battle, the survivors of which were even now back at Carthage preparing to defend against the anticipated Roman assault.[12] Carthage still had available to it some 256 ships after Ecnomus, and though many of these would have been damaged, some could have been repaired, and thus a probable majority would have been battle worthy. The Carthaginians therefore retained over 70 per cent of the fleet that it had brought to the engagement of Ecnomus, and some 110,000 men had survived the battle. Carthage had been badly wounded, but was not at all dead.

What then can be made of the recall by Rome of almost its entire fleet and all but 15,500 of its troops? If the order was not the result of colossal overconfidence (and it might well have been) on the part of the Romans thinking that the

Carthaginians were finished, then alternatively, it is possible that Rome simply could not keep so many men away from Italy for so long. Her reliance upon allies for supplying crews for her warships was likely an irritant in Rome's relations with other Italian states, which understandably wanted their men back home.

Carthaginian minds were tightly focused on the danger at hand. They did not attempt to prevent a Roman landfall on the African continent despite the opportunity to do so. Diodorus says that this was because of their diminished morale. 'No one is so shattered in spirit by defeat as are the Carthaginians', he wrote.[13] The possibility of a strike at the Roman invasion fleet was there. The Roman ships that first touched in Africa were few in number, just thirty, and might have been annihilated had the Carthaginians applied themselves more assiduously to the task. The Roman fleet had arrived in disorder as a result of heavy winds, and was very vulnerable as it drew near to the coast. The Carthaginians certainly had the means to act aggressively with the ships remaining to them. Notwithstanding that some of these may have been too badly damaged to be of any use in battle, many others would have been capable of some kind of action. The Carthaginians were suffering more from the psychological shock of their defeat, and mentally were perhaps unprepared to undertake naval operations that might have produced beneficial results in the wake of the Ecnomus fight. Also, the overriding fear of the Carthaginians was that the Romans would descend directly on Carthage, and so they concentrated their attention there, in front of their home city.

Hasdrubal, the son of Hanno, and Bostar, were appointed as generals over the army. Hamilcar was recalled from his base at Heraclea Minoa in Sicily, bringing with him 5,000 infantry and 500 cavalry.[14] Regulus, in the meantime, had departed his camp and was looting the countryside and capturing towns. A Carthaginian force appeared close to the town of Adys, which the Romans had under siege. They lacked the strength to raise the siege, and instead kept the Romans under observation from a nearby ridge, where they established their camp. The Carthaginians had the edge over the Romans in cavalry and elephants, but their occupation of the steep and rough ground of the ridge negated this advantage. The Romans, seeing that the terrain hindered the best elements of the enemy army, chose to attack.

With their horses and elephants stymied by the unfavourable terrain, it was up to Carthage's mercenaries to resist the onslaught of the Roman legionaries. This they did with great bravery, driving the men of the First Legion away. The mercenaries pursued the legionaries too enthusiastically, however, and became separated from the rest of their comrades. Another part of the Roman army surrounded them. Carthaginian defences crumbled, their camp was captured, but their horsemen and elephants managed to escape. The Romans resumed their raiding without fear of Carthaginian reprisals, and took several cities, including Tunis. To make matters worse for Carthage, the ever-dangerous Numidians seized the opportunity to devastate Carthaginian farmland.[15]

Regulus now exhibited the poor judgment that was endemic among the Romans on account of the nature of their system of command. It was all well and good that consuls should be elected annually; that there should be two of them so that each could watch and if need be guard against overreach by the other. In the primitive days of Rome, when its enemies were just a few miles or so away, this was not too problematic. The Romans were republican to their core, and nothing horrified them quite like the despotic power of a king. Command authority over an army was of limited duration, coterminous with the duration of a consulship. Once the term of the consulship was completed, a new consul would take command of the army.

Regulus could smell the blood in the water. He knew that the Carthaginians were close to defeat, and he could just taste the triumph that would be held in Rome in honour of his capture of their city. But his time was running out. What if his term ended and Carthage had not been taken? Regulus would be forced to give up his command and hand the greatest victory of Rome's history to his successor. There was no way he could not do so. For a consul to refuse to obey one of the most solemn laws of the Republic would be so horrendous a crime as to be unthinkable.

Let's get this over with now, Regulus must have thought. Perhaps the Carthaginians would talk, and make peace right away. Carthage was teeming with refugees from the Roman assault, and they were hopeless as the Romans approached. Seeking to spare themselves a siege, the Carthaginians sent negotiators to speak to the consul.

Regulus had a victory without further bloodshed in his grasp. A submission from Carthage would have garnered him the triumph he knew he deserved. But he fumbled his chance and displayed the tactless insensitivity of conquerors in all times and places. 'Woe to the conquered' was the Roman maxim for expressing the helplessness of the defeated. Diodorus writes that the Carthaginians asked the consul 'to treat them with moderation and in a manner worthy of Rome'.[16] Regulus had forgotten, however, that Carthage had not yet been conquered, and the terms that he now proposed to them were so dire that the Carthaginians realized that it would be better to die than accept them, and they departed. Regulus demanded that Carthage give up its fleet but for one ship, except when Rome called upon it to provide fifty of them for service with Rome's navy. They were to give up Sicily and Sardinia, and pay an indemnity to Rome too. It is no wonder that the Carthaginians baulked. Regulus had not truly offered them terms, but instead dictated the impositions of a nearly unconditional surrender.

The Carthaginians knew that they were in trouble. Diodorus writes that 'all men are apt to be mindful of divinity in times of misfortune, and though often, in the midst of victories and success, they scorn the gods as myths and fabrications, yet in defeat they revert to their natural piety'.[17] With overwhelming Roman power darkening their door, the Carthaginians quickly rediscovered their religious feelings. They began to conduct again the sacrifices that they had neglected for many years, and gave the gods the rightful honours due to them.[18] Their prayers were answered when help arrived in the form of a talented Spartan officer named Xanthippus. He had been recruited by the Carthaginians in Greece, along with a number of other troops, to supplement Carthage's limited manpower. Xanthippus inspected the tottering army, and gauged the soldiers to be sound, but their generals to be poor. He told the government what he believed to be the problems facing the army, and offered himself as the solution. The Spartan must have been a great talker because he was put in command by the very generals whose skills he had criticized. The Carthaginians were desperate, however, and Xanthippus offered them that most precious of things: hope.

Xanthippus proved to be one of the great hires of that or any other age. He drilled the moribund Carthaginians in the state-of-the-military-art tactics of the Hellenistic world, and had them ready to face down the Romans again. The armies of the Macedonian successor kingdoms of the Greek East utilized tactics that were descended from those developed by Philip II of Macedonia and his son, Alexander the Great. They employed combined arms, heavy infantry, light and heavy cavalry, along with light skirmishing infantry to knock an opponent off balance and ready him for the killing blow. Roman tactics consisted primarily of a ferocious frontal assault.

Once in charge, Xanthippus showed the Carthaginians how to defeat the Roman bull. He taught them how to manoeuvre on the battlefield, and also to believe in themselves again. He became the hero of the Carthaginian soldiers, who were now straining to get another crack at the Romans. With Xanthippus in command they knew that they would win.

There was no room for error. The Carthaginians had been reduced to a small army of 12,000 footsoldiers, 4,000 cavalry, and about 100 elephants.[19] In spring 255, they marched out to fight with Xanthippus as general. The audacity and unexpectedness of the Carthaginian move made the Romans blink. The enemy was marching and camping on level ground, and not trying to avoid a direct confrontation. The Romans held up and established their own camp a mile from the Carthaginian force.

Xanthippus ordered a general assault with the elephants deployed in a line across the front of the Carthaginian citizen phalanx. These men were not hired mercenaries, but genuine Carthaginians, who were fighting in defence of their home. Xanthippus placed bodies of cavalry on both wings, in keeping with standard Hellenistic practice, and these were supported by his nimble light infantry.

The Romans were themselves ready for battle, and drew themselves up in a line, with their horse on the wings, that was shorter but deeper than that of the Carthaginians. Both sides advanced, with Xanthippus sending his elephants smashing through the Roman centre, while his cavalry flanked the Romans on the wings. The Romans held up the elephant charge, despite heavy losses, but the Carthaginians won the crucial contests on the wings. Their cavalry greatly outnumbered the Roman cavalry, which fled from the field. The Carthaginian horse then struck at the Roman rear, and the encircled Romans were crushed by the elephants, the cavalry, and the citizen phalanx.

Carthaginian losses were minimal, with just 800 mercenaries dead. Of the Romans, whose army had numbered over 15,000 at the start of the campaign, a mere 2,000 survived. Regulus was taken prisoner and hauled back to Carthage. '[O]nly a little while before [he] had refused any pity or mercy to the vanquished', Polybius wrote. Now Regulus was being 'led captive and pleading before his victims for his life'.[20] He deserved his fate. It was his hubris and harsh terms that had caused the Carthaginians to recoil from a negotiated peace and make a 'last stand' in defence of their city. Diodorus wrote that Regulus had 'dictated terms so harsh that the gods themselves were roused to just anger'.[21] His defeat by Xanthippus was simply 'the punishment that his arrogance deserved'.[22]

Some of the blame must be attributed to the Roman system of command, which had clearly outgrown its origins. The Roman army was no longer a communal militia. Its commitments were now far larger, and campaigns could not always be won in the short time allotted to a consul. The Roman Senate may also be faulted for reducing the strength of the African expedition by recalling Manlius and his troops to Italy. The senators appear to have believed final victory to be inevitable, and unwisely weakened the army.

Nonetheless, the imperfections of Roman command and any errors made by the Senate can't excuse Regulus' misjudgment. The great weight of fault must be attributed to him. It was his decision to place his hunger for personal glory ahead of the interests of his country. There is no doubt that he had seen the triumph that had been granted to Duilius just a few years before. The one that awaited the man who brought a victorious conclusion to the war would have dwarfed it. Duilius' achievement had been commemorated with a marble statue of the man and numerous honours. Until the end of his days a torchbearer always walked before Duilius, and a flute-player accompanied him home from dinner.[23] Regulus must have become enamoured by the thought of the same kind of glory accruing to him, and so squandered the great naval victory of Ecnomus and all the benefits that it could have brought. Rome had gained mastery at sea. It had found a way to neutralize the superior seamanship of the Carthaginians and opened the sea lanes to Africa. All of Rome's tremendous exertions, all of the costs that it had borne, the ghastly price it had paid in blood, were tossed away because Regulus had to have his triumph. Maladroit diplomacy and unforeseen enemy genius restored Carthage's sinking fortunes. The Carthaginian army had been revivified from an almost comatose state. Regulus' defeat throws into stark relief a fundamental limitation of seapower. The decisive result must be sought on land, since that is where the enemy resides. A loss on land can undo the patient labour, tactical brilliance, and valour of a navy at a stroke.

With the battle won, and the Roman campaign in Africa in ruins, Xanthippus chose this moment to leave Carthage. Like a lawman of the Old American West, he had come into town, done his job, and departed a hero.

The war would continue for another fourteen years.

Chapter Eleven

The Battle of Cape Hermaeum, 255 BC

The news of Regulus' defeat arrived in Rome with a definite thud. The Romans had been confident of victory. The defeat outside Tunis was an unwelcome surprise. Their first concern was to assemble a fleet to sail to the rescue of their stranded legionaries in Africa. These were the remnants of the army that had made their way back to the town of Aspis. They repulsed attempts to take the city, and the Carthaginians instead focused their attention on preparing their own fleet for battle with the Roman one that they knew would soon be coming to collect them.

In early summer 255, the Roman fleet numbered 350 ships, a figure that should not have been too difficult to reach given the strength at Ecnomus and that their losses had been for the most part confined to the legions, not the navy. Opposing this were some 200 Carthaginian galleys, some repaired, some newly-built. It was an impressive total when considering the losses of the previous year. It did not help them much. The two fleets met off Cape Hermaeum (the modern Cape Bon) and the Romans were no less capable in this naval battle than they had been at Ecnomus. They inflicted a devastating defeat on the Carthaginians, capturing 114 enemy ships along with their crews.[1] The corvus had done its work once more, and the Carthaginians had found no nautical Xanthippus to provide them with a counter.

Polybius' description of the titanic battle at Hermaeum is meagre. What actually happened in this engagement? Polybius merely states that the Carthaginians 'presented no problem' but does not explain the reason for either Rome's victory or Carthage's defeat.[2] A clue may be found in the number of prizes taken by the Romans, an astounding figure of 114, but with no sinkings reported. One scenario is that the Carthaginians were caught completely off guard, and so were unable to mount an effective resistance to the Roman assault. Another possibility is that the Carthaginians were pushed very close to the shore by the Roman advance, and thus were forced to beach themselves. As seen at Ecnomus, the greater part of the captures made there occurred when the Carthaginian left found itself trapped between the ships of the Third Squadron and the two consular squadrons. All of this took place near to the coast and so with scant room to manoeuvre, they were captured in a bunch. At Cape Hermaeum, the Carthaginian fleet had positioned itself to wait for the Roman rescue fleet that they knew was coming to Aspis, but perhaps did so too close to the shore.³ Their ships may have found themselves pressed shoreward, with similar results.

A further alternative is that Carthaginian seamen were not as skilled in 255 as they had been in 256. In this view, the ships that Carthage sent to watch for the Roman rescue fleet were either hurriedly built or patched up vessels, and that their crews were only half trained.⁴ Many of the Carthaginian galleys on hand for Hermaeum may indeed have been newly-built, but we lack specifics as to how many of the ultimate force of 200 were new, and how many had been repaired. It is worth noting that the Carthaginians were compelled to construct new ships to reach the 200 mark, though they had over 250 surviving warships from Ecnomus. Some of these older ships had likely been dispersed to other bases, and the Carthaginians may have discovered that some of their ships were no longer worth refurbishing, thereby necessitating new construction. It is needless, however, to infer poor workmanship on these new vessels as a reason for Carthaginian defeat. Also, the conjecture that the Carthaginians' crews were somehow inferior to those of the previous year is not easily supported by the evidence. Most of the Carthaginian fleet had escaped the battle, and these men would have been available for service in 255. There is no reason to suppose that they had collectively diminished in rowing skill.

The Carthaginians may have been hindered in fighting back against the Romans during boarding actions by the need to maintain a stout defence on land. They had performed relatively well at Ecnomus. They had sunk twenty-four Roman galleys to about thirty or more of their own sunk. Bearing in mind Polybius' figure for the total shipborne manpower of the Punic fleet of 350 warships at the earlier battle, which was 150,000, it is evident that the Carthaginians had put large numbers of marines, in the range of 120 or more, aboard each of their ships to fight the Romans in boarding actions. These men had probably been withdrawn from the fleet and were thus not available for shipboard service once Rome had carried the war to Africa. If Carthaginian galleys were lacking marines, then they may have been afraid to engage the Romans aggressively out of fear of their boarding-bridges. This may help explain the debacle.

The Storm

It seemed that luck was once again favouring the Romans, and that there might be a chance of renewing their assault on Africa. The Roman fleet, under the command of the consuls Marcus Aemilius Paullus and Servius Fulvius Paetinus Nobilior, and now numbering 364 ships, recovered the legionaries holding out in Aspis. It then made its way back to Italy, sailing eastward along the southern coast of Sicily. When it was close to Camarina, a tremendous storm hit, causing catastrophic losses. Out of the entire fleet just eighty ships were spared destruction.

The loss of life was calamitous. The weather had done to the Romans what the Carthaginians could not. Assuming that the Romans were still outfitting their ships with a maximum number of marines, as they had at Ecnomus, the loss of a single ship meant the deaths of well over 400 oarsmen, sailors, and marines. A conservative estimate of the casualties gives at least 100,000 dead.[5] This was one of the worst losses of life that Rome's military would ever experience. It eclipsed other Roman military catastrophes, such as Cannae and Adrianople, which today loom so much larger in modern consciousness. Polybius places the blame for the Camarina disaster squarely on the pigheadedness of Roman commanders, not on chance misfortune. They wilfully ignored their pilots who warned them again and again of the dangers of sailing in the waters off Sicily's southern coast during the season. The period was that 'between the rising of Orion and that of Sirius'.[6] This correlates to 4 July to 28 July in the modern calendar.[7] For the experienced mariners with Rome's fleet, it was a time in which sailing in these waters was to be avoided. But the Romans took no heed of their misgivings. The pilots may themselves have not been Roman, perhaps they were Greeks from southern Italy, and easy for the Romans to discount. The Romans wanted to use the impressive size and strength of the fleet to overawe coastal Sicilian towns into submission. This needlessly exposed it to the storm that overwhelmed it. Polybius observed that 'the Romans rely upon force for everything. They feel obliged to finish anything they start and regard nothing as impossible once they have made up their minds.' Such obstinate determination often brought them success on land, but not at sea. 'On land, against human beings and their artefacts, they are usually successful ... because they are employing force against people with similar capacities and resources to their own, but they come off by far the worst when it is the sea and the weather that they take on and try to subdue by main force.' The Romans were bound to suffer such misfortunes 'until they restrain the kind of reckless arrogance that makes them fail to recognize any obstacles to their sailing and travelling whenever they feel like it'.[8] Roman resolve and grit was no match for the power of nature.

Of the mighty fleet that had assembled at Ecnomus, and won such a crushing victory, there must have been little left. Regulus' African army was gone completely. Of Manlius' troops we have no word of where they had been deployed upon their return to either Italy or Sicily, but we can presume that many of these men would have taken part in the rescue operation to Aspis, and thus that many would have perished in the storm as well.

Carthage had been granted a second miracle. From a purely military standpoint, it is hard to fault the Carthaginians for taking advantage of the hammer blows dealt to the Romans to go on the offensive. The calculus of power had changed greatly. But the war need not have gone on. The Carthaginians could have seized upon the opening provided by the psychological shock to the Romans of such severe losses to seek a settlement. There is no report of them sounding out the Romans on this possibility. There is no record of any Carthaginian peace initiative being rebuffed by the Romans at this juncture. Instead, the Carthaginians began to build a new fleet of 200 ships and sent their general Hasdrubal to Lilybaeum for a renewed offensive in Sicily.[9]

It must be noted here that a Roman tradition of uncertain origin exists that Regulus was later released on parole by the Carthaginians so that he could relay in person in Rome their desire for a peace settlement. According to this story, once back in Rome, Regulus advised the Senate against making any peace with them. Nonetheless, Regulus was bound by his agreement with the Carthaginians to return to Carthage, which he did. He was thereafter put to death. This dubious tale does not appear in the pages of either Polybius or Diodorus. It is extremely improbable that such an embassy by a released Regulus would have been ignored by both historians. Each devotes considerable attention to the man when criticizing his missteps in Africa. Had he been a part of any kind of peace initiative by Carthage it is difficult to see why it would have garnered no mention. The story is thus almost certainly an ahistorical invention of no veracity.

Carthage's strategic position was hardly worse off now than it had been at the start of the war. It still held several important strongholds in Sicily, including Lilybaeum and Drepana. From these bases a counterattack to regain lost territory in the island could be mounted, but a breathing space would have been welcome. Given the later difficulty that the Romans had in besieging Lilybaeum, a well-fortified stronghold city, these places could have been reinforced during a period of peace to make them even tougher. Africa was safe, for the time being, from Roman invasion. The Carthaginians still held their overseas empire. It was time to recoup and reorganize.

The Carthaginians can't be blamed for rebuilding their fleet, since warships could not be magically created in the event that they were needed. A perceptive, clear-eyed Carthaginian policy, however, would have recognized that Carthage had also suffered terrible hurts of its own in nine years of war. Their losses in manpower and money were more critical than a few cities in Sicily. Dissatisfaction with Carthaginian rule, to put it mildly, was already a reality among the subject Libyans. Diodorus recorded that the Libyans, who were not Carthaginian, hated them 'with a special bitterness because of the weight of their overlordship'.¹⁰ The taxes and other harsh exactions being placed upon the peoples of Libya would bear bitter fruit later in the war and in the post-war period.¹¹ If the Carthaginians believed that they could somehow eject the Romans entirely from the island then they were being too optimistic. The Romans were there to stay, and even an uneasy coexistence on the island would have brought more benefits to Carthage, at least in the short run, than more war. As it turned out, the continuation of the struggle for Sicily would entail enormous additional costs for Carthage, and bring tragedy to it. The Romans were not the only participants in this war to miscalculate badly.

Chapter Twelve

Rome Tries Again

Though the Romans were still reeling from the devastation of the storm, their determination was unshaken. Another fleet of 220 ships was constructed in the space of only three months. When it was ready, it set sail under the command of the consuls for the year 254, Gnaeus Cornelius Scipio and Aulus Atilius Caiatinus. The fleet put in first at Messana, incorporated the eighty ships based there, and then departed for the Carthaginian stronghold of Panormus. This city was besieged and the section known as New Town was taken by assault. Old Town Panormus then capitulated and a garrison was put in place before the fleet went back to Rome.[1]

In 253, the consuls for the year were Gnaeus Servilius Caepio and Gaius Sempronius Blaesus. They took the whole of the Roman fleet on an expedition to Africa. The goal of this endeavour seems to have been to conduct raids along the coastline, and it did not accomplish much. If the Romans had hoped that the Carthaginians would issue forth to give them a major naval battle they were disappointed. One theory that has been advanced to explain their strategy for this year was that they hoped to induce the subject African cities of the Carthaginian Empire to revolt by means of these raids. If so, then this did not have the desired effect, though the consul Blaesus was granted a triumph, which would indicate that he did inflict considerable damage in Africa.[2] The most noteworthy event of the campaign was the grounding of the Roman fleet on shoals. The ships were helpless at ebb tide, and were only refloated by tossing overboard heavier items and waiting for the tide to come in once more. The Romans were lucky to have survived this self-inflicted injury, but not so lucky on their voyage home. They reached Panormus safely, but then set out once more for Rome. On this leg of the journey, another storm struck. The fleet lost over 150 ships, and another disaster on such a scale was too much even for the Romans. Depending upon whether the Romans had their full complements of marines or had disembarked some of them at Panormus for further land service in Sicily, Roman losses may well have been in the 50–60,000 range.

This too was a loss at least as great as those incurred in Rome's most terrible defeats on land. Many of the dead men would of course have been drawn from Rome's Italian allies, and the loss of life from this storm and that off Camarina made the continuation of Rome's offensive naval policy impossible. The

Romans put an end to their shipbuilding programme and instead put all of their energy into the defeat of Carthage on the ground in Sicily. A small fleet of just sixty ships accompanied the army sent to the island under the consuls of 251, Lucius Caecilius Metellus and Gaius Furius Pacilius, to aid in its supply.[3] That the Romans had chosen to put an end to their feverish ship construction is not difficult to comprehend. Four major naval efforts had been made in 256, 255 (the relief effort), 254 (with the fleet of 220 built to replace those lost in the Camarina storm); and 253, which resulted in another fleet wrecked by bad weather. The loss of life had been tremendous, causing more deaths for Rome than the Carthaginians ever had. The cost in treasure spent on the ships rotting at the bottom of the sea was immense. What did Rome have to show for all of its struggles to gain command of the sea? Not much really. They had shown themselves to be more powerful than the Carthaginians whenever they had met in battle. There was no Carthaginian counter to the corvus that could prevent a Roman naval victory. Yet in spite of all they had achieved by employing their simple but effective tactics, they were no closer to winning the war. The Carthaginians again liked what they saw when they considered the strategic picture in Sicily. They had command of the sea, even if this was due more to storms and forfeiture than by their own efforts. The source of this command did not matter, only that they held it in the absence of a Roman fleet to challenge them.

Having turned their attentions to victory on land, Roman fortunes in Sicily in 252 and 251 were disappointing. Though they took the cities of Therma and Lipara by siege, fear of Carthage's corps of elephants kept the Romans from giving battle. The devastating impact of these animals had been experienced first-hand by the legionaries, and they sought the protection of the mountains and uneven terrain. The elephant, in a way, had become the Carthaginians' corvus, a weapon so daunting that it diminished the enemy's willingness to fight.

The year 250 saw a modest construction programme of just fifty ships and the recruitment of rowers.[4] This was a small effort compared to the major armaments in the past. The difficulty that the consuls of that year, Gaius Atilius Regulus, victor of Tyndaris, and Lucius Manlius Vulso, hero of Ecnomus, faced in obtaining enough men for their small fleet is a strong indication that Rome and its allies had become deeply disenchanted by the prospect of further sea service in the Sicilian War.

The Carthaginians were aware of the Romans' uncharacteristic hesitancy in offering battle on land, which was a stark change from 258 when it had been the Carthaginians who had dared not emerge from Panormus to fight the Romans. Their commander on the ground was Hasdrubal, and he timed his campaign for the period when one of the consuls and his portion of the army rotated out of Sicily back to Italy. With Rome's manpower on the island now cut in half, Hasdrubal marched out of the fortress city of Lilybaeum and made camp near to the border of Panormitis. Caecilius Metellus, the consul who had stayed behind with his half of the army, refused to leave the safety of Panormus where his troops had been stationed to protect the crops of Rome's Sicilian allies during harvest time. Hasdrubal set his men loose destroying these crops while Metellus remained shut up inside Panormus. This was not done out of fear of the Carthaginians, but was instead a stratagem designed to lure them into a trap. The overconfident Carthaginians brought their elephants too close to the city, where the Romans had dug a moat. The Romans sprang their trap, which was a deadly hail of arrows and javelins that struck the animals. Once wounded, the elephants rampaged through their own lines, which dissolved in chaos. Metellus ordered a countercharge, and this saw the Carthaginian army crushed. Even more importantly, the entirety of the Carthaginian elephant corps present was captured, thereby diminishing this threat to the legions.

Rome made yet another bid for control of the sea. A fleet of 200 ships under the command of both consuls made its way to Sicily where it blockaded Lilybaeum. On land, the city was besieged by the legions. Lilybaeum was well-defended, with a strong wall and a moat. Approaching the city from the sea was rendered difficult by shallow and treacherous waters all around. These required a high level of skill and experience to navigate successfully. The Romans set up camps on both sides of Lilybaeum. These were connected by a trench, a palisade, and a wall. They deployed all of the myriad siege engines known to their military science, including battering rams, covered sheds, towers, catapults. To prevent the reinforcement of the city from the sea, the Romans sank fifteen light craft at the harbour's entrance.[5] The Romans patiently advanced their siegeworks toward the wall of Lilybaeum, beginning with the tower nearest to the sea. Day after day this continued, with the siegeworks slowly extended to other towers in succession. Seven were undermined in this way, and then the Romans mounted a full-scale assault on all of the others. They had enough success that Roman siegeworks were moved forward into the city itself, but the Carthaginians, under their resourceful commander Himilco, were able to contain the Romans just enough to prevent the city from falling. It was dirty, bloody work, a war of mines and countermines and hastily improvised defensive walls.

There were 10,000 mercenaries defending Lilybaeum, but the greatest share of the credit for its defence lay with Himilco. Every day he launched a sortie against the Roman siegeworks, astutely keeping the besiegers off balance.[6] The Roman force, if Diodorus is to be trusted, numbered 110,000 men.[7] This total also included oarsmen from the fleet serving as part of the besieging troops.[8] The claustrophobic stress and terror of tunnels, parapets, ditches, assault sheds, battering rams, and siege towers must have reminded Roman rowers of their own nasty, filthy world of wooden ships.

The Carthaginians soon had a problem besides the Romans. The officers of her mercenary garrison were not quite as attached to Lilybaeum as their paymasters, and did not wish to perish in it. Several sneaked out to speak with the Romans about betraying the city to them. Himilco learned of the plot and moved quickly to shore up the loyalties of the rest of the garrison. When the traitorous mercenary officers returned from their talks and tried to speak with their men about Roman terms, they found themselves shut out of the city and were driven away by a shower of missiles.[9]

Carthage had long since decided that it would forego any other military activity in Sicily and instead devote all of its resources to sustaining the garrison of Lilybaeum. At this stage of the war, Carthaginian territory in Sicily had been reduced to just Lilybaeum and nearby Drepana. Retention of just one of these places would be enough for Carthage to one day mount a counteroffensive to regain the lands that it had lost. A relief expedition of fifty ships was fitted out under the command of Hannibal (another Hannibal) with 10,000 soldiers embarked. This fleet stopped first at the Aegates Islands and waited for a favourable wind to arise. Once this arrived, Hannibal's fleet raced straight for Lilybaeum's harbour mouth. The Carthaginian ships sped right past the Roman ships lying offshore, which were caught off guard.

With Carthaginian morale improved by the unexpected appearance of the fleet, and reinforced by the 10,000 additional troops that had come with it, Himilco attempted to destroy the Roman siegeworks that were slowly strangling the city. This was repulsed by the Romans only with great difficulty. Hannibal then made his way out of the harbour and escaped the waiting Romans' ships again, going now to join forces with the Carthaginian admiral Adherbal at Drepana.[10]

Further contact with the garrison in Lilybaeum was prevented by the siege and accompanying blockade. Some time passed without any word emerging, and the Carthaginians needed to know what was going on within it. A Carthaginian captain named Hannibal (yet another Hannibal) and nicknamed 'the Rhodian' on account of his fine nautical skills, offered to undertake a daring mission. He would take a single ship to Lilybaeum, and with the help of a favourable wind, sail right past the Romans into the harbour. Once he had taken stock of the situation inside the city, he would sail out again and give a report.

One can imagine Carthaginian jaws dropping at such a bold and seemingly foolhardy offer. They accepted it in any case, as they had no other option available. Hannibal proved to be as successful as he was brave, and took his ship into Lilybaeum's harbour while the incredulous Romans waiting on either side of the harbour mouth watched. He had a special route through the shallows into which the Romans, with their heavier vessels, could not follow. Polybius says that he made his 'approach from the direction of Italy, with the sea tower over the prow of his ship and hiding from view all the rest of the towers on the Libyan [African] side of the city'.[11] He benefited from the long experience of the Carthaginian sailors with the waters around Lilybaeum. Hannibal did not intend to stay within it for long. There can be no doubt that Himilco conveyed the desperate nature of his situation, and requested more help from Carthage. The Romans were waiting outside the harbour with ten of their swiftest galleys to prevent Hannibal from slipping past. These were stationed on either side of the harbour entrance with their oars at the ready. Their preparation was for nothing. Hannibal again dashed past the Roman ships, which could not catch him.

Hannibal's feat encouraged several other Carthaginian captains to attempt the same deed along the same route through the shallows. Roman ships were too heavy to enter these waters and a number of blockade runners made it into Lilybaeum's harbour despite Roman knowledge of their intentions. The Romans did their best to stop them by filling in the water around the mouth of the harbour but they achieved little because the water was too deep and the fill material that they deposited was dispersed by the roughness of the waves. In one place, however, they did manage to make a higher bank, and an unlucky blockade runner grounded upon it. The Romans captured this ship, said to be a quadrireme, or four, of excellent construction. They placed a picked crew of rowers and marines aboard it and kept watch for other Carthaginian blockade runners to appear. That same night Hannibal the Rhodian had himself returned and made his approach. He spotted the quadrireme and understood that something was amiss. He tried to flee but the pursuing ship with its well-trained Roman crew was too fast to escape. Hannibal turned and fought it out instead, but he had no chance against the more numerous Roman marines. He was taken captive and his ship, an exceptionally well-made quinquereme, was used by the Romans to stop the other blockade runners.[12] The Carthaginians must be applauded for doing their utmost to help the besieged garrison of Lilybaeum. The courage and talent of their captains was beyond question, and their navigational skill was top-notch. But they were tempting fate by running the blockade again and again into the same city along the same route. Their predictability allowed the Romans to adapt and implement an effective countermeasure. What was really needed was an expedition to lift the siege entirely, which was not forthcoming.

The stalemate at Lilybaeum continued. The Romans would advance their siege works but then Himilco would then contain them with his own counterworks.

The weather intervened against the Romans once more. A wind came up that blew so strongly that it toppled the Roman siege towers. The Carthaginians used this moment to launch a surprise assault on the Roman lines and set them alight. The Roman siege equipment was old and dry, and with the wind blowing so strongly, the flames raced along the length of the Roman siegeworks. The besiegers could do nothing to douse the flames because they were blinded by the enormous cloud of smoke blowing into their eyes. The siegeworks suffered total destruction as a result of this attack, and the Romans quit their lines and retreated to their fortified camp, where they brooded on what to do next.

Once more there had been a shift in fortune that changed the complexion of the war. Rome had seen the progress made in its long and tiring siege of Lilybaeum reversed in a single day. Lilybaeum was not safe, but it was not in imminent danger of falling. Rome had been hurt in another way. Some of the men who had prosecuted the land siege of Lilybaeum had also been rowers with the fleet, and many of these had been killed in the attack on the siegeworks. Another 10,000 rowers were hastily recruited, and these were dispatched to the Roman camp outside of Lilybaeum. For 249, a new consul was sent to take command of the war in Sicily. This was Publius Claudius Pulcher. At this time, what Rome really needed was a fireman to put out the blaze in Sicily. Instead, it got an arsonist.

Chapter Thirteen

Drepana, 249 BC

Pulcher had a reputation as a martinet and instituted severe disciplinary measures once he had assumed command. Diodorus says that he 'applied the traditional punishments unmercifully to soldiers who were Roman citizens and flogged the allies with rods'.¹ This sort of behaviour was in keeping with the reputation of the ultra-patrician Claudii clan for haughtiness and wilfulness.² 'The distinction of his clan and the reputation of his family had so spoiled him', Diodorus concluded, 'that he was supercilious and looked down on everyone'.³ To Diodorus, Pulcher was 'naturally hot-blooded and mentally unstable' and 'his conduct of affairs often verged on the lunatic'.⁴ Pulcher also spoke scornfully of the efforts of prior commanders of the siege. He said that 'they had been remiss in their handling of the war, drunkards who lived lives of license and luxury, and that on the whole they had been the victims of a siege rather than the besiegers'.⁵ As obnoxious as Pulcher was, on that last point he was more right than wrong. The long siege of Lilybaeum had been a bloody fiasco. In spite of his unpleasantness, he convinced his officers that an attack on Drepana, one of Carthage's two remaining holdings in Sicily, would be a good idea. The time was ripe for a strike at the city, Pulcher said, because their admiral there was unaware that the Romans had received new rowers in camp to replace those lost in the siege lines of Lilybaeum, and thus would not be expecting an attack. A move against Drepana would have the benefit of surprise, and would possess an additional advantage in that the Carthaginians would have taken no measures to defend themselves from an assault.

A Roman fleet numbering at least 123 ships departed Lilybaeum at night, with the best of the legionaries, enticed by the prospect of booty, embarked to serve as marines. It sailed northward to Drepana, with the coast to starboard. It reached Drepana at sunrise, and the Carthaginians were taken completely off guard by the appearance of a large Roman fleet on their doorstep. Adherbal's first move was to get his fleet of about 100 ships out of Drepana's harbour before it could be blocked inside. The summons went out to his crews and his mercenary soldiers who assembled promptly. He warned them of the danger of being shut up within the harbour, and how painful a siege of Drepana would be. With his crews fired up for a fight, they boarded their ships, and with Adherbal in the lead ship, headed out of the harbour along the northern edge, heading west.

Pulcher, meanwhile, was stationed at the rear of the Roman line, heading north to Drepana. He had not expected a fight, presuming that the city would capitulate once he appeared offshore. By the time that Pulcher was close enough to see what was occurring, the Carthaginians were already departing the harbour, rowing out to sea. The lead Roman ships had themselves entered the harbour via its southern approach, and Pulcher hastily recalled these vessels. The order wreaked havoc with the Roman fleet, with several ships colliding with others as they tried to comply with Pulcher's recall. While this was going on, the Carthaginians had extracted their fleet from the harbour, and were now formed out to sea, with the Romans between them and the shore just south of Drepana. Pulcher managed to get his ships into a semblance of a battle line, but they were in a tactically inferior position, despite their initial advantage of total surprise. The shore was at their backs, leaving them no room in which to retreat. For all intents and purposes, it was as if the Romans themselves had been caught by surprise. Adherbal ordered an attack on the Roman line, which was still incomplete as it was waiting for stragglers from the harbour to join it.

Pulcher's overconfidence had ensnared his fleet. The Carthaginians, when under pressure during the fight, simply backed off to the open sea behind them. The contest was even for a time because Rome had the best of her legionaries acting as marines, and these were still fearsome in a boarding action no matter who was commanding the fleet. But Carthage's rowers showed much greater facility than their green Roman counterparts. Just as Hamilcar's ships had once done at Ecnomus, Adherbal's galleys retreated out to sea, luring the Romans to pursue them. Once they did this, the Carthaginians' ships turned around and delivered powerful ramming attacks to the sides and sterns of the Rome galleys. The Romans could not counter these strikes because of the inferiority of her crews and also because her ships were heavier and less manoeuvrable than those of the enemy. The Carthaginians could also lend assistance to any of their number that was in trouble by sailing around their own ships across open water. The Romans meanwhile were hemmed in by their terrible position between the enemy and the Sicilian coast. Several of their ships became stuck in the shallow water there or deliberately grounded themselves to escape the Carthaginians.

The entire day was an unmitigated failure for the Romans. Pulcher fled with about thirty of his ships on the Roman left, but the majority of his fleet was not so fortunate. Ninety-three quinqueremes were captured, and this figure does not include the unknown number of ships that may have been sunk by Punic rams during the fight.[6] For Carthage, Adherbal was the hero of the hour. On account of his quick thinking and energetic leadership, he had averted not only defeat but had won a great victory over the Romans. In terms of ships sunk or captured, the Carthaginians had inflicted losses on the Romans equivalent to those that they themselves had sustained at Ecnomus. He was aided in this grand achievement by Pulcher's own ineptitude. The consul had evidently sailed to Drepana expecting that the enemy would do something that it did not, which was give up. His handling of his fleet once it was clear that the Carthaginians had decided to fight was poor, and is a cautionary example of the adage that no plan ever survives contact with the enemy. Unfortunately for the Romans, Pulcher seems not to have had a back up plan in case the Carthaginians chose to fight it out. There was no reason why the Romans had to arrange their line so close to the shore while also allowing Adherbal's ships to escape the harbour and form a line out to sea. Why did Pulcher confine his own ships as he did? A clue may be found in Diodorus, who writes that the consul, 'finding himself overtaken he fled for refuge to the shore, for he regarded the terrors of shipwreck more lightly than the risk of battle'.[7] An immediate albeit disorderly attack on the Carthaginians while they were still making their way west out of the harbour might have paid better dividends than the actual battle that was fought with more formal battle lines. Rome might also have been better served if Pulcher had instead ordered whatever ships which were not yet inside the harbour to turn hard to port and head westward out to sea, thereby preventing the Carthaginians from sandwiching them all between their ships and the shore.

For Pulcher to have made what might have been better decisions, however, he would have had to be at the head of his fleet, not trailing at the rear. It may have been the case that Pulcher took the hindmost position in the Roman line because he was concerned about shepherding the stragglers of his fleet.[8] This position cost him invaluable time in which he could have issued new orders and possibly averted disaster when it was evident that the Carthaginians were leaving the harbour to do battle. Pulcher either ignored or overlooked every fundamental of naval combat that day. This should not be taken to lessen Adherbal's victory in any way, but it must always be borne in mind that battles are two-sided affairs, and it helps to face an incompetent opponent.

Pulcher returned to Rome wrapped in the foul odour of defeat. He was held at fault for the disaster, an accurate assessment. Pulcher 'fell into disgrace', Polybius wrote, and 'was attacked on all sides for his conduct of the battle'.[9] He was put on trial, found guilty, and smacked with a heavy fine. His only solace was that he was not also executed for his poor judgment. A legend arose concerning the battle and the cause of the disaster. The historian Suetonius relates that the sacred chickens carried aboard Pulcher's flagship refused to eat the food that had been presented to them as part of the taking of the auspices before the battle. Pulcher, it is claimed, then grabbed the birds and hurled them overboard. 'Ii they will not eat', the impious nobleman cried, 'let them drink!'[10] It is tempting to think that Pulcher doomed Rome's chances by behaving so irreligiously, and that perhaps he was even held up at the rear of his fleet while he waited for the chickens to have their fill. The Romans took religious matters very seriously, and would never consciously perform or condone such sacrilegious acts.

The sincerity of the horror felt by the Romans for a lack of respect for proper ritual should not be dismissed. Though it may appear to be a needless superstition, for the Romans ritual was of the utmost importance, and Pulcher's crass impiety would have offended all, thus explaining the survival of the tradition regarding the sacred chickens. The orator Cicero relates a story in which consul Tiberius Gracchus the Elder was found to be at fault for improper ritual observance. A ballot collector had died in the midst of the election for consul in 162 BC, and the Etruscan priests called in to determine the cause had blamed a failure of ritual observance. Naturally, Gracchus, who was also an augur (a type of priest) himself, was extremely angry with the Etruscans, since he was especially attentive to proper observances. Nevertheless, he let the voting continue, resigned as consul, and took up the governorship of Sardinia. Once he had reached that island, he realized that he had indeed made a ritual fault, as he had, just prior to the election, unintentionally crossed the *pomerium*, or sacred boundary of the city of Rome, and had neglected to take the auspices before crossing back out again. Since proper ritual had not been observed, the election of the consuls for 162 was judged invalid. He duly informed the Senate, the current consuls resigned, and new ones were elected. All this was done because of a simple ritual fault.[11]

Such strict attention to detail also had the benefit of providing a ready explanation for disaster. The sacred chickens story perhaps had more of an explanatory purpose than a basis in actual fact. It was not to be thought that the Romans had lacked courage or had otherwise come up short in battle (an admission of which would only serve to dishearten the people) but instead the fault could be placed squarely upon the magistrates who had somehow been remiss in observing proper ritual.

The Drepana campaign, like the seemingly endless siege of Lilybaeum, had been a calamity for Rome. Much autonomy was granted to the consuls who directed the legions and the fleet. Some exercised good judgment; others, such as Pulcher and Regulus, did not. But what was Rome's alternative? Under Rome's republican constitution, the consuls were the replacements for the king. Each consul stood as a check on the ambitions and excesses of his colleague. Command of the army had once been the prerogative of the king. It was now the duty of the consuls to lead the army in wartime. This opened the door to military amateurs gaining what was, in effect, the supreme command of the Republic's armed forces as a result of a purely political selection process.

Appointment to high command was not based upon proven military acumen. There is no doubt that by the time that a man could achieve the consulship he would have obtained extensive military experience in his younger days. Serving with a general was not itself a guarantee, however, of genuine ability. Pulcher made a mess of things by not taking the lead of his fleet and allowing the foremost ships to enter Drepana's harbour. He then failed to contain the Carthaginian fleet while it was trying to get out of the harbour. Unintentionally, he had obliged the Carthaginians by forming his line so close to shore that he had repeated the blunder of the Athenians who had trapped themselves in the constrictive confines of the harbour of Syracuse. That Pulcher was not truly inside Drepana's harbour was immaterial. He had deprived his own fleet of any room to retreat out of danger or go to the assistance of overwhelmed ships. Also, for the first time, the Roman edge in fighting boarding actions seems to have been dulled. The Romans were able to hold their own for a while, but it was not enough to secure victory.

Pulcher was psychologically unprepared for a fight, having assumed that the city would surrender on his arrival there. He may not even have had a battle plan, though his arrangement of his ships in a line with their prows facing the enemy complied with standard Roman tactics. The Romans had succeeded before against bad odds and in a bad position, as at Tyndaris. Their marines were still excellent fighting men. Surely the defeat should not have been so terrible, given Roman performance in previous battles with the Carthaginian navy. Could the catastrophe really have been the result of the gods punishing Pulcher?

Whither the Corvus?

A more reasonable explanation for Pulcher's defeat at Drepana, apart from the inferior tactical position of her ships, is that the Romans had given up the great equalizer that had allowed them to make up for their lack of manoeuvring skill. It was the corvus, when combined with the effective Corinthian-style prow-first ramming tactics, that made the Romans masters of the sea. Strangely, the corvus receives no mention after its use in the great victory at Ecnomus. Though its disappearance from Roman ships is not remarked upon by contemporary historians, the conventional explanation given in modern times for its non-appearance is that the corvus was removed because it contributed to making Roman ships top-heavy, and thus fatally unseaworthy in rough weather. The extraordinary, even horrifying, number of ships and men lost to storms after Ecnomus would seem to support this theory. In this view, the Romans had a device on their ships that gave them an enormous tactical advantage in battle, but when the ships ran into bad weather, they were very prone to capsizing because of that same device. The corvus had to go.

This theory has the virtue of being entirely logical, and neatly conforms to the evidence as it exists. The Romans encountered bad storms after the Cape Hermaeum fight in 255, and these storms killed more men than the Carthaginians ever did in battle with the Roman fleet. The corvus was not mentioned as being used at the Battle of Cape Hermaeum, but that battle was itself described only briefly by Polybius, and was such a lopsided victory that it is generally assumed that the weapon was still in use. Whatever benefit the corvus might have brought before, it was a terrible liability now. That is why the corvus is not found deployed at Drepana in 249, even though it might have saved some of the Roman ships that had been penned against the Sicilian shoreline.

An argument against the top-heaviness theory is that the corvus need not have been always erected on the decks of the ships when it was not in battle. This is never said in the sources, but it stands to reason that the corvus should have been a device that could be removed and stowed or at least lowered while the ship was underway. The masts of ancient galleys and their sails could be lowered or taken off before going into battle, and doing so does not seem to have been an enormous challenge. Why should the corvus, which was essentially a mast with a boarding-bridge attached, have been so impossible to remove that it could not have been disassembled and stowed while the galley was travelling with no battle expected? It would have made little sense to retain the corvus in its upright position at all times. Not only would this have made the ship more top-heavy than it need have been, but it also would have meant a significant amount of weight placed directly at the prow of the craft, making it bow-heavy too. The more one ponders the corvus as described the more it seems to have been a piece of equipment intended to be used in battle but not kept erect at all times. This is merely a supposition, but it would seem to weigh against the logical but otherwise unsupported notion that the corvus was a great and irremediable liability in poor weather. Further, even if the corvus made the quinquereme dangerously top-heavy in stormy weather, the same could be said even more truly about the large number of marines that the ships carried. If a full complement of 120 marines is taken to have weighed about several metric tons, then a 24ft pole and its associated boarding-bridge are not likely to have been the difference maker in such conditions.

Notwithstanding the great quantities of ink spilled in connecting the putative disappearance of the corvus from the decks of the warships of the Roman navy with an alleged top-heaviness, there are still other explanations as to why they receive no further mention after the fight at Ecnomus. These may supplement, if not necessarily supplant, the tradition provided by Polybius, who goes to great lengths to describe the importance of the corvus in enabling the inexperienced Romans to even the odds during the early sea battles with the Carthaginians. It may be that Polybius, as an author, did not see any reason to belabour the point after clearly establishing the worth of the device in combat. The corvus is not mentioned because there is no longer a need to describe it or what it did. This could explain why he did not mention its use at Cape Hermaeum, a great Roman victory. However, that the corvus is not mentioned *ever* after, by any other author, weighs against this theory.

It is also possible that the Carthaginians themselves developed an effective countermeasure to the corvus. The corvus was a large and bulky platform that had to be deployed onto the deck of an opposing craft to allow the legionaries to cross, and this may have been a weakness that the Carthaginians at last exploited. Perhaps they found a way to detach the corvus, or maybe they used pikes to prevent it from lodging itself in the decks of their warships. This explanation, however, raises the question as to why the Carthaginians had not employed such measures sooner, since, as Polybius writes, the device was first employed at Mylae in 260, and was found to be still very effective at Ecnomus in 256.

A further explanation is that the corvus was no longer in use because it was no longer needed. Polybius presents the corvus as equipment meant to turn a naval battle, which favoured the Carthaginians, into a land battle, which favoured the Romans with their edge in face-to-face combat. Other gear, such as grappling hooks, which had been used before in sea warfare, may have now been employed in preference to the corvus, which may indeed have been heavy, slow to operate, and vulnerable to Carthaginian attack. The use of a spiked boarding plank that slammed onto an enemy deck had at least a theoretical vulnerability in that the Carthaginians could have installed a railing or some other impediment along the edges of their own ships, taller than the (unknown) length of the spike, which could have interrupted the rapid descent of the bridge, making it less likely to implant itself firmly, if at all.

Following on from this, Roman skill in sea war had certainly improved in the decade since Mylae, even when taking into account the result of Drepana. It may therefore be that the corvus was not seen as being necessary for victory because the Romans themselves had gained the experience and confidence in naval encounters that they had lacked when they built their first fleets. The Romans put up a stiff fight at Drepana in the early stage of the battle because their ships had their best legionaries aboard. This can only mean that the Romans were holding their own in the boarding actions that were clearly taking place. Conventional ramming and boarding tactics, *sans* corvus, may now have been preferred. The corvus was gone because it was obsolete for the purpose for which it had been originally used. That the Romans lost the Drepana fight shows only that the tactical position they assumed there, one perilously close to the Sicilian shore, was the major cause of Roman defeat.

Supply Expedition to Lilybaeum

Pulcher's colleague as consul for 249, Lucius Iunius Pullus, was next sent with a fleet of sixty warships to lead a supply convoy to Sicily. He collected a further sixty vessels at Messana, and then sailed on to Syracuse with his augmented fleet and about 800 supply transports. Some of these ships were sent ahead to carry supplies to the legions fighting in the siege at Lilybaeum while Pullus waited in Syracuse for the rest of his straggling ships to arrive and to wait for more grain to come in from Rome's Sicilian allies. Those ships that had continued on to Lilybaeum found their comrades under attack by a Carthaginian fleet of 100 galleys under the command of Carthalo. These vessels were busy either burning or towing away the Roman ships lying offshore. Himilco, still holding Lilybaeum, heard the clamour of the Romans as they struggled to go to the aid of their ships and ordered an attack on their camp. Carthalo departed after damaging or capturing some Roman ships, and on his way, ran into the scout ships of the Roman supply fleet. With the consul still in Syracuse, the fleet was under the command of a few lower-ranking officers, who did not like their chances against the strong Carthaginian force in front of them. They beached their ships and set up a fortified base protected by catapults and ballistas. Carthalo appeared but was unable to dislodge the Romans from their position. Diodorus relates a more detailed version than does Polybius, with a much more serious outcome. He writes that the Romans sought safety at the city of Phintias, and there Carthalo's ships sank seventeen Roman warships and disabled fifty large freighters. A further thirteen freighters had their timbers smashed in and were 'rendered useless'.[12] Carthalo snatched a handful of transport ships from the Romans and then moved off a short distance to wait for the Romans to come back out to sea. Pullus at last arrived from Syracuse, on his way to Lilybaeum, and his approach was spotted by Carthaginian lookouts. Pullus saw the enemy fleet too, and refused to do battle with such a large force. His ships were slower than those of Carthalo, and there was no way that he could outrun them. Instead he chose to take his ships very close to a rugged and dangerous section of the coast, where he moored them.

Carthalo would not approach the Romans so near to the forbidding coastline, and anchored his fleet off a nearby headland for safety. The weather soon turned bad and Carthalo, on the advice of his helmsmen, took his ships away and rounded Cape Pachynus where he found a safe anchorage. The Romans were not so fortunate. The storm that rose drove their ships onto the rocky shore, and the ships of both of their flotilas were wrecked. In Rome, the devastation was so appalling that they gave up their quest for control of the sea for a second time.

Pullus had made a great error in sending only some of his ships ahead while he stayed with the remainder in Syracuse. He cannot have known that the advance fleet would run right into Carthalo's ships outside Lilybaeum, but the strength of the Carthaginian fleet at Drepana should have given him pause. The portion that he sent ahead was too small to be of any use against the Carthaginians, and even if it had been large enough to make it a contest, there was still no sound reason for Pullus to divide his forces, and thereby surrender the advantage of numbers. Had both flotillas remained together and made the journey to Lilybaeum en masse, they might have stood a chance. Once Pullus did arrive, his own flotilla was also too small to fight the Carthaginians, and was too slow to run away. He sought the protection of the Sicilian shore but this proved fatal once the storm came up. Carthalo must also be credited with having the wisdom to listen to his pilots and refrain from needlessly pursuing the Romans when he had the advantage over them. The Carthaginians again proved that they were the superior mariners, as their speed convinced Pullus that he had no chance of escaping, thereby compelling him to go too close to the rugged coast that proved to be his fleet's undoing.[13]

The Carthaginians also showed that they had a better intelligence picture of what was happening around the island. It can be no coincidence that Carthalo arrived at Lilybaeum just in time to also intercept the Roman supply fleet. It is more than probable that Carthaginian spies, look-outs, or scouting ships had notified Adherbal in Drepana of the sailing of this convoy. There could be no mistaking its destination, and so Adherbal gave Carthalo thirty ships to supplement the seventy that he already had brought to Drepana, and ordered him to attack Lilybaeum, destroy the ships there, and then wait for and wipe out the supply fleet.[14]

We can only guess at what made the consul behave so imprudently and send his supply transports ahead to Lilybaeum while he stayed in Syracuse. Perhaps word had arisen of dire circumstances among the legionaries outside Lilybaeum and that they could not bear to wait much longer for food. Diodorus claims that the Romans were on reduced rations, and sickness had broken out among them, with many dying in the period following the destruction of the siegeworks.[15] Whatever their state of privation, even if these men were starving, they were ill-served by the dispatch of a weak supply fleet. Pullus' decision to split his fleet was made for the questionable reasons of waiting for straggling transports to arrive there and to wait for more supplies to reach Syracuse from the Sicilian interior. These ships and the supplies that they carried were in any event lost in the storm and so Pullus' delay in Syracuse did not bring any benefit at all.[16] To put the need for the entire mission into question, the besieging Roman forces outside of Lilybaeum were to be adequately provisioned by overland routes after Pullus' voyage had failed.[17] This major naval enterprise need not have been undertaken at all.

Chapter Fourteen

The Debut of Hamilcar Barca

Pullus sought to redeem himself for the loss of his fleet by taking Eryx by storm. Along with it he took Mount Eryx, which rose above the city on its slopes. Pullus established a garrison on the summit, and another along the road leading to Drepana, which was still in Carthaginian hands.[1] Carthalo mounted a naval raid against Italy in 248. Zonaras says that Carthalo's goal was to draw some of the Roman forces in Sicily back to defend Italy. Failing this, he sought to do whatever damage he could. The approach of a Roman force made him hurry back to Sicily.[2] The most significant change for Carthage at this time was the appointment in 247 of Hamilcar Barca to the command the Sicilian war. He was audacious and talented. Diodorus, who had an extremely high opinion of the man, wrote of him that: 'Even before he became a general Hamilcar's nobility of spirit was apparent, and when he succeeded to the command [of the Sicilian war] he showed himself worthy of his country by his zeal for glory and scorn of danger. He was reputed to be a man of exceptional intelligence, and … surpassed all his fellow citizens both in daring and in ability at arms.'[3] Though 'Barca' is often used as a surname for Hamilcar and his sons, it was not a family name, but more of a nickname. The derivation of Barca seems to actually mean 'lightning', from the Punic *baraq*, with his name probably being a reference to the speed with which he conducted his hard-hitting raids against the Romans.[4] It was a fitting appellation.

Hamilcar launched naval raids on Italy and then landed his fleet at Mount Hiercte, which he fortified and turned into a fleet base. Hamilcar's move was a bold one. At a stroke he had effectively outflanked the Romans by taking up a position so near to them, albeit one in an easily defensible spot. He turned this station into a staging point for further raids against the Italian coasts. With the Romans close by, he engaged them in numerous skirmishes. His logic seems to have been that the cost of holding the site at Mount Hiercte was worth its usefulness as a naval base. By establishing this stronghold where it was, he simultaneously threatened Panormus, now in Roman possession, and took some of the pressure off Lilybaeum and Drepana.[5] Hamilcar's seaborne raids against Italy, which ranged as far north as Cumae, in Campania, however, did not bring about any weakening of Roman forces in Sicily. The Romans were content to let the municipalities of Italy look to their own defence, though they did plant a few colonies to help out. Crucially, they did not shift their forces back to Italy to protect it from Hamilcar's reaving galleys.[6]

Polybius describes the years of war following Drepana in only the broadest of outlines. He likened the struggle between the Carthaginians under Hamilcar and the Romans to one between 'a pair of exceptionally brave and skilful boxers fighting it out in a contest for first prize'.[7] This could well have described the entire war up to this point with its abrupt changes of fortune and seemingly endless nature. The war in Sicily was now a vicious affair of ambushes and bloody skirmishes. The opponents 'tried everything - traditional ideas, improvised tactics dictated by particular circumstances, and schemes that involved risk and aggressive daring - but for many reasons decisive success eluded them'.[8] One would have hoped that Polybius would have gone into greater detail about what must have been a fascinating period of the war. It is one of the chief frustrations of Polybius that at times (most of the time) he does not provide the kind of specific information that would clear up much of the confusion and ignorance that surrounds the First Punic War, such as the use of the corvus and why it disappeared. It must be remembered that Polybius was not writing a military history. Relating such material, he thought, would be 'boring and totally unprofitable'.[9] That may have been an accurate assessment concerning his readers of the second century BC, but it is our loss in modern times.

This period of guerilla-style warfare continued for about three years until Hamilcar captured Eryx, the same city that Pullus had taken back in 248. Diodorus says that the intrepid Hamilcar brought his ships there by night and led the attack on the city himself.[10] This placed the Carthaginian garrison between the summit of Mount Eryx, which the Romans still held, and the Roman camp at the base of the mountain. Furious Roman attempts to root them out over the next two years were unsuccessful. Hamilcar was too clever and resourceful, and displayed great tactical acumen in fighting the Romans from his stronghold. Barca was a canny operator, who, like Napoleon, played his cards close to his vest. Diodorus says that 'he revealed to no one what had been planned; for he was of the opinion that when stratagems are imparted to one's friends they either become known to the enemy through deserters or produce cowardice among the soldiers by their anticipation of great danger'.[11]

Chapter Fifteen

Endgame: The Battle of the Aegates Islands, 241 BC

The Romans decided to try to win the war once more by gaining mastery of the sea. Hamilcar's superior generalship and the toughness of the Carthaginian troops convinced them that a third major effort there might bring victory. Their strategy was to cut off the Carthaginian force at Eryx from resupply by sea. If this lifeline could be cut, the garrison would wither and die. Rome would need to build new ships to enforce this blockade. She also had a more immediate problem than constructing them. Rome was flat broke. With the public treasury emptied by over two decades of war, the Republic turned to her foremost citizens, solid and patriotic, to pay for the building of new quinqueremes out of their own pockets, either individually, or in conjunction with a few others. In exchange they received only the promise that they would be compensated if the undertaking met with success.

Rome's fiscal situation must have been truly parlous for it to rely upon (or perhaps demand) such contributions from its private citizens. The Romans lacked the concept of the funded debt, and could not float bonds, which are essentially promises to pay a certain sum of money at a future date, to provide for the war against Carthage. As late as 169 AD, we find that a shortage of money forced Emperor Marcus Aurelius to auction off in Trajan's Forum furniture taken from the imperial palace to pay for Rome's military expenses.[1] The need to resort to such extraordinary measures, whether the auctioning of interior furnishings or relying on the gifts of private citizens, highlights a major fiscal problem that faced an ancient state at war. There may have been great wealth within the polity, in private hands, but the government could not get at it to use it to pay for its wars.

The origin of the idea to rely upon private subscriptions to build ships is not known. Centuries before, the 400 wealthiest citizens of Athens, known as trierarchs, had each been obligated to both outfit and captain a trireme every year.[2] Public participation in such matters was thus not completely novel. Zonaras writes that in the period just before the new fleet was created Rome was enjoying some encouraging success at sea in the form of privateers that raided the Libyan coast.[3] As far back as 247, some state-owned ships had been granted to the privateers on the condition that they restore the vessels to seaworthy condition. They would then be allowed to keep whatever plunder they obtained and a successful raid against Libya was mounted.[4] It is clear then that someone had money to spare to undertake these privateering expeditions. It may be that the value of these privately-managed citizen efforts showed that war-worthy ships could be constructed if private wealth could be made to serve a public purpose. Their accomplishments may also have shown the Romans that Carthage's vaunted navy was not what it once was.

The new fleet of 200 quinqueremes was built between 243–242 using this method of payment. The Romans again used a captured Carthaginian ship as the model for their own. The type specimen was the fine ship of Hannibal the Rhodian that the Romans had taken in 250 at Lilybaeum.[5]

Command of the new fleet was given to consul Gaius Lutatius Catulus, with his second in command being the senior praetor, Quintus Valerius Falto. Ordinarily, Catulus' colleague in the consulship for 242 would have been expected to command the fleet alongside him, but in this case, Aulus Postumius Albinus was also a priest, a *flamen martialis*, and he was denied permission on religious grounds from departing from Rome.[7] Carthaginian intelligence seems to have failed miserably to discern where this fleet was headed. In early summer 242, Catulus descended upon Sicily while the Carthaginian fleet was still laid up at Carthage. He took the roadsteads at Lilybaeum and sailed straight into the harbour at Drepana, with far more success than Pulcher, and surrounded that city with siegeworks. Catulus was aware that the outcome of the war would depend upon a decisive battle at sea, and he drilled his men constantly in anticipation of the match that he knew was coming. This period of intense training was an important difference from prior Roman efforts. By insisting upon lengthy instruction for his oarsmen they attained a level of rowing proficiency that no Roman fleet had before possessed. These rowers could also make proper use of their skill because their ships, based as they were on the specifications of Hannibal the Rhodian's excellent quinquereme, were fully suitable for sophisticated manoeuvre tactics.

Word now arrived in Carthage of the appearance of the Roman fleet in Sicilian waters. It seems less than believable that the Carthaginians could have been caught so flat-footed by the movement of the Roman fleet to Sicily. The construction of so many new galleys was a great undertaking that could not have been hidden. The Carthaginians had to have been aware of the Roman building programme. They were probably preoccupied elsewhere during this period. Further, it is probable that they were having great difficulties finding enough men to crew their ships. The dearth of manpower slowed their reaction to this new threat. Polybius seems to exaggerate the alacrity with which the Carthaginians responded to Catulus' move to Sicily. The Roman consul sailed there in the early summer of 242, but the Carthaginians did not mount a resupply mission to the garrison at Eryx until March of the next year, a lapse of perhaps eight or nine months.[8] If rowers and marines were not available in quantity until March 241, then there was no chance of an expedition to Sicily before then. This delay gave Catulus ample time in which to train his fleet.

At last, once the fleet was ready, the Carthaginians set sail for Sicily. Their ships were filled with food and other supplies for Hamilcar's men at Eryx, the destination of the expedition. Hanno's plan was to make a fast run into Eryx and dump his supplies. He would then take aboard Hamilcar and the best of his troops to fight as marines. Hanno seems to have had a force comprised mainly of warships, and perhaps a few transports. The manpower situation may also have been so dire that he could not find enough rowers for his galleys except by denuding the merchant fleet of its sailors. That he had burdened his warships with supplies was probably due to an inability to crew both them and the freighters that were more appropriate for the movement of cargo. The whole affair smacked of desperation. Hanno did not even have aboard sufficient marines to go head-to-head with the Romans in boarding actions. For them, Hanno had to hope that he could reach Eryx safely and then embark Hamilcar's men.

Hanno waited at the Sacred Isle, the modern Marettino in the Aegates Islands, for an opportunity to steal into Eryx. But Catulus learned of his arrival, and he sailed to Aegusa, an island near Lilybaeum. Aboard his ships were the cream of his own legions to serve as marines. Then came an ill-omen. The weather, ever the bane of the Roman navy, turned bad. The sea became rough, and the consul was presented with a dilemma. The strong wind that was blowing favoured the Carthaginians, while his own men would have to struggle through heavy swells. On the other hand, if he allowed Hanno to gain entry into Eryx, he would then have to confront enemy warships that had been lightened of their cargo and had also embarked Hamilcar and his battle-hardened mercenaries. Catulus made perhaps the most fateful decision of the war. He chose to go into battle immediately and take his chances with both the rough weather and an encumbered Carthaginian fleet. There was so much riding upon this decision. If Rome suffered a defeat after having exhausted its treasury and tapping its citizens for funds, then it would have been next to impossible to sustain the war in Sicily for much longer. It would have been especially hard for Rome to convince its allies to give up yet more of their sons. Defeat might even have precipitated a revolt. Catulus had made one last roll of the dice for Rome.

On 10 March, 241, the Carthaginian fleet was sighted, and Catulus put to sea. His oarsmen's extensive training paid off. They powered their way through the waves and formed a line of battle, with their prows toward the enemy fleet.[9] The Carthaginians spotted the Romans, and lowered their masts. They were not ready for the battle that ensued. Their galleys were laden with supplies, their crews were green, and the marines that they had aboard were untried. It was a different story entirely for the Romans. Their finest soldiers stood on their decks, their crews had been trained to a peak of perfection, and most notably, their ships were sleek and light in comparison to the sluggish vessels of Carthage. Polybius writes that the Roman ships had been offloaded of 'everything heavy apart from what they would actually need for the battle'.[10]

The battle was a resounding success for the Romans. The Carthaginians were overmatched in every way. Fifty of their ships were sunk and seventy others were taken by the Romans, including some 10,000 prisoners. Polybius gives no losses for the Romans, a practice common with him, while Diodorus says that the Romans lost thirty ships, with another fifty being badly damaged.[11] Hanno escaped the scene and returned to Carthage, but suffered crucifixion. It was a harsh and unfair punishment to mete out to Hanno, who had been dealt a weak hand by his government. His ships were slow and his rowers were poor. He lacked the marines to fight the Romans in the boarding actions that were bound to happen. This was a fleet that was incapable of doing much more than ferrying supplies. It should never have been risked in a confrontation with a Roman fleet. Polybius suggests that the Carthaginians had simply underestimated Roman ability. '[T]he Carthaginians had expected the Romans never to challenge them again for mastery of the sea',' he wrote, and so 'they had come to dismiss the Romans' naval capabilities as no threat at all'.[12] They paid dearly for that misjudgement.

The Battle of the Aegates Islands should never have been fought. It need never have been fought. Hamilcar's campaigns against the Romans at Eryx during the 240s now seem like a misguided, quasi-private war that brought no real benefit to his homeland. The raids that he had mounted on Italy out of his base at Hiercte had no appreciable effect on the Romans, and these stopped as soon as he moved to Eryx. Simply maintaining himself in this new and hazardous position may have required too much of him and his men to dare to send ships to attack Italy as they had once done. So while the Romans in Sicily were harried mercilessly by Hamilcar's mercenaries, the shores of Italy remained safe from seaborne raids. To the Romans, this must have seemed to have been a fair trade. In five years of bitter campaigning, Hamilcar had not accomplished anything substantive that brought victory any closer.[13] There seems to have been little strategic point to holding Eryx aside from taking some of the pressure off Drepana.

Ironically, Hamilcar's bold actions around Eryx seem to have persuaded the Romans to renew their offensive at sea, thereby bringing about another Roman challenge on what had been a Carthaginian preserve for much of the decade. His fighting there, for all that it may have done the Romans some hurt, does not seem to have altered their strategy or dispositions in any appreciable way. Though his operations in Sicily showed him to be a fine tactician, he did not devise any means to bring about victory over Rome.[14] The brilliance of Hamilcar Barca seems to have been geared toward the survival of him and his men, not achieving any larger Carthaginian war aims.

But the Eryx garrison did become a dangerous liability when Carthage had to fight Rome for control of the sea again. Once the Romans had put to sea with a new fleet, the supply situation of the troops there was bound to become untenable. This is what brought about Hanno's mission, and saw the destruction of the Carthaginian fleet.

Given the state of the navies at the outset of the war, when Carthage enjoyed unchallenged naval dominance, and even the decade after Drepana, in which Carthage had chased the Romans from the sea, the failure of the Carthaginian navy at the Aegates is astonishing. Polybius, as we have seen, attributed a laxity to the Carthaginians arising out of their belief that the Romans would not fight for the sea ever again. Nonetheless the neglect of the fleet has to have deeper roots than simple complacency. The Carthaginian Empire was a maritime state, and armed ships were useful not just for fighting Romans but also for fighting pirates and other nations that might trouble Carthaginian commerce. It seems that there was a desperate and unsatisfactory scramble to fully crew their warships for the mission to Eryx. They could not have been short of ships, barring inexcusable neglect of their condition. So many had been ready for action at the start of the decade for use at Drepana, about 100, plus the 93 Roman captures, that there should not have been a problem in fitting out a fleet for battle in 241. The real problem lay in finding enough men for the ships, not ships for the men.

Where were these men? Carthage had not had a serious problem in manning its fleet beforehand. Though it could reasonably be argued that she may have been running low on funds, the undermanning of the fleet with poor oarsmen and insufficient marines seems to have had more to do with finding bodies than cash. Apart from the belief that the sea war was over, the Carthaginians may also have considered the war itself to be mostly over, with just a simmering conflict of small guerilla actions taking place. Too, there were problems with the subject peoples of North Africa that seem to have preoccupied Carthage during the 240s. We have seen that the Numidians raided Carthaginian territory in 255 while Marcus Atilius Regulus was busy devastating Africa. Also, in 247, Hanno the Great, a Carthaginian general (but not the Hanno crucified for his defeat at the Aegates) laid siege to the city of Hecatontapylus (modern Tebessa) in Numidia.[15] He was renowned for his actions against both the Numidians and the inhabitants of Libya, and was later chosen to command Carthaginian forces when large swathes of North Africa rose in revolt against Carthage. The basic grievance that these peoples had against Carthage, both during the First Punic War and afterward, while in revolt, was the harshness of the Carthaginian regime. Carthage levied heavy taxes and took much of the produce of these regions for itself. It stands to reason that the situation in North Africa in the post-Drepana period was far more serious than is commonly acknowledged, and may have occupied the minds of the Carthaginian government more than the war in Sicily did.

The war in North Africa may even have been pursued as an *alternative* to the war in Sicily. Many leading Carthaginians seem to have given up on Sicily, the retention of which was so costly and entailed an endless struggle with Rome for dominion. Expansion in North Africa promised more rewards than could ever be had in Sicily. Apart from the capture of the aforementioned Hecatontapylus, which lay some 160 miles south-west of Carthage, Hanno also took the city of Sicca, about 100 miles to the south-west of Carthage. This indicates the existence of a genuine plan of territorial aggrandizement, perhaps demonstrating that a powerful Carthaginian faction had chosen to set its sights on North Africa as the more attractive option. In the third century BC, the rural population of Carthage's African hinterlands appears to have been on the increase, along with a concomitant rise in agricultural output. This territorial expansion may have been undertaken in conjunction with the wars against the Numidians to the west, with Carthage's farmers taking over land acquired by force. Connections with Sicily were conversely on the wane and Sicilian imports to Carthage had declined as the war developed; no doubt because as a battleground whatever foodstuffs that Sicily produced were consumed by the armies and garrisons scattered across the war-torn island. Also, Carthaginian amphorae, earthenware jugs used as the common shipping container of the ancient world, appear more strongly in the archaeological record of the island, indicating that Carthaginian agricultural surplus was now being sent to Sicily.[16]

So Carthage let the war there go on, permitting Hamilcar Barca to tie up the Romans with his mercenaries while other forces acquired lands in Africa. It has been suggested that the two-headed nature of Carthaginian policy was personified in their foremost commanders. Hamilcar, the master of the war of raids in Sicily, represented the Carthaginian commercial faction which had interests across the Mediterranean and saw Carthage as a mercantile empire dominating the cargo trade. This one wanted to expand Punic territory around the sea. Another faction, championed by Hanno the Great, instead sought to increase Carthaginian holdings in Africa.[17] This made for a divided strategy, and the situation could not continue much longer once the Romans had built a new fleet. Then the Carthaginians were presented with an insoluble dilemma.

Barca was now effectively stuck behind enemy lines and was in need of resupply. The best man that Carthage could have chosen to conduct such a hazardous rescue mission would have been Barca himself, but he had been allowed to take up such a dangerous position at Eryx that he was the one in need of rescuing. Instead the Carthaginians were forced to rely upon Hanno, who was not nearly the commander that Hamilcar was. There may not have been any winning formula that Carthage could have applied when the Romans threatened again at sea. Hamilcar's conduct of a private war and the lack of attention that Carthage paid to it was to prove its undoing.

Since the Carthaginians were fighting an expensive war in North Africa while also fighting a costly war on land on Sicily, they may have withheld further support for the fleet during these years when the Romans themselves had given up on fighting for its control. The swift rearmament of 243–2 in which Rome built a new fleet must have caught the Carthaginians off-guard, and unable to withdraw enough troops from other fronts to meet this new challenge. There is also the matter of the loss of recruiting grounds for her military. Carthage's manpower shortage can only have been exacerbated by its conflicts with the subject peoples of North Africa. From these folk they would normally have recruited men for its army and fleet. Strife in Africa would have cut off the supply of the very men that she required to fend off the renewed Roman offensive at sea.

The shortage of men also highlights a deeper deficiency in the Carthaginian war effort. In its hour of need, with a large Roman fleet based in Sicily and the war heating up, Carthage's policy of not insisting upon the compulsory service of its citizenry in the armed forces showed itself to be a serious obstacle to victory. The direct involvement of its citizens, apart from the officer corps, was very slight during the war. The citizens took part in the defence of the homeland during the Roman invasion of Africa in 256–255, when Regulus brought the war to their doorstep.[18] But this was unusual. They may not even have appeared for service in Hanno's fleet in 241. Carthage ordinarily refused to conscript its citizens into the military, and perhaps feared the consequence of a revolt if it did.[19] The war, for Carthage's citizens, with the exception of the years of the Roman invasion, was always a distant one. This distance was not merely physical, but psychological as well. Their brothers, sons, fathers, and husbands were not off fighting the Romans. That was being done by mercenaries, foreigners, and 'other' people. Zonaras notes that Hanno's ships at the Aegates battle were also carrying money, which must have been placed aboard to pay the troops at Eryx.[20] Carrying coin cannot have made the ships any faster. The necessity to pay the soldiers was detrimental to Carthaginian success in this crisis. Soldiers fighting out of patriotic duty would have been much preferable.

For Carthage's citizenry, the war does not seem to have been allowed to burden them as individuals, except to the extent that it cost them money to pay for it. This was the fundamental difference between Carthage and Rome, one that Carthage did not transcend even in so desperate a time. Carthage was a nation of merchants, of civilians. Rome was a nation of soldiers.

Chapter Sixteen

Peace

Bereft of seapower in the wake of the defeat at the Aegates Islands, Carthage recognized that she could not supply her holdings in Sicily. Now that Rome controlled the sea, it was time to seek peace. Hamilcar, at the behest of his government, dutifully entered into negotiations with the Romans. Though he carried out the wishes of his superiors, he was never reconciled to the peace that followed. Zonaras says that the only term that Hamilcar managed to keep out of the agreement was the dreadful indignity of having his garrison at Eryx depart 'under the yoke'.[1] This was a punishment in which a surrendered army was made to pass under a low spear by the victor as a sign of its utter humiliation. Polybius gives the outline of the draft terms as follows, all of which were subject to the approval of the Roman people: (1) the Carthaginians were to evacuate Sicily; (2) they were not to make war on Hiero, Syracuse, or any of Syracuse's allies; (3) Roman prisoners were to be turned over without payment of any ransom; (4) the Carthaginians were to pay an indemnity of 2,200 Euboic talents over 20 years (later the payment period was reduced to 10 years and an additional 1,000 talents were to be paid immediately).[2] Another modification was that the Carthaginians were compelled to evacuate all of the islands between Sicily and Italy, which could have been used as naval bases from which to mount attacks on the Italian peninsula.

Diodorus preserves an alternate story of the peace process. Though some of the terms given by Diodorus differed somewhat from those reported by Polybius, the essence of the story is in keeping with all that we know of Barca and later his son Hannibal. Certain parts of the negotiations with the Romans seem to have been carried out by others, especially Gisgo, another highly regarded Carthaginian officer in Sicily. Hamilcar, it is said, listened to Gisgo read him the terms of the peace agreement that he had reached in stony silence, but when he heard that they were to surrender their arms and hand over their deserters (which are not the same as prisoners) he reacted angrily. He would sooner 'die fighting rather than agree through cowardice to a shameful act; and he knew that Fortune shifts her allegiance and comes over to the side of men who stand firm when all seems lost'.[3] Hamilcar's wish to continue was not granted. Carthage had been soundly defeated. After twenty-three years the war was at last over. Eryx was given up, as were Lilybaeum and Drepana, none of which had fallen to

Roman arms despite the most intense pressure, but instead were lost on account of Rome's control of the sea.

At least one counterfactual is worth contemplating. What would have been the result for Carthage had it earlier sought a peace agreement with Rome from a position of strength as opposed to weakness? She had the opportunity to do so in the wake of the various naval disasters that befell the Romans in the mid-250s when Rome had lost hundreds of ships and tens of thousands of men to storms off the Sicilian coast. Her financial situation was deplorable, if a story reported by Appian is to be believed. Around 252, Carthage sent a delegation to Egypt to request a 2,000 talent loan. King Ptolemy, who was on good terms with Rome as well as Carthage, refused, and is said to have replied: 'It behoves one to assist friends against enemies, but not against friends.'[4] Instead she was encouraged by Roman distress at their multiple setbacks and chose to continue the fight. She also had another golden opportunity to solidify the status quo in the aftermath of the Battle of Drepana. Once again, Carthage failed to use the opportunity to seek an end to the war. Her expenditure during the 240s in Sicily seems to have been minimal, more of a holding action than a dedicated attempt to eject the Romans from the island.

There is also the sneaking suspicion that a war set at a low temperature may have suited some of Carthage's generals on the island very well. While there, they were far from the oversight of their putative civilian masters in the mother city. They were the paramount rulers of their own domains, with private armies at their command. If and when the war ended they would have to relinquish that power, return home, and give an account of their conduct of their part in it. They were only too aware of the ugly fates of others who had held military command on behalf of Carthage, and how utterly ungrateful she could be to her generals. With resources for a major offensive against the Romans not forthcoming, and the spectre of crucifixion looming in the event of failure, it is small wonder that the Carthaginians seem not to have pressed the Romans too much, apart from the guerilla campaign being waged by Hamilcar Barca at Eryx.

This stalemate was not a durable peace, however, and as long as Carthage was at war she was still subject to the same vicissitudes of fate as was Rome. Rome's retreat from the sea for so many years after Drepana and the disastrous Pullus expedition contributed to an overconfidence that left her vulnerable to one more big Roman naval effort. Had the war been ended in the period after Drepana, perhaps confirming the territorial boundaries as they stood, Carthage would still have held important footholds in Sicily; Sardinia would have been hers; and there would have been no crippling indemnity to pay to Rome. She could have concentrated her energy on restoring her strength, increasing her commercial ties with other lands, and improving the defences of her holdings in Sicily.

Rome might have been willing to accept a division of the island after the shocks of the storms and the loss at Drepana, thereby concluding the war before Carthage's strategic situation deteriorated so miserably. These opportunities for peace settlements were not explored notwithstanding the unbelievable tale of the return of Regulus. The reasons for this are not examined by Polybius, but the same underlying cause that hindered the Carthaginian war effort, a lack of direct involvement on the part of her people, was likely to blame. The war did not touch the citizenry very much, and so there was little impetus to end the low-boil struggle being fought by mercenaries in Sicily. Then, after Rome had taken again to the sea and won at the Aegates, it was too late.

Sicily would ultimately be incorporated into the Roman dominion as its first province. This was the beginning of the eventual Italicization of the island. It was important too as a model for how other lands outside of Italy would be brought into the expanding empire. Cicero wrote many years later that Sicily was 'the first to teach our ancestors what a fine thing it is to rule over foreign nations'.[5] The Roman appetite for empire had been whetted. It would be a long time before it was satisfied.

Chapter Seventeen

Was Seapower Worth The Cost?

One might expect that Rome's acquisition of naval power and its critical contribution to its ultimate victory over Carthage in the First Punic War would place its value beyond question. The Romans, despite the terrible destruction caused to their fleets by storms, lost only a single battle at sea to Carthage during the entirety of the conflict. On balance, the Romans were far more successful at sea warfare, swimming chickens notwithstanding, than the Carthaginians were. Though Rome did in fact use its fleet to defeat Carthage, had she really needed a fleet to do so? Rome's strength had always been her legionaries, the building blocks of her armies. By going to sea in such a big way, did Rome err by shifting its resources to a venue where her enemy had the advantage? If so, did the shift detract in a substantial way from Rome's continued success in Sicily? Were the Romans being strategically clear when they built their large fleet, or did they allow the frustration that they experienced during the early years of the war, when Carthage detached a number of coastal cities from Roman orbit, to distract them from the real mission of the war, which was the control of the land of Sicily, and not its surrounding waters?

There can be no doubt that Carthage at the outset was the nation of superior mariners. Her oarsmen were better trained and her ships swifter and more finely built. The Romans were fully aware of this, and how could they not have been? Carthage possessed the large maritime empire, not Rome. Seaborne trade was the lifeblood of Carthage's economy, whereas Rome's was limited to Italy.

The viewpoint that holds that Rome's decision to fight Carthage at sea was a mistake argues that Roman seapower was not needed to win the war in Sicily. Rome was certainly superior in land warfare, and what it actually needed to do was take and hold a number of cities in the west of the island. Instead, the acquisition of a big fleet took on a life of its own. Not only did it drain men and money from the army, but it also encouraged the Romans, by their mere possession of so many ships, to conduct peripheral operations against Carthage in many places (Sardinia, Corsica, and Africa) besides the primary theatre of Sicily.[1] The Romans at times would use their fleet wisely, as they did when they captured Panormus in 254, but then would waste it on the fruitless (and embarrassing) 253 excursion to Africa that did nothing to advance their cause in Sicily.

There is much to be said for this argument, and its does encapsulate well the counterfactual scenario in which Rome devotes all of its resources and energy to the reduction of Carthage's Sicilian holdings from the land. Since the Romans did choose to construct a navy instead of maintaining a purely land strategy, we must ask what motivated this move. Were the Romans the victims of their own muddled strategic thought? Or were there good reasons to do what they did?

There are a few that seem to justify Rome's decision to build its ships. The first is that Roman land power was simply not as unequivocally supreme in Sicily when Carthage's seapower is factored in to the equation. Polybius cites Carthage's detachment of a number of coastal Sicilian cities from Rome's orbit because they 'were overawed by the Carthaginian fleet'.[2] This transfer of loyalties occurred over the course of just a few months following the fall of Agrigentum. There can be no doubt that the loss of several coastal cities in such a short span impressed upon the Romans that there could be no final victory as long as the Carthaginian fleet was free to descend at will on Sicily's shores. A fleet was needed to break the deadlock.

Further, there was the matter of Carthaginian naval raids upon the Italian mainland. Polybius mentions these raids in conjunction with the stalemate in Sicily as another factor in Rome's decision. Italy suffered while Rome could do no harm to Carthage's home soil in return. Polybius says little beyond that Italy was devastated by them. We can imagine, fairly, that the raids were possibly more destructive than Polybius acknowledges. It is likely that many of these Italian cities complained to their Roman overlords about the damage being inflicted upon them.

In addition, these raids may have raised the spectre of a detachment of the Greek cities of the Italian south from alliance with Rome via the same process of intimidation that had won Carthage the coastal cities of Sicily.[3] Alliances are political constructs just as much as they are military associations. Absolute military necessity often must take a back seat to the maintenance of the political ties that bind states together. The protection of these Italian cities now in league with Rome from sea raids had probably risen very high in the strategic calculus of the Roman Senate. A big Roman fleet would, in this regard, compel the Carthaginians to concentrate their own ships together for fear of an engagement with the Romans, and perhaps spare Italy's shores from attack by small raiding squadrons. The Romans may have been forced in part by diplomatic considerations to engage Carthage at sea to preserve the Italian confederation of which it was now the head.

There was also Carthage's continued threat to Roman logistics. Just as Carthage's fleet had attempted to stop the Romans crossing to Sicily in 264, it would have retained the unhindered capability to disrupt, if not cut altogether, the supply lines to Italy if the Romans had not built ships to match it. It should be recalled just how dire Rome's supply situation was in Sicily in the 260s before Hiero of Syracuse came to the rescue and gave them enough to get by. That this problem existed at all was due to the Carthaginian fleet's control of the sea.

Carthage's seamen retained the nerve and daring to attack Italy whenever the Roman fleet was not around to stop it. Hamilcar Barca's raids in 247 against the Italian coast up to Cumae evidence an understanding of what their ships could achieve when unrestrained by the enemy.[4] It is noteworthy that these attacks gathered momentum in the aftermath of Rome's loss of its fleet to storms, and its unwillingness to immediately build another fleet to replace it. This left the sea open to Carthage. Had Carthage been left with a free hand there from the start it is very possible that Roman armies in Sicily would have found themselves marooned, dependent upon the vagaries of supply from their allies, and with reinforcements from Italy slowed to a trickle.

It is always difficult to assess a 'what if' scenario fairly. A counterfactual can never provide the same evidence on which to make a reasoned judgment as actual fact. Controversy still surrounds the decision of the British and Americans to devote such massive resources and manpower to their bomber offensive against Germany during the Second World War. The argument against the strategic bombing campaign is that it was too costly in lives and machines, and did not harm the Germans nearly enough to be worth the cost. Germany's output of weaponry actually increased through the later years of the war, despite the intensity of the bombing of its factories by day and night. What this counterfactual can never prove is whether Allied victory would have been more likely by concentrating on other means of fighting Nazi Germany than by the use of heavy bombers. Might the Luftwaffe, now freed from their defence of German cities and industry have intervened more effectively in either Russia or the Western Front, and thereby stalled the great drives that finally saw the Third Reich fall? Would German industry have managed far more startling feats of production if it had been left untouched by Allied air attack?

What we are left with is history as it happened. With regard to the First Punic War, Rome *did* go to sea, and lost heavily in both ships and men, but it did win the war in the end. A land-only strategy was never tried, and can't be properly assessed. In retrospect, it may be fairly said that Rome had very good reasons to mount a naval challenge to Carthage that went beyond the purely tactical. Surely, the Romans would have preferred to fight on land, where they were predominant, but they must also have believed that they had no choice but to take the fight to the Carthaginians at sea too, for the reasons set forth. That does not mean that the Romans handled their fleets well at all times or made optimal use of them during the course of the war. They did allow themselves on occasion to become distracted from Sicily, and such distractions, such as the 253 raid on Africa, were only possible because they now possessed the ships to take them on adventures distant from it.

For their part, the Carthaginians seem to have suffered from a deficiency in their own conduct of the naval war against Rome. There is no doubt among the ancients that the Carthaginians were the better mariners from the outset, and that the Romans only achieved superiority in naval skill, as measured by their ability to row and manoeuvre their ships, at the very end of the war during the Aegates campaign. The Romans had nevertheless gained the upper hand at sea relatively quickly, once they had built their own ships and placed the corvus devices aboard them. The size and scope of the Roman naval challenge was a novel thing for Carthage. It has been argued that she had never before fought a major naval war.[5] That depends on the definition given to 'major', since Carthage had certainly fought powerful enemies at sea, such as Agathocles, prior to encountering the Romans. Yet the bulk of her experience of sea warfare had come fighting pirates and commerce protection. Her own wartime efforts seem to have been at times half-hearted, aside from the occasional excellence of admirals such as Adherbal and Carthalo. The Carthaginian strategy was to hang on to their remaining bases in Sicily, something that had been learned as a viable plan over long years of war with Syracuse. The fleet was not often employed as an instrument to achieve dominance over the Romans. It was rarely used as aggressively as it might have been. This was due in large part to the Carthaginian failure to come up with a counter to the corvus.

The enduring mystery is why the Carthaginians were unable to devise an effective response to it. If they ever did, something not even hinted at in the sources, it certainly took them a long time. Between its first attested employment at the battle of Mylae in 260, and the last attested usage at Ecnomus in 256, the Carthaginians had approximately four years to find a way to neutralize the corvus boarding-bridge. The actual time in which the corvus was in use may have been longer, if it was employed at Cape Hermaeum in 255, which is highly probable. Hamilcar's tactics at Ecnomus certainly seem to have been enacted with an eye towards drawing the Roman war galleys out of position, and thus reducing the threat of their bow-mounted corvi. This was not a direct counter to the corvus, and in the end failed to bring victory to Carthage. The only full-fledged naval battle won by Carthage during the twenty-three year-long war was at Drepana, a fight in which the Roman fleet lacked the corvus and had been mishandled badly at the tactical level by an incompetent admiral. Had a more effective answer been found to the corvus earlier in the war, then the outcome of the conflict, which was decided by naval power, might have been very different.

The Romans won the first naval battle that they ever fought because of the corvus. They were then victorious at Sulci and Tyndaris, and later won the gigantic Ecnomus and Cape Hermaeum encounters too. Rome had just five years of real naval experience by the time of Cape Hermaeum, and yet had proven superior in battle against the Carthaginians who had centuries of nautical experience on which to draw. Had these early battles turned out badly, the Romans might have quickly given up on seapower, much to the benefit of Carthage's overall strategic position.[6] The war might never have lasted so long if the Romans had been badly beaten at sea in these years. Roman tenacity being what it was, there can be no certainty in this regard, but it is worth contemplating just how valuable the corvus was in negating Carthage's edge in naval power during the first half of the war.

Yet the corvus itself does not explain the whole of Carthage's lack of aggression at sea. It is probable that the corvus was gone from Roman ships before 249. In both the Drepana battle where the impressive Adherbal was in command, and the subsequent convoy engagements fought by Carthalo against Pullus' divided fleet, the Carthaginians had shown that they could succeed against Roman galleys. It was certainly not beyond Carthage's resources to construct a fleet large enough to defend its holdings in Sicily, of which there were not many, and mount naval raids against Italy. Carthalo did this in 248, as did Hamilcar Barca for a time while operating out of his base at Hiercte. Once he had moved to Eryx, a move occasioned perhaps because Carthage was unwilling to continue putting resources into the naval campaign against Italy, thereby reducing the value of Hiercte as a forward base, these raids ceased. We have seen that Roman strength in Sicily was not reduced to counter these raids. Did Carthage end its raids because they failed to bring about the reduction in Roman pressure in Sicily that they had hoped for? Did they stop because they were uninterested in pursuing an expensive policy for seemingly little gain? Or was it perhaps that they were unwilling to pay the price to construct a fleet powerful enough to inflict such pain on Italy that the Romans might be made amenable to a negotiated end to the war?

The Carthaginian outlook was fundamentally different from that of the Roman. At root, this is traceable to the merchant mentality of the Carthaginians, who were focused upon trade and profit, not military achievement. The Carthaginians rarely fought for themselves, and used their money to purchase the services of soldiers from around the Mediterranean world. They do not seem to have ever determined a strategy that would have brought victory, and also failed to seize various opportunities for a negotiated peace when Rome reeled from severe naval disasters such as the Camarina storm and the Drepana fiasco. The Carthaginians appear to have been fighting not so much to win, but instead not to lose. The Romans proved more willing to shed their own blood to gain victory, and this ability to outlast an opponent, not merely physically, but also morally, was the crucial difference between the two peoples.

Part III

Conflicts Between the Wars

Chapter Eighteen

Illyria and Gaul

Rome had at last come to the end of a long, bloody, and extremely costly war. The Roman mentality would never allow them to rest, however. There were too many other enemies to fight, too many scores to settle. The circumstances surrounding Rome's intervention in Illyria in 229, which lay just across the Adriatic, were far different in scope and peril from those that existed at the time of the first crossing to Messana back in 264. Yet it was another overseas deployment of the Roman army, and it would not be the last. Rome's interests could never again be limited to just the Italian peninsula, and over the course of the following decades she would again and again send armies far outside of Italy's boundaries to do battle with her enemies. Perhaps most importantly, Rome had proven to herself that she had the mettle to weather the most devastating reverses. Her staying power was extraordinary.

The war with Illyria began in a similar fashion to the First Punic War. An obstreperous group of Gallic mercenaries had seized control of the city of Phoenice, in Epirus, from their former employers, the people of Phoenice. They made common cause with a warband of some 5,000 Illyrians that had been dispatched on a raiding expedition by their Queen Teuta. The Gauls betrayed the city that they had been hired to protect to the Illyrians. A relieving force of other Epirotes was mauled by the barbarian coalition, and Phoenice was only returned to its citizens upon the payment of a heavy ransom. Had the Illyrians confined themselves to despoiling Epirus or other Balkan lands Rome might never have gotten involved. Teuta, however, overreached herself by making an enemy of the Romans. She did this by failing to take into account the concerns of what was now the most powerful state in the known world, and one that was just across the Adriatic. Apart from the raiding of Epirote lands, Teuta's people had also been busy conducting piratical attacks on Italian shipping. Robbing Italian seafarers was bad enough, but Teuta was careless of the concerns of the Romans who were now the unchallenged overlords of Italy. Many Italians were taking their grievances with the Illyrians to the Senate, and so it became a problem that the Romans would have to contend with. Polybius writes that in 'the past the Roman government had always ignored complaints made to them about the Illyrians'.[1] That neglectful stance was about to come to an end.

Two commissioners were sent by the Senate to Illyria on a fact-finding mission. The Roman giant had been roused, and was not happy. The Romans would like the situation even less when their commissioners arrived in the arrogant Teuta's court. She dismissed Roman concerns too easily, saying that while she would ensure that they would receive no injury from her own forces, it was not the custom of the Illyrian kings to stop the piratical activities of their own subjects. The Romans saw this (correctly) as a distinction without a difference. One of the commissioners warned the queen that the Romans would 'do our utmost, and that very soon, to make you reform the dealings of the Kings of Illyria with their subjects'.[2] Teuta expelled the commissioners from her court, and Polybius even claims that she had the commissioner who had spoken so boldly in her presence assassinated as he sailed for Italy. The Roman people were so incensed by Teuta's murder of one of their ambassadors that they quickly mustered their legions and readied their ships to sail to Illyria. The Roman war machine had a new target.[3]

Queen Teuta readied her navy for further operations. Her war galleys struck at Epidamnus and these were repelled with great difficulty by its people. After this the Illyrians landed on Corcyra and began a siege. The Corcyraeans appealed to the Achaeans and Aetolians of Greece for help, and this was sent in the form of ten Achaean ships. In the meantime, the Acarnanians allied themselves with the Illyrians and sent seven of their own galleys to the join the force besieging Corcyra. The two small fleets met in the waters off the nearby Paxi Islands. The Achaeans and Acarnanians fought inconclusively, with just a few casualties on either side. There was a different outcome in the fight between the Achaean ships and the light galleys of the Illyrians. These had been lashed together in groups of four, and were oriented so as to present an inviting broadside target for the rams of the approaching Achaean galleys. The Achaeans predictably went right in for the kill only to discover that, once they had rammed, their ships were entangled with the lashed-together Illyrians' vessels, and they were unable to extricate their rams from their stoved-in timbers. The Achaeans' ramming attacks had been of use only to the Illyrians, who now sent their embarked marines across to the decks of the Greek ships, which they quickly overwhelmed by weight of numbers. Four Achaean quadriremes were captured as a result of this ruse, and one was sunk with all aboard lost. The success of the Illyrians again showed the effectiveness of simple, straightforward boarding tactics when employed against the supposedly more sophisticated Athenian-style ramming tactics. As long as a ship could be held in place, it could not manoeuvre, and it became easy prey for enemy marines.

After suffering this defeat, the Achaeans decided that discretion was the better part of valour, and nobly abandoned their Corcyraean allies to their fate.

The Illyrians resumed their siege untroubled by outside intervention. Without support, the Corcyraeans soon lost heart and made a peace agreement with the enemy. The Illyrians were to place a garrison in the town in exchange for lifting the siege. The Illyrians then left, and sailed back to Epidamnus where they readied another blockade of the city.[4]

It was at this juncture that the Roman military made its first appearance on the scene. Consul Aulus Postumius was given command of the army, while his co-consul, Gnaeus Fulvius, took command of the fleet. Sailing from Rome, Fulvius took his ships to Corcyra in the hope of lifting the siege. Corcyra, however, had in the meantime made its peace with the Illyrians, and though a relief operation was now not possible, Fulvius decided to go to the island anyway. The command of the new garrison at Corcyra had been given to Demetrius of Pharos. He was not too attached to Teuta. Polybius writes that he was afraid of what the queen might do to him (the reasons for his fear are not explained) and so he had opened up a channel of communication with Fulvius even before the Roman fleet had departed from Rome. Demetrius, not blind to Corcyra being the obvious target of the Roman navy, wisely sought terms from the consul. To Fulvius he offered to turn over Corcyra as well as the garrison. Once the consul had appeared in Corcyraean waters the island's citizens happily became a protectorate of Rome and Demetrius found a new line of work as an adviser to Roman forces during the campaign.[5]

From Corcyra the fleet moved on to Apollonia, while the Roman army of 20,000 infantry and 2,000 cavalry sailed from Brundisium across the Adriatic. This army linked up with the fleet at Apollonia, which was also made a protectorate. Once news arrived of the siege of Epidamnus, the Romans moved on again to go to its aid. The Illyrians fled once they became aware of the Roman approach. Epidamnus was also placed under Roman protection, and the legions next struck inland.

The navy took several coastal cities by assault, but was repulsed at Nutria, where it lost many legionaries and officers. The Romans nonetheless had the better of the fighting at sea. The light Illyrian galleys, so useful in raiding, were no match for the bigger Roman quinqueremes, which took twenty of them in action during this period. Teuta saw that her lack of forethought had caused the collapse of her kingdom. She had angered the greatest power of the day all for the meagre benefits of some captured Italian merchantmen. With the Roman legions marching throughout Illyria and the navy in control of the coastal waters, she too fled, making her way to the fortified town of Rhizon.[6]

With the Roman mission for the most part accomplished, Fulvius returned to Rome with the bulk of the fleet and army, leaving just forty ships in the hands of his colleague Postumius, who wintered at Epidamnus. It made good sense to reduce the naval commitment for the winter too, as the logistical effort of keeping a fleet of 200 manned was enormous. At full strength such a force would have required some 60,000 rowers alone. The Romans were spared the cost of making another such great effort in the following year. Teuta sued for peace in the spring, and under the peace terms she lost control over most of Illyria, was compelled to pay a stiff tribute to Rome, and the activities of the Illyrian navy were strictly circumscribed.[7] The Illyrian problem had been solved, but the continued Roman presence in the Balkans would cause friction with Macedonia that would bring about war several years later.

The Gauls also caused difficulties for Rome during the interwar period. Several tribes combined their might and mounted a major invasion of Italy in 225. Relations between Rome and the Celtic Gauls had never been good. The Gaul was the traditional bogeyman of the Roman imagination, and had been so ever since the Gauls had sacked Rome in the early fourth century BC. The fear engendered by this descent of the Gauls into Italy was so great that it united the Italians firmly behind Rome for the coming fight. 'Help was readily provided on all sides', Polybius writes, 'for the other inhabitants of Italy were so terror-stricken by the invasion of the Gauls that they no longer thought of themselves as allies of Rome, nor regarded this as a war to uphold Roman hegemony. On the contrary, every people saw the danger as one which threatened themselves and their own city and territory. For this reason they responded to the orders from Rome without a moment's hesitation.'[8] Polybius' statement is revealing. It is worth comparing the alacrity with which the Italians responded to Rome's call to arms in the face of the Gallic threat with Rome's dragging effort during the long war against Carthage. Recruitment for that foreign war (even if it was taking place mainly in nearby Sicily) must have appeared to have been for the primary benefit of Rome, while the defence of Italy would have been considered of benefit to all the Italians.

Rome, in conjunction with her Italian (and some Gallic) allies, amassed an astounding force of men under arms. Polybius gives extremely detailed figures, as he had access to the surviving muster rolls of the period. Between the Romans proper and their various allies they had some 700,000 foot and 70,000 horse ready for the upcoming war.[9] This is an extraordinary but still very believable total, and shows the kind of manpower that Rome was capable of drawing upon when the situation was dire enough.

An initial battle at Faesulae was fought and this went badly for the Romans, who lost 6,000 men, which was well over a legion's worth of soldiers. The Gauls plundered as they marched throughout Italy, and were for the time being satisfied with their haul of booty. They decided to return home with their loot and then invade Italy again. A separate Roman army now approached them, under the command of the consul Lucius Aemilius Paullus. He chose to avoid an immediate battle, and instead shadowed the Gauls with the intent of picking off stragglers and regaining some of the plunder. His colleague, consul Gaius Atilius, had arrived from Sardinia at Pisae (Pisa) with his own legions. His scouts captured some Gallic foragers near the town of Telamon and from them he learned of the result of the earlier battle and also that they were being followed by Paullus' troops. Atilius immediately occupied some nearby high ground, both as a tactical move, knowing that the Gauls were on the way, and also because doing so would enable him to begin the battle, with the barbarians, and thus secure for himself the greatest share of the credit for the result.[10] The Gauls soon found themselves trapped between two Roman armies, and the contest followed closely the standard literary tropes found in classical descriptions of battles with the barbarians. Savage ferocity was pitted against the discipline of civilized soldiers.

The Romans had the best of the encounter at Telamon, their arms and equipment being more useful than those of the Gauls, who chose to fight naked. Though the glory-hungry Atilius (not to be the last of such consuls) lost his life in the battle, the Gauls suffered a terrible defeat. Polybius reports their losses as 40,000 slain and another 10,000 captured.[11] The Romans would continue their operations against the Gauls in northern Italy for several more years, and with much success. By 220, Cisalpine Gaul had been brought firmly within Rome's power. The Gauls further north were still a threat, but Italy, for the time being, was safe.

Chapter Nineteen

The Mercenary Revolt 240–238 BC

The interwar years were hardly less troubling for Carthage and left it in a worse position. Much of her trouble was to arise out of the mishandling of relations with her mercenaries. These were men who had ably served Carthage in her darkest hours, and it was on account of their skills and bravery that Roman legions were not now camped amid the ruins of that city. Certainly these men deserved their full pay, which was now deeply in arrears. They had earned it.

Hamilcar Barca, who should have been more conscientious, had quickly given up his Sicilian command in disgust with the peace with Rome. So it was left to the Carthaginian general Gisgo to oversee the dicey logistical effort of demobilizing 20,000 soldiers in Sicily and sending them to Carthage to collect their money. Gisgo, with the foresight of one who understood the psychology of men under arms, had the intent to send them back in small groups to be compensated and then sent off to their homelands before the next group arrived. This would avoid having too many foreign troops gather all at once in Carthage. Unfortunately, the officials back in the mother city lacked his apprehension at what 20,000 mercenaries might do if displeased. The merchant mentality of the Carthaginians seems to have asserted itself at the worst possible moment. Yes, it was true that the treasury was close to empty, but it was sheer madness to make these soldiers wait until the entire army of Sicily had arrived in the belief that (as a group) they might be persuaded to take less than what they were due.[1] Hamilcar himself seems to have made many promises about the rewards that awaited them for their service, promises that his government would now have much trouble keeping. The Carthaginians were being penny wise, but in the end turned out to be disastrously pound foolish, in their dealings with their mercenaries. These men not only knew how to fight, they also wanted their money, and as events would show, they were prepared to use violence to get it.

It is remarkable how often cities in the ancient world were betrayed by the very mercenaries that were hired to protect them from external threats. Time and again wealthy cities were seized by unruly soldiers for hire, their citizens slain, and their property stolen. The First Punic War itself began on account of one such insurrection, in Messana. Another such seizure had occurred about the same time in Rhegium, just across the Strait. That it had happened at Phoenice decades after the two aforementioned rebellions shows an unwillingness to learn from the mistakes of others. Mighty Carthage had come to rely very heavily upon the services of mercenaries to make up the shortfall of manpower that its own citizens either could not, or more likely, would not, make up. It cannot be a coincidence that the Roman legionaries acting as marines, raised on a national territorial basis, proved more ferocious in boarding actions than the mercenaries bought by Carthaginian gold.

It may be legitimately argued that Carthage had successfully employed mercenaries for hundreds of years, and that their use allowed her citizens to use their skills at commerce more fruitfully than they otherwise would have if they were compelled to spend time in the ranks soldiering. Further, it may also be argued that the surprising (to us) number of mercenary uprisings in various cities of the Mediterranean reflects merely the limited record of negative outcomes, and that the use of mercenaries as defensive garrisons was actually much more positive than the various reports of insurrections that have come down to us would appear to indicate. Mercenaries may have been employed in so many cities that a few such relationships were bound to end badly for their employers, while most may have been profitable for both parties.

Yet this view misses the salient point. The safety of one's home city had to be the paramount concern of its citizenry. Avoiding the duty to defend the state in order to engage in mercantile pursuits or to simply enjoy one's wealth was an invitation to disaster. Apart from the fiascos at Messana, Rhegium, and now Phoenice, we should also add the troubles engendered by the mercenaries at Syracuse who were craftily annihilated by Hiero in battle prior to the start of the First Punic War.

Mercenaries fought for gold, and even if their relations with their paymasters might be good, they were not tied to them by patriotic feeling. If the gold ever ran out, so too would their willingness to fight. These men bore weapons, and had the necessary skills to use them effectively. When hired as a garrison force it is easy to understand how the temptations of the great wealth amassed over generations that surrounded them in a city of unwarlike citizens would have become irresistible. Some of these mercenaries made rebellion a habit. Polybius tells us that the same Gallic mercenaries who betrayed Phoenice had earlier, when in the employ of Carthage as the garrison of Agrigentum, revolted and pillaged that city over a pay dispute.[2] It may be a wonder that more such seizures by mercenaries did not occur.

That the Carthaginian authorities thought that it was a good idea, in any sense, to allow their mercenaries to collect themselves in Carthage shows a deep lack of understanding of the soldiers' mindset. It was also a serious blunder. It would seem impossible for the sophisticates of Carthage to so seriously underestimate the dangers that such a large body of men with no enemy to fight (and no money in their pockets) might pose. Yet Polybius assures us that the Carthaginians initially kept these soldiers confined to the city.³

The Carthaginians soon saw their error for what it was. The bored and insolent mercenaries began committing crimes while they lingered for their payment. They were convinced to leave the city and go to the town of Sicca, each man with a gold coin apiece, there to wait for their full compensation. While there, still unpaid and without the military discipline that war instils, the soldiers began to demand exorbitant sums from Carthage for their services. A Carthaginian general, Hanno, arrived at Sicca to discuss matters with the mercenaries. His visit turned out poorly. His appeal to the men to reduce their demand in consideration of the massive indemnity that the Romans were forcing Carthage to make, as well as Carthage's depleted treasury, fell flat. These soldiers had only just been resident in Carthage and doubtless were aware of the richly appointed mansions of the merchants and the other great wealth of the city. Hanno's cry of poverty was not merely unwise, it was untrue, and was made to men who were bound to know better. Mutiny was the result.⁴

Polybius writes that Carthage's attempts to quell the pay dispute also suffered from its reliance upon mercenaries recruited from so many nations. The men were in a frenzy and could not be calmed because they had no common language in which matters could be explained to them all at once. 'These are the kinds of troops', Polybius wrote, 'that once infected with anger and hostility towards someone, do not stop at the worst a man can do, but sooner or later behave in a deranged fashion, like the most savage of beasts.'⁵ Such was the penalty for relying so heavily upon mercenaries and not insisting that the natives of Carthage fight for the empire in greater numbers. Hanno then tried to talk to the officers to convince them to accept his proposals. Yet even among these select men communication was problematic. It is more than likely that many of these officers had a good enough grasp of the Punic language to comprehend and convey orders. Understanding the words of Hanno concerning their pay was another matter entirely. This lack of facility with Punic also impeded them in accurately explaining the Carthaginian offers to their countrymen. Relations between the soldiers and the Carthaginians collapsed. The mercenary army set out against Carthage for a reckoning and made their camp at nearby Tunis.⁶

So now it was Carthage's lot to be assailed by an army that she had once trusted with her safety. These men were veterans of the wars with the Romans, and were far superior than the citizen troops that Carthage could muster on her own. The Carthaginians also lacked bargaining power over the mercenaries. The authorities had rashly forced the dependents of the men to leave the city and go to Sicca with their menfolk, their thinking being that having their wives and children with them would deprive the mercenaries of a reason to return to

Carthage. This also served, however, to deprive the Carthaginians of potential hostages for the mercenaries' good behaviour. There was, for all intents and purposes, a hostile foreign people established within easy reach of the capital. Carthage was faced with a mortal peril in the form of these disgruntled soldiers.

Matters went from bad to worse. The Carthaginians tried to placate the mercenaries by sending supplies to their base in Tunis, but this policy of appeasement only made the men more grasping, and encouraged them to insist on ever greater payments. They accepted a proposal to put the matter before an arbitrator on the condition that he be a general who had served in Sicily, just as they had. They rejected outright the name of Hamilcar Barca, who was held at fault for abandoning them in Sicily and for not seeing to their welfare once they had arrived in Carthage. Instead, they accepted Gisgo, a veteran of the war in Sicily and an officer in whom they had some trust.[7]

Gisgo arrived at Tunis with some money and heard out the mercenary officers. He next addressed each national contingent in turn, and promised to pay each group what was owed to it. Polybius claims that any chance of this settlement holding was undone by a runaway Campanian slave named Spendius. This man feared that his former master would come and take him, an unhappy prospect because Roman law allowed masters to torture and kill their runaways. So Spendius agitated against any kind of amicable agreement between the mercenaries and the Carthaginians. Another opponent of the agreement was Mathos, a soldier from Libya. His great worry was that he would be punished for being an instigator of the mercenary uprising. This was a not unreasonable fear, since Mathos would be much more vulnerable once the greater part of his mercenary comrades had departed and the Libyans were left alone to face the Carthaginians' vengeful wrath. Gisgo clearly had good intentions, and was sincere in his desire to come to terms with the mercenaries, but the crisis had persisted for too long for his good faith gestures to defuse it. The mercenaries took what pay Gisgo offered in the interim, before a final settlement was reached, but then they started complaining that compensation for their horses and the promised grain allowance had not been provided. Discipline broke down, and several men who had come forward to talk things over were stoned to death by drunken fellow soldiers. This force was not much better than a mob, and in the chaos that prevailed Mathos and Spendius were voted generals of the nascent mercenary army.[8]

Gisgo had grossly miscalculated in his dealings with the soldiers. The Libyan contingent came to him, wanting to be paid. He foolishly told them to look to 'General Mathos' for their pay, a waspish remark that ignited a looting spree. Mathos and Spendius seized Gisgo and several other Carthaginians in his entourage. This was the final break with Carthage. The Mercenary War had begun. Other Libyan cities joined the uprising, seeing the revolt of the mercenaries as an opportunity to rid themselves of Carthage's oppressive rule. Rome was not the only imperial city to be resented by those she had made subject to her will. Carthage too was ready to exploit her subjects in Libya as harshly as she could as part of her war effort against Rome. She had taken no less than half of the farm produce of Libya for herself and had levied taxes at twice the normal peacetime rate on its towns and cities. The Libyans saw a chance to win their freedom and gave what they had left to the mercenary cause. Mathos and Spendius, perhaps not the most deserving recipients of this largesse, were recipients of it nonetheless, and had enough to pay all of their troops what they were owed by the Carthaginians. More importantly, they also had enough to fund the continuation of the war against Carthage.[9]

The Carthaginians reacted to the outbreak of full-scale war by placing the blunder-prone Hanno in charge of the army. Hanno had put down a revolt prior to this at Hecatontapylus, so the city's elders may have been encouraged by his experience. Alternatively, there may have been no one better on hand. Hanno began organizing the citizen infantry and cavalry, and of course, again recruited mercenaries, whom we would think must have seen the irony of the situation. The army of rebellious mercenaries by now had swelled greatly, augmented by 70,000 Libyans who had flocked to their standards. The cities of Utica and Hippo Acra, which had remained loyal to Carthage, were besieged. The hinterlands of Libya came under the control of the rebels and Carthage itself was placed under siege.

Hanno had drilled his army well, but his leadership on the battlefield left much to be desired. He had enough elephants to roll over the mercenaries outside of besieged Utica, and drive them off. He was unable to make use of this success because he underestimated the men whom he fought. He thought he had won the day once the mercenaries had fled, but they had not broken. Instead, they took refuge on a hilltop. Polybius says that they 'were men who had been schooled by Hamilcar Barca's daring'. They were conversant with the tactic of retreating and then counterattacking, and were far from beaten. Hanno had not even considered the possibility that these soldiers represented a continuing threat, and did nothing to guard against an attack by them. The mercenaries struck at the Carthaginian camp, which was disorganized and full of soldiers expecting a victory celebration, not a fight. These men were routed, and Hanno's siege equipment and baggage train were captured.[10]

The authorities in Carthage did the sensible thing and relieved Hanno of command. In his place they set Hamilcar Barca. His army was very small, just 10,000 men drawn from all sources – citizens, mercenaries, and deserters from the enemy – but he also had a corps of seventy elephants. He struck immediately at the force under Spendius outside Utica and lifted the siege, slaying 6,000 mercenaries and taking 2,000 of them captive. Hamilcar took several other rebel-held towns in the region, and then defeated the mercenaries again with the help of newly arrived cavalry from Numidia. Another 10,000 mercenaries perished (using the term 'mercenary' as a catch-all for all those now part of the revolt against Carthage) and 4,000 others were taken captive. To these men Hamilcar astutely offered an olive branch allowing them the chance to join his army. Those who declined his offer he allowed to depart, but under the threat that if they were ever captured again under arms and fighting Carthage there would be no mercy for them.[11]

Mercenaries elsewhere in Carthage's vast domain saw the example of their brethren in Africa and followed it. Some of these men took part in an uprising in Sardinia against their masters there. A relief expedition under Hanno (this was another Hanno) reached the island but the mercenaries whom he had brought with him deserted to the rebellious mercenaries. Hanno was captured and crucified. These vengeful men set about slaughtering the Carthaginian residents of the island, and their reign of terror was only ended when the native Sardinians themselves rose in revolt and expelled them.

Hamilcar's policy of clemency began to pay dividends. Mathos and Spendius correctly saw this leniency as a threat to their rebellion and worried that the less belligerent of their number might seek to end their part in the war on Hamilcar's terms. They invented a conspiracy that was alleged to have been a plot by some in the mercenary army to set free Gisgo and the other Carthaginians being held captive. A Gallic mercenary named Autaritus who had served for a long time with Carthage publicly argued against any compromise with their former masters. Giving his argument an Orwellian spin, he claimed that anyone who disagreed with him should be considered a traitor to the mercenary cause. Autaritus' speech was especially effective because he spoke Punic so well as a result of his many years of service in the Carthaginian army, and so more of the assembled soldiery could make sense of his words than any other speaker. Gisgo and the other Carthaginians should be tortured and killed, he insisted, along with all the other Carthaginians that they captured in the future. From the point of view of Mathos and Spendius, this horrific act would be an irrevocable break with Carthage that would end at a stroke any chance of a peaceful resolution. Their own personal survival depended upon the continuation of the war, and for that they needed the army to stay loyal to them, even if it meant committing an atrocity that would make the war into one fought without mercy.

In the chaotic atmosphere of the mercenary camp, murder prevailed. Some of the men came forward to plead that Gisgo should at least be spared from torture, as he had been good to them before the war. The mentality of the mob was such that it would countenance no such thing, and these well intentioned men were themselves stoned to death by their bloodyminded comrades. Gisgo and the other captives, of whom there were approximately 700, were next. The mercenaries, in the throes of a wild and deadly rage, severed the hands of Gisgo and his compatriots, mutilated them still further, broke their legs, and then hurled the still living men into a trench.[12] The galvanizing effect of this atrocity on Carthage was predictable. Hamilcar and Hanno combined their forces in an effort to crush the mercenary revolt once and for all. Their attempts to act in concert were stymied by their inability to decide upon a strategy. Their quarrelling placed Carthage's forces in jeopardy on occasion, causing the authorities back in Carthage to give sole command to Hamilcar. Carthage had still other problems. The cities of Utica and Hippo Acra, which had resisted the mercenaries earlier in the war, defected to the mercenary side, and an important supply fleet was lost in a storm. Carthage was again besieged by Mathos and Spendius, and the situation seemed so dire that Hiero of Syracuse and even Rome sent aid. Hamilcar attacked their supply lines, and this forced the mercenaries to raise the siege of the city, but their army, numbering about 50,000, was still very large.

Hamilcar's superior generalship got the better of the mercenaries in the period of campaigning that followed. He besieged the mercenaries under Spendius and Autaritus in their camp and waited for them to eat up their food. When they had consumed the last of their stores, they resorted to eating their Carthaginian prisoners, and then ate their slaves in their desperation. The mercenaries' officers concluded that once the slaves had been finished that they would be next on the menu of their hungry soldiers. No relief from the rest of the mercenary army in Tunis was in sight, so they decided to open negotiations with Hamilcar before they ended up as a cannibal's supper. Spendius, Autaritus, and eight others were granted permission to treat with Hamilcar. Hamilcar's proposal was that he be allowed to pick the ten men he wanted from the enemy camp as prisoners; the remainder would be free to lay down their weapons and leave. Spendius and the others rashly agreed to this term, and as soon as they had done so Hamilcar selected the party of ten standing before him. With the high command of the starving mercenary army now captive, Hamilcar struck at the leaderless mercenary camp and slew the entirety of the army, which Polybius says numbered 40,000 men.[13]

Though the peace talks with Hamilcar had ended poorly for the mercenaries, there was still the matter of Mathos and his men holding out in Tunis. Hamilcar's follow-up was to move against this position and crucify Spendius within sight of the city's walls. One of Hamilcar's officers, another Hannibal, failed to safeguard his own camp during the investment of Tunis, and Mathos struck at it hard. Many Carthaginians were either slain or driven off, and Hannibal was himself crucified on the same cross upon which Spendius had been nailed. After this disaster, Hamilcar was forced to give up his siege.

The end of the war was nevertheless approaching. Carthage summoned the last of its military age citizens, and her authorities insisted that Hamilcar and Hanno be reconciled, as their feuding was dangerous to the survival of the state. Staring into the abyss seems to have focused their minds, and from then on the two generals worked together well, having left behind the acrimony that had hampered their previous operations. The Carthaginians had the upper hand. Several small encounters went against the mercenaries and Mathos decided to seek out a decisive battle, a move that pleased the Carthaginians, who were depleted of manpower and treasure. A major battle at least offered the chance of a quick resolution to the ruinous conflict, which by now had gone on for years. The mercenaries were defeated, and Libya was brought back into the Carthaginian fold.[14]

Hamilcar had again proved himself to be Carthage's best general. It was largely by his efforts that Carthage had survived the mercenary uprising, though the entire affair might have been avoided had he not laid down his command in Sicily in a fit of pique and thereby abandoned the very men who had served under him there. In doing so, he opened the door to their being swindled by the authorities in Carthage. However painful it might have been to pay the mercenaries what they had been promised during the war, that cost paled in comparison to the price paid in blood and treasure by Carthage fighting the men who had once marched beneath her standards. Carthage was saved, but it had been severely weakened by this unnecessary struggle.

When in 239 Carthage made preparations to retake Sardinia, which had been the scene of a mercenary revolt of its own, the Romans claimed the muster was being made for an attack on Italy. Though this was perfect nonsense, it served as a pretext for Rome's own conquest of that island.[15] Polybius, who normally was defensive of Roman actions, couldn't help but call the taking of Sardinia 'an act of sheer injustice'.[16] Rome had improved its strategic position by grabbing the island. It sat alongside the sea routes that led to her western shores, and in Carthaginian hands it could have been used as a naval base from which to harry Italy. There can be no doubt that the Romans had sound reasons for doing what they did, but the effect on Carthage was dire. Her people were incensed, Hamilcar not least among them. Though it would still be several years before Rome and Carthage would do battle again, the theft of Sardinia was yet another important step along the road to a second war.[17]

Part IV

Strangling Carthage

Chapter Twenty

The Second Punic War, 218–202 BC

'It was not before the Carthaginian soldiers that Rome was made to tremble', wrote British military theorist Major General J.F.C. Fuller, 'but before Hannibal.'[1] Hannibal was born in the city of Carthage in 247. He would have been too young to personally remember much, if anything, of the First Punic War, but he would certainly have recalled the years of difficulty and strife with the mercenaries that followed. His father Hamilcar never reconciled himself to the loss in Sicily. He seems not to have even considered it a loss, inasmuch as he had never been defeated in the field and had only quit his base at Eryx at the behest of his government. In 237, when he was 9 years old, Hannibal went with his father to Spain. Most of his formative years would have been spent in the camps of his father's army there. Polybius reports a story in which Hannibal assured Antiochus the Great, king of the Seleucid Empire, that he was trustworthy. 'He said that he was there, by the altar, aged nine, when his father was about to launch his campaign in Iberia with his army … [Hamilcar] called Hannibal over and asked him kindly if he would like to join him on the expedition. Hannibal eagerly said yes … So his father led him by the right hand up to the altar, and told him to place his hand on the victim and swear unremitting hatred for the Romans.'[2]

Over the course of his life Hannibal never displayed anything but hostility to Rome and her people. He sought to fight them long after his home city had made its peace with Rome. As late as 190, Hannibal was commanding a Seleucid fleet against Rome's Rhodian allies at the Battle of Sîde in the eastern Mediterranean. Hatred for Rome was not merely a means for Hannibal to rally his soldiers and win over disaffected Gauls and Italians over to him. It was an *idée fixe* that had strong religious underpinnings.

There was never any real chance of a lasting peace with Rome. Just as many Germans, in the aftermath of the First World War, had refused to believe that they had actually been defeated, so too there must have been many Carthaginians, Hamilcar Barca foremost among them, who would not accept that they had lost the first war. The extraction of harsh indemnities and Punic lands as part of the 'peace' evoked similar feelings of anger and a desire for revenge.[3]

The Barcid Dominion in Spain

In ancient times, the Spanish peninsula was known as Iberia. The Romans called it Hispania, and it is from this word that the modern English name 'Spain' is derived, though the geographical entity so identified also included modern Portugal at that time. For the sake of simplicity, in this work, Spain will be used to refer to the entirety of the peninsula. The Carthaginians had longstanding trading contacts with the peoples of Spain, and had established a network of trading posts and colonies, including a major port at Gades (Cadiz), to extract the riches of the country. Spain, though very much a frontier land, was hardly empty. There were three main types of inhabitants. The oldest were the Iberians. Later to come to the land were the Celtic tribes. The fusion of the older natives and the newcomers produced a hybrid cultural type known as the Celtiberians.

Hamilcar conceived of the creation of a power base in Spain around the time of the Roman seizure of Sardinia. Spain was to become the great imperial recruiting ground for a rebuilt Carthaginian army. Politically, Hamilcar and his party represented the commerce-minded class which wanted Carthage to once again dominate the Mediterranean carrying trade.[4] This group had obtained the upper hand over the Africa-centred faction led by Hanno the Great. The taking of Sardinia had been a psychological shock that convinced many Carthaginians that another war with Rome was inevitable, and for that a powerful army was needed. Hanno's party declined in influence, with Rome's high-handed action winning the argument for Hamilcar.

Polybius writes that once he had put down the mercenary rebellion, Hamilcar then 'devoted himself to subduing Iberia, with the intention of using it as a springboard for war against Rome'.[5] To create a new army Hamilcar needed soldiers and supplies, and to obtain those he would need money. There were many fine soldiers to be found among the warlike tribes of Spain and Hamilcar would be able to train his new army there.[6] Money he had too, as he could draw upon the land's mineral riches to provide sufficient coin. Spain's silver mines produced an estimated 2,000 to 3,000 talents in yearly revenue for Carthage, an extraordinary amount.[7] With Spain as its base, the Barca clan came close to holding an independent state within the larger Carthaginian Empire, distant from the motherland in North Africa.

For Hamilcar, at least, the idea of an eventual war of vengeance against Rome can't be discounted. Even if the stories that surround him and his son concerning their hatred of Rome are exaggerated, and they probably are not, Hamilcar was clearly an implacable foe of the Romans. The entire Spanish project is itself strong evidence that he had a showdown with Rome in mind.

Hamilcar's 'personal resentment [of Rome] was fed by the anger all his fellow citizens felt' at its theft of Sardinia.[8] That he might lead a Carthaginian army stronger than the smallish force that he had at Hiercte and Eryx during the latter years of the First Punic War can't have escaped his mind. When he went to Spain in 237 he was, at about 38 years of age, still in the prime of his life. His work in Spain was conducted according to a plan, and one of its chief aims was to alter the balance of power in favour of Carthage. The scope and extent of his project indicates that he was preparing for war with Rome.

In this effort he had the support of his government.[9] Hamilcar was not a rogue general conducting an Iberian mission unauthorized by Carthage. Zonaras holds that Hamilcar embarked on the Spanish expedition 'contrary to the wishes of the magistrates at home'.[10] Yet it is difficult to see how such a large mission could be undertaken without the support of the government. Carthage was almost bankrupt after years of war with Rome and her own former mercenaries. The whole point of expansion, whether in Spain or in Africa, was to secure enough money to restore Carthage's devastated economy, which was also labouring under a crushing Roman indemnity. In time the money that he gained from the Spanish protectorate that he established would grant him a freedom of action from the home government, which was effectively bought off once the Spanish wealth began to arrive, but not quite yet. Hamilcar would have required some kind of 'seed money' for this great project. This initial funding would not have been forthcoming if his superiors had been against his mission. Africa could very well have provided the agricultural produce to revitalize Carthage economically, and the soldiers too, but Hamilcar's Spanish strategy won the day. There were still those in Carthage who would have preferred African expansion to the Spanish endeavour, collected around Hanno the Great, but the wealth that soon flowed from Hamilcar's new dominion in Iberia was enough to give the expansionist party the upper hand.[11]

Hamilcar did not simply set foot in Spain and begin hauling away treasure. Hard fighting was required. After his fleet put in at Gades, an old Phoenician foundation in Spain, he marched to the 'land of the Tartessians', who may be identified with the tribe of the Turdetani, and captured the valuable silver and copper mines in the area.[12] Hamilcar was far from chivalrous in his treatment of the natives whom he fought. It may be argued that the years of war in Sicily, and the bloody struggle against the mercenaries afterward, induced in him a harshness that was hardly commendable. Diodorus relates the grisly tale of his treatment of Spanish leaders in 235. In the Baetis River valley of southern Spain he had faced and defeated a Spanish tribal army of 50,000 under the command of a native chieftain named Indortes. This man was captured along with 10,000 of his men. On Hamilcar's orders, Indortes' eyes were put out, he was mutilated, and finally crucified in front of his horrified troops. These men were, however, shown clemency, and allowed to return to their homes. By this gesture, Hamilcar had demonstrated that he could be merciful, but if crossed he would exact the harshest of punishments. The freed soldiers spread the story of their crucified commander and the general who had let them go just as effectively as if Hamilcar had paid them to do so.[13] Those who resisted would run a dire risk, while those who cooperated would be rewarded. The Turdetani tribe soon gave up the struggle, indicating that Hamilcar's ruthless methods were working.[14]

Extracting the mineral wealth of Iberia was a laborious undertaking. The older system in which the native peoples did the mining and then traded their production to the merchants in the trading posts was replaced by one in which the Barcids took direct control of the mines. The scale was increased greatly and the operation became more sophisticated. Slaves were used to do the grunt work. The courses of underground rivers were changed and passed through tunnels and shafts, while pumps were installed to remove water. The silver ore-bearing rock was combined with lead, pulverized in running water, and then passed through sieves several times. The ore was then heated in a kiln to separate the silver from the rock and the lead. The resulting product was then sent to the larger cities on the coast.[16] Hamilcar was even minting his own silver 'Barcid' coins as early as 237. The portrait on the obverse of the coin has been identified with the syncretic deity Heracles-Melqart, a useful reminder to all of the Barcid connection with the god and the religious dimension of their endeavour.[17] He carefully spread the wealth around to make his own position in Spain easier to maintain. Appian writes that 'whatever property he took he divided, giving one part to the soldiers, to stimulate their zeal for future plundering with him. Another part he sent to the treasury of Carthage, and a third he distributed to the chiefs of his own faction there.'[18] These were intelligent distributions. He kept his soldiers happy, the government of Carthage mollified, and his own political supporters in the home city strong.

Hamilcar kept up his offensive. Once he had subdued the south, he advanced his forces northward along the eastern coast to Akra Leuke, near modern Alicante, where he built a fortress. The Greek city of Massilia (Marseilles), in southern Gaul, was deeply troubled by Carthaginian advances. This surge was a threat to their trading interests in the region, where they had established their own colony of Emporion (Ampurias) to the north of the Ebro River. Carthage had been fighting various Greeks for commercial position for centuries. Massilia was right to be worried that they would lose out. Carthaginian expansion was bringing their army ever northward towards Emporion. The Massilians had already had to give up on a settlement at Akra Leuke to the south of the Ebro because of Carthaginian pressure.[19] This prompted them to complain to their chief ally, Rome. In 231 the Romans sent a delegation to find out just what Hamilcar was up to. The Carthaginian general cannily answered that he was merely fighting the Spaniards to obtain money to repay the indemnity that Carthage owed to Rome. The Romans cannot have been completely deceived by Hamilcar's obfuscation, since the scope of the Carthaginian operation in Spain was so undeniably large, but their attention was occupied by brewing crises elsewhere, and they left.[20]

Hamilcar died fighting a Spanish tribe somewhere in Spain. He was laying siege to a certain town, which may have been Helice, the modern Elche, close to Alicante, and was waiting for the appearance of reinforcements in the form of a friendly tribe, the Oretani. Once they had arrived, Hamilcar, anticipating that he could rely upon them to continue the siege, sent the bulk of his mercenary troops home. Once these men had departed, the chief of the Oretani turned on the Carthaginians and launched an assault not on the town, but on the small contingent of Hamilcar's men who had been left behind. Hamilcar saved the lives of his two sons, the 18-year-old Hannibal and the younger Hasdrubal, whom he sent down one road while he drew the pursuing Oretani down another. His sons got away, but Hamilcar died while crossing a river in a vain attempt to escape. The great Hamilcar Barca was no more. He was just 46.[21]

But the project continued on without him. Hasdrubal, Hamilcar's son-in-law, succeeded him in the Spanish command. According to Diodorus, the Carthaginian army under Hasdrubal numbered some 50,000 footsoldiers, 6,000 horse, and a powerful corps of 200 elephants.[22] All of these expensive mercenaries were paid for by the precious metals being extracted from Barcid mines.

Chapter Twenty-One

A Second War with Carthage

After Hamilcar's death, Hasdrubal continued with the Iberian project, and his outstanding achievement was the foundation of New Carthage, modern Cartagena, in 228.¹ This port city became the main base for Carthage in the peninsula, and was of immense military importance to the furtherance of its dominion there. During his governorship he and the Romans entered into a treaty by which Carthaginian advance north of the Ebro River was forbidden.² The Romans correctly understood that Carthage was busily creating a powerful army that could be a threat to them, especially since trouble was brewing with the Gauls in this period. Had the Romans not been preoccupied by the Celtic menace to their north, they would likely have moved against Carthaginian interests in Spain, but the treaty was the most that could be done at this point. Hasdrubal was assassinated by a Celt in 221. Polybius' summation of his eight year governorate is positive. Hasdrubal 'hugely advanced Carthaginian interests, not so much by military means as by diplomacy with various Iberian rulers'. Upon his demise Hannibal took over the army in Spain. Hannibal's openly stated goal was a war with Rome.³ It is worth pondering how history might have differed had Hasdrubal remained in power and continued to strengthen Carthage's hold on the country.

When war at last came, it seems that Hannibal was somewhat surprised, not expecting that the Romans would draw the line when and where they did. He had spent his early time in command subduing Spanish tribes. It was when he set his sights on the city of Saguntum, the last unsubdued state south of the Ebro, that the Romans declared war. Saguntum was not a genuine Roman ally, but Hannibal's attack on the city gave Rome the *casus belli* that she needed. Hannibal had tried to forego an attack on Saguntum so that Rome would not go to war just yet, before he finished his subjugation of Spain. But his conquests had roused the Romans to take action, and they sent an embassy to him at his winter quarters at New Carthage after receiving frantic appeals from Saguntum to do something, anything, about the Carthaginian general. The Romans delivered their warning to him to take no action against Saguntum. Hannibal was dismissive, saying that he was merely protecting his own Spanish subjects from Saguntine aggression. Hannibal set out for Saguntum and besieged the city. His thinking was that war was inevitable in any case, and that capturing

Saguntum would deprive the Romans of an Iberian base from which to make war. Saguntum fell in 219, while Roman forces were busy securing their eastern flank in Illyria.[4]

Expecting that the coming war would be fought far from Italy, in Spain, Rome had turned first to suppress her former ally Demetrius of Pharos, who was now capturing Illyrian cities that had been placed under Roman protection. Lucius Aemilius Paullus, consul for 219, was sent to Illyria to put down Demetrius. Demetrius had become close to King Antigonus Doson of Macedonia, and was now firmly allied with that kingdom. Rome's troubles with Carthage and the Gauls had made their Illyrian possessions appear vulnerable. Demetrius sailed with fifty *lemboi* past Lissus, forbidden by treaty, and had raided the Cyclades too. Paullus made short work of the Illyrians, taking the well fortified city of Dimale in just seven days. Other Illyrian towns now came forward to surrender to him. Paullus next moved on to the city of Pharos on the island of Pharos where Demetrius was based. The city was strongly fortified with a powerful garrison, and Paullus recognized that the city would not succumb easily to assault, and decided upon a ruse. He landed most of his army on the island some distance from the town. With just twenty galleys he sailed to the harbour closest to Pharos. Demetrius, seeing how few the Romans were, sailed out of the harbour to prevent the Romans from landing. These two groups fell to fighting, and the full complement of Demetrius's troops left the city to come to his aid. The rest of the Roman army appeared, having approached along hidden trails, and took up position on a hill between the harbour and the city. The Illyrians were caught between both Roman forces and were routed. Pharos then fell on the first assault.

Demetrius and his entourage escaped from the disaster at Pharos in *lemboi* he had placed in a secluded cove in case of an emergency. That emergency was now upon him. He made his way to the court of the young Philip V of Macedonia, Antigonus Doson's successor, and remained there until his death in 214 during his attack on Messene. Crucially for the course of the coming war with Carthage, Polybius blames Demetrius for goading Philip into making war on the Romans when they were 'down and out' after the many defeats that they received from Hannibal in the first years of the war.[5]

A Roman embassy was sent to Carthage. They offered two unpleasant choices to the Carthaginian government. Either it would give up Hannibal and his supporters, or find itself at war with Rome. It was an ultimatum that backed Carthage into a corner, and she chose war. Hannibal meanwhile made preparations for his great expedition to Italy. He readied his brother Hasdrubal for taking over the governorship after he left, and sent some troops back to Libya to defend the homeland from the expected Roman attack there. His own army he organized for the expedition against the Roman enemy that he had been contemplating since he was a child.

Of the many dramatic moments of the Second Punic War, perhaps the most famous occurred at its beginning, when Hannibal led an army out of Spain across southern Gaul to cross the Alps and invade Italy. He did this in the belief that only by striking directly at Rome in Italy could he deliver a death blow to the Italian confederation which it commanded. Without the manpower of other Italian states to supplement its armies, without other peoples to crew its war galleys, Rome would be fatally weakened. In outline his plan was simple enough. He would go to Italy with his small but highly trained army and defeat the Romans so profoundly that their allies would desert and come over to the Carthaginian camp.

Hannibal first had to get to Italy to enact his plan of destruction. Here the possession by Rome of unchallenged seapower made itself felt in how Hannibal was compelled to reach Italy. An attempt to sail there with his soldiers and horses embarked upon transports was out of the question. Significantly, he had also left behind in Spain a sizeable fleet of fifty quinqueremes, two quadriremes, and two triremes in the hands of his brother Hasdrubal Barca. Polybius notes though that only thirty-two of the quinqueremes and five of the triremes had crews. These were certainly insufficient to make a crossing to Italy, and they were of no use to Hannibal.[6] Roman control of the sea was too strong. Hannibal would thus have to make his way through Gaul to come to grips with Rome's main strength. Polybius tells us that he began his march through Spain to the Pyrenees with about 90,000 infantry and 12,000 cavalry.[7] The route out would not be uncontested. There were unfriendly tribes in his path, Polybius names the Ilourgetes, Bargusii, Aerenosii, and Andosini, and Hannibal fought several battles against them. These are described by Polybius as being 'major' battles, which together resulted in 'severe loss of life' to Hannibal's expeditionary force.[8]

Hannibal left some 10,000 infantry and 1,000 cavalry behind in Spain under the command of Hanno, and released an indeterminate but evidently sizeable contingent of Spanish troops from his service, allowing them to return to their homes. He departed Spain with a greatly reduced force of 50,000 infantry and around 9,000 cavalry.[9] From there he made his way across the south of Gaul, and upon reaching the Rhone River he now captained an army of just 38,000 infantry and about 8,000 cavalry. Not all of the Celtic tribes that he encountered were friendly, and this cost him the lives of many of his soldiers. His traversal of the Alps was terrible, and cost him yet more men. Polybius, who based all of these figures upon an inscribed bronze plaque made by Hannibal that he viewed at Cape Licinium, writes that Hannibal at last escaped those mountains with just 12,000 Libyan troops, 8,000 Spaniards, and a cavalry force of about 6,000.[10]

Since these numbers come from a reliable eyewitness, we can consider them to be accurate, and use them to come to a reasonable conclusion concerning the overland journey to Italy. Before Hannibal had even encountered a single Roman army in battle, his own had lost *over half of its strength*. Even when taking into account the departure of the Spanish troops before he crossed the Pyrenees and the 11,000 other troops who remained behind with Hanno, there can be no doubt that Hannibal's army had been badly mauled by Spaniards and Gauls and sorely depleted by the wretchedness of the march.

Roman arms had not directly caused the deaths of any of these men. Indirectly, however, this great weakening must be attributed to Roman seapower. Hannibal had to make his way across Europe through hostile tribes because he could not deliver an army by ship. With control of the sea and sufficient transports Hannibal could have taken his army to Italy by water, and reached it in days. But Rome's control of the seas north of a line cutting across Italy to Sardinia and then Spain, made such a voyage impossible.[11] Rome's acquisition/theft of Sardinia may have made the second war more likely, but its possession, along with Corsica, denied their use by Carthaginian ships and shut what would otherwise have been a yawning gap in Rome's naval defences. The seapower that Rome had developed in the First Punic War at such great expense in lives and resources was of invaluable strategic benefit to it in the second war with Carthage. This point cannot be stressed too much. Hannibal would never have enough troops to occupy all of Italy, and every dead soldier decreased his ability to take and hold ground. It would remain to be seen whether such dire losses would be fatal to his ambitions once he descended from the Alps to the Po Valley and did battle with Rome's field armies.

Roman strategy at the outbreak of war was clear-sighted, in that it was understood that though Hannibal's intent was to invade Italy, Carthage itself would be vulnerable elsewhere once his army had left Spain. The Senate dispatched an army to Spain under the command of Publius Cornelius Scipio and another to North Africa under Tiberius Sempronius Longus. Scipio, with a force of sixty ships, would go to challenge Carthaginian dominion in Spain, while Sempronius' fleet of 160 ships would land in Africa and assault Carthage directly. Sempronius began assembling an invasion army at Lilybaeum, Carthage's former stronghold in western Sicily.[12] The Carthaginians, though clearly outnumbered in ships, still acted aggressively, perhaps as a means of dissuading them from mounting an invasion of Africa, and a raid is reported to have taken place in the vicinity of Vibo on Italy's Tyrrhenian (western) coast.[13]

Scipio sailed from Pisae and four days later found himself at Massilia in southern Gaul, a distance of about 250 miles. This was a move at a speed that Hannibal could have only wished for, but the rapidity of Hannibal's land-only movement through Gaul still astounded Scipio. He discovered that the Carthaginian army had already crossed the Rhone and was well on its way to Italy. He sent ahead his brother Gnaeus Cornelius Scipio with the army while he returned to Italy to take command of Roman troops there and meet Hannibal as he descended from the Alps. Word of Hannibal's speedy progress also reached Rome, and they recalled Sempronius and his troops. His entire expeditionary force, instead of sailing for Carthage, went to Italy, with the troops pledging that they would meet again at Ariminum.

In the first years after his arrival in Italy, Hannibal inflicted upon the Romans a series of crushing defeats of rare and devastating brilliance. At the Trebia River in 218 he worsted a Roman army, and at Lake Trasimene in 217 he smashed another. Hannibal's evident superiority in head-to-head encounters caused the Romans to avoid pitched battles. This strategy came to be embodied by Marcus Fabius Maximus, called the 'delayer' because of his refusal to do battle with Hannibal's main force. He instead shadowed it and picked off smaller foraging Carthaginian parties.[14] Hannibal's continued depredations in Italy caused the Romans to abandon this judicious strategy in favour again of a direct contest. This led to the unparalleled disaster of the Battle of Cannae in 216, in which a huge Roman army was nearly annihilated in a cunning double envelopment. Three major Roman armies had now been shattered, their legions rendered impotent in the face of a reborn Carthaginian army and its spellbinding general. Any neutral observer in Italy would have almost certainly predicted an eventual Carthaginian victory over Rome. That this did not occur, that Rome would in fact triumph, was due in no small part to Rome's possession of seapower and the flexibility that it granted in the making of its strategic plans for coping with Hannibal in Italy and Carthage's other forces around the Mediterranean.

Chapter Twenty-Two

Hannibal in Italy

After Cannae, it seemed as though Rome's days were numbered. But she held on long enough to survive the period of crisis that ensued and recover her balance. Cannae in fact was the high watermark for Carthaginian fortunes in the war. Hannibal could not have known this at the time. He fully expected that Rome's Italian allies would soon break away and that a peace agreement that neutered Rome would be made. Many of the Roman-hating peoples of Samnium, Lucania, Bruttium, and the Greek cities of the Italian south did go over to him, but the expected collapse of the Italian confederation never materialized.

That he did not march on Rome immediately following his success at Cannae in Apulia has brought him in for much criticism. In hindsight, only the occupation of the city of Rome promised a certain victory over the Romans. Hannibal did not believe this at the time. He was not dissuaded from besieging Rome on account of a lack of siege equipment, which could have been constructed on the spot when needed. Other factors may have weighed on his mind. He had inflicted enormous losses on the Romans at the Trebia, Trasimene, and Cannae, but his army too had been severely handled by Rome's legions. Even in total defeat, as at Cannae, the Romans were a tough bunch, and inflicted many casualties. Though Rome's losses there as reported by Livy had been in the range of 50,000, these men could and would be replaced.[1] Hannibal's losses were not so easily made good. Livy gives Hannibal's losses as 8,000. Polybius gives a smaller figure of 5,700, but whatever the losses incurred by the Carthaginian army, it cannot be doubted that Hannibal had won a costly victory. Hannibal's unwillingness to go to Rome was influenced at least in part by the mauling that his own force had received at Roman hands, leaving it too weak for Hannibal to contemplate a siege at this point. Though the tactical brilliance of his double envelopment at Cannae had led to the destruction of a large Roman army, the Romans had fought back with the ferocity of trapped animals, and bled the Carthaginians heavily before they were slain. His army was too small now and too wounded to bring about the end of Rome by its capture, if that had been even possible before Cannae.

There were also political aftershocks to Cannae. The Campanian city of Capua, seeing Rome faltering, became dismissive of her and went over to

Hannibal in 216. But by and large, the cities along the Campanian coast stood by Rome.[2] The result was a stalemate as Hannibal, unbeatable in the field, was kept at bay by the more numerous Romans. Hannibal's army was scarcely reinforced by Carthage, and it shrank every year as losses went unreplaced. He never had sufficient troops to fight the Romans in a major battle and also garrison multiple cities in the south of Italy, where he was mainly confined. His Italian allies soon learned that Hannibal could neither defeat Rome outright nor protect them from Roman vengeance. Capua was placed under siege by the Romans and taken in 211.

In 212 the Italian Greek city of Tarentum came over to Hannibal through treachery. Hannibal's primary hope for the city was that it would become a port useable by Philip V of Macedonia, with whom he was now allied. Philip's naval crossing did not take place, and the city proved to be of little worth because a Roman garrison remained in control of the citadel within it with enough food to sustain itself for a very long time. The position of the citadel controlled the entrance to the harbour, and the harbour was not of much use without the citadel. If the citadel fell, then Hannibal might have a functional major port on Italy's southern coast. An attempt to storm the citadel was repulsed, and Hannibal instituted a blockade to shut the garrison up and away from supplies and reinforcements. The blockade itself was weakened because the Tarentines' own ships were bottled up in the harbour by the Romans in the citadel. What they needed, to make the blockade work, was a squadron of ships on the seaward side of the harbour to close off the Romans' access to the sea.

Hannibal improvised. He noted that the streets of Tarentum were flat and wide. The Tarentine galleys could be moved along these streets if they could be set upon wagons. Wagons were brought from all over the city, and the ships were set atop them. Within a few days, the Tarentine galleys had been hauled across the city to the sea, where they took up position at the harbour entrance.[3] The contest now began to see whether the Romans could recapture the port before the garrison was starved into submission.

The Carthaginian admiral Bomilcar made a voyage to Tarentum after the fall of Syracuse to the Romans in 212, and in the next year was either still there or had perhaps made a second trip to it. Though the Carthaginian ships were helpful in preventing supplies from reaching the Roman garrison in the citadel, the sheer number of men who crewed a fleet of war galleys proved to be a major logistical hindrance. Supplying an ancient fleet was not really any different from that of provisioning an army. There were many hungry mouths that needed to eat. The sudden appearance of tens of thousands of crewmen in a city such as Tarentum that was already having trouble feeding itself only made the food issue more severe. Livy writes that while grain could be imported through ports under Carthaginian control, the amount collected that way never equalled what the Carthaginian crewmen ate themselves.[4] In contrast, the Romans, because of their limited number, were making do for the time being on the food that they had stored in the citadel with them. So having worn out its welcome, the Carthaginian fleet at last departed, though this did not much alleviate the food supply problem since the Tarentines were unable to continue to import their food without the protection provided by the Punic warships.[5]

With Tarentum in Carthaginian hands, the condition of the Roman garrison there steadily deteriorated as gnawing hunger took its toll. It needed to be reprovisioned with food soon or else it would succumb to starvation just as surely as if it had been overrun by enemy troops. In 210, a Roman supply fleet of twenty warships and a number of cargo freighters under Decimus Quinctius gathered at Rhegium and sailed for Tarentum. Just five of these warships seem to have been Roman. The other fifteen were vessels supplied under treaty by the allied communities of Rhegium, Velia, and Paestum. Quinctius took his ships to Sapriportis where he was waylaid by 'a like number of Tarentine vessels' under the command of Democrates.[6] It is clear that Quinctius had neither expected nor readied his ships for a fight because his sails were still filled with wind as he made his way to Tarentum. With a fight looming, Quinctius was fortunate at least in that he had found full crews for his ships along the way from the region of the south Italian cities of Croton and Thurii. The wind died away as soon as the Tarentine fleet was spotted, and the Romans hurriedly took down their sailing rigging and made their ships ready for battle.[7]

The ensuing engagement was especially vicious. 'Rarely have conventional fleets clashed with such ferocity', Livy remarks.[8] The Tarentines were fighting to preserve their liberty after almost a century of Roman domination. If the Roman supply ships could be stopped then the citadel with its Roman garrison would soon fall. The Romans had their own desire to show that the loss of the city had been accomplished by trick and not by courage. The nature of the fight itself bore all of the hallmarks of the engagements of the First Punic War. The Roman and Tarentine ships collided, prow-to-prow, and there was no opportunity to manoeuvre. Each ship was grappled by another, and held fast. Boarding actions followed in the tight confines into which the two fleets had become packed.

At the forefront of each squadron were the ships of Quinctius and his Tarentine opponent, a man by the name of Nico. Nico nurtured an ardent hatred of Rome, and he engaged Quinctius at the prows of their ships while the Roman was occupied with ordering his men about. Nico 'took [Quinctius] by surprise and ran him through', writes Livy.[9] Quinctius fell head-first over the prow of his own ship, and Nico jumped across to the enemy vessel while the stunned Romans looked on. He and his men worked their way down the length of the enemy galley, pushing the Romans steadily back to the stern. A second Tarentine trireme made contact with the Roman ship, which was quickly taken. The capture of the flagship caused the rest of the Roman fleet to flee. A few were sunk out in the open sea while others beached themselves where they became prey for the peoples of the nearby cities of Thurii and Metapontum. Luckily for the Romans, most of the freighters escaped the scene, but the supply mission was a total failure.[10] Oddly, the Romans had been defeated by the Tarentines with the same combination of Corinthian-style prow-to-prow ramming tactics and Roman-style boarding tactics that they had successfully used against the Carthaginians for decades.

Hannibal's war in the years that followed Cannae became progressively more confined to the territories that he and his allies in the south of Italy could control. The Romans were content for the most part to keep Hannibal penned up in Bruttium, where the inhabitants were particularly ill-disposed toward Rome. Hannibal enjoyed only limited success in convincing Italic peoples to come over to him, and these were primarily the Italian Greeks, Samnites, and other south Italians. The Samnites had a long and bitter history of war with Rome, and the Greeks of the south had only been brought under Roman dominion within living memory. Their dissatisfaction with Rome should also come as no surprise when it is remembered that the burden of naval service and the horrific losses suffered by the Roman navy during the First Punic War had fallen heavily upon them.

Chapter Twenty-Three

Holding the Line in the Adriatic: The War with Macedonia

The political picture for Rome became complicated in the wake of its defeats by Hannibal in the years 218–216. Philip V, the 21-year-old king of Macedonia, was encouraged by Hannibal's victory at Trasimene in 217 and most of all by the result of Cannae in 216 to go to war with Rome. Philip saw his chance to eject the Romans from Illyria, where they had been established since the previous decade. He ended his hostilities with other Greek states and waited for an opportunity to strike. He also sought an alliance with Carthage and sent envoys to Hannibal in Italy with the remit to negotiate a pact on his behalf. Together they made a treaty containing a clause that the Romans would be compelled to relinquish all of their Illyrian possessions and shed all their alliances there as part of any prospective peace with Carthage.[1] Philip built himself a fleet too, but this was never meant to be a match for the Roman navy. Instead it was more of a transport force with most of the ships being *lemboi* biremes of the smaller Illyrian type, swift and useful for raiding but not nearly large enough to sustain combat with the larger Roman quinqueremes.[2]

The alliance with Carthage took so long to achieve that the crisis period after Cannae passed without Philip making any kind of contribution to Hannibal's war effort that might have made a difference. This was in large part because the vagaries of war bear little relation to the overall measures of power or the disposition of forces. In 215, Philip's first group of envoys made its way to Bruttium in Italy to seek out Hannibal in Capua to open talks. These men ran straight into the Romans, and in a masterful bluff convinced the Roman commander at Luceria, Marcus Valerius Laevinus, that they were in Italy to form an alliance with Rome. This was accepted by the praetor, and he gave them directions to the rest of the Romans' positions and also the location of Hannibal's men too. Laevinus bid them goodbye, and they of course made for Hannibal, with whom they conducted their real business. With three Carthaginian envoys in tow, they began their return by sea to Philip, but their ship was stopped by a Roman naval patrol under the command of Publius Valerius Flaccus. The Macedonians again gave out their improvised cover story that they were there to make an alliance with Rome, but the presence of the Carthaginians belied that tale, their treaty documents were discovered, and they were sent to the Senate under guard. One of the envoys managed to escape from his captors, and found his way back to Philip, who then dispatched a second delegation to Hannibal to learn what the first had agreed to. Under the terms of the agreement, the Macedonians were to assemble the biggest fleet that they could, anticipated to be about 200 ships in number, and then cross to Italy, harry its coasts, and conduct further land and naval operations. As noted earlier, once victory had been had, all of Rome's Illyrian holdings would go to Philip, and Hannibal would then aid Philip in defeating his enemies in Greece.[3]

This second party, having visited Hannibal, and with the details of the agreement now known, returned home without incident. However, the delay occasioned by the first party's capture cost so much time that when the matter had at last been resolved the Romans had strengthened their naval guard in the Adriatic.[4] Despite the looming threat of a war with another major power, and with Italy still suffering from foreign invasion, the Romans considered an offensive response. They increased the size of Flaccus' Adriatic squadron to fifty-five ships and tasked it with patrolling the coast out of the base at Tarentum and Flaccus with learning what he could of Philip's war preparations. If Philip appeared to be serious about war with Rome, then Laevinus was to proceed to Tarentum also and make ready to cross to Macedonia with his troops to keep Philip occupied on his own territory. Rome's old ally, Hiero of Syracuse, again demonstrated his loyalty and worth by supplying this force with 200,000 measures of wheat and 100,000 measures of barley.[5]

In 214 open hostilities flared at last. Laevinus at Brundisium received envoys from the Illyrian city of Oricum warning that Philip had attacked Apollonia with 120 light biremes. His assault on the city had not been successful, and so he moved against poorly defended Oricum, which fell immediately. Valerius agreed to come to its aid, and after leaving behind a garrison under the command of Flaccus, he departed for Oricum, where he arrived the next day. The Macedonian garrison there was insignificant and the city was rapidly taken. Delegates from Apollonia now appeared, begging Laevinus' help for their city which was still under siege. An elite force of 2,000 soldiers under Quintus Naevius Crista was sent to the city, which got inside during the night without alerting the besieging Macedonians to their presence. The Macedonians maintained terrible security procedures, and Crista took his men out on a night-time raid on the king's camp. One thousand Romans had made it over the enemy's camp ramparts before the alarm was raised. They killed or captured some 3,000 Macedonians, with Philip escaping only by fleeing in his bedclothes to his ships moored nearby on the river. News of the encounter was brought to Laevinus, who moved his fleet to the mouth of the river and bottled up Philip's fleet there. The king, despairing of succeeding against the Romans, burned his ships and marched back to Macedonia. The Roman fleet went into winter quarters at Oricum.[6] Laevinus' command was continued into the next year, 213, and then the next.

The Macedonian theatre was quiescent for some time after the fight at Apollonia. Philip was engaged in fighting Illyrian tribes, and the Romans, preoccupied with so many pressing matters elsewhere, were content to maintain the status quo in the region. In 211 Rome made an alliance with the Aetolian League, a collection of Greek city states. The nature of the agreement indicates that Rome saw itself as a limited partner in the alliance, and that the Aetolians, as well as any other Greek states that wished to join it, would bear the greater share of the burden in fighting Philip.[7] The king by this time was not seen to be a mortal threat, but it was still highly desirable that he be kept out of Italy. So Laevinus' conclusion of an alliance with the Aetolians, building upon their longstanding conflicts with the Macedonians, was a shrewd and inexpensive move. Rome pledged to send twenty-five quinqueremes to support the Aetolians and to help them conquer Acarnania.[8] Rome had opened up a second front against Philip on the cheap, thereby preventing him from causing trouble for them in Italy while Hannibal was still at large.

Once the alliance had been established, Laevinus attacked and took the island of Zacynthus and the two Acarnanian towns of Oenidae and Nassus, which were annexed by the Aetolians. Having punched Philip in the nose, and ensured that the king was involved in a war serious enough to keep him away from Italy, Laevinus took his forces to winter at Corcyra.[9] The next spring Laevinus left his base and besieged Naupactus, which fell in just a few days. Laevinus was elected to the consulship not long afterward, and went back to Rome where he gave his report on events. Based upon the success of hemming in Philip, the Senate decided to withdraw the single legion there and leave the small fleet to guard against Macedonian intervention in Italy.[10]

The future conduct of the war involved the Romans to only a small degree. In 208 Philip scored a minor success against plunderers from the Roman fleet based at Naupactus on the Gulf of Corinth, who were caught wandering the countryside near Corinth with their booty. The desire for plunder in fact seems to have been the other great motivating element in Roman involvement in the war with Philip, which was clearly a secondary theatre once the Aetolian alliance had been made. Later that same year a Roman fleet of just fifteen quinqueremes under Publius Sulpicius Galba landed with 4,000 soldiers at Cyllene and drove the king off the battlefield at Elis.[11] As Philip went from potential threat to Roman survival to mere local Greek problem, Rome's interest in the fighting waned considerably. An army of 11,000 and a fleet of 35 ships was dispatched to Greece in 205, but this was done more to keep Philip occupied while Rome prepared for an invasion of Africa.[12] In the same year a peace was concluded between Rome and Macedonia. Philip had made several acquisitions of his own during the long war, but these were hardly consequential to the Romans, who had achieved their overarching goal of disrupting any cooperation between Philip and Hannibal.[13]

The alliance with Philip never produced the benefits that Hannibal had wished for. It was probably, all told, more trouble than it was worth. It is not even clear whether the agreement reached between Hannibal and Philip involved the Carthaginian government proper. Had Philip not allied himself with Carthage while it was at war with Rome it is doubtful that Rome would have intervened in the theatre. Rome did so, but with only limited forces, and this did not reduce the pressure on Hannibal in any appreciable way. The conclusion of the pact may instead have harmed the Carthaginian effort against Rome. If Philip had concentrated first on taking control of Greece, without also at the same time making enemies of the Romans, he might have defeated the Greeks and then been in a position to shut down their ports to Roman trade and only then intervene in Italy. Instead, the Romans were induced by the Macedonian threat to send sufficient forces to the theatre to sustain Philip's enemies and keep those shipping lanes open. Rome was able to import food supplies along them after Sicily's farm produce was denied to it by events there.[14]

Chapter Twenty-Four

Sicily and Sardinia

Roman control of the sea did not extend as far as the waters that lay between Sicily and Africa. Carthage was able to keep open its communications with its forces there for years.¹ It is hard to see how Rome could have done much to stop this when it was preoccupied with operations in several other theatres, not the least of which was Italy. Africa was much too close for transit between them to be shut down entirely.

At the opening of the war, the consul, Sempronius, had gone to Sicily to arrange an invasion of Africa with a large fleet. Even before his recall to confront Hannibal in Italy Sempronius' planned attack on Carthage had gotten off track. A minor Carthaginian naval raid on Lilybaeum had resulted in seven Punic ships lost and the remainder, some twenty-eight vessels, running away. Another Carthaginian raid had been disorganized by a storm and three of its ships were captured outside of Messana. Sempronius was far more worried about the threat of Punic naval raids than was warranted by these ineffectual attacks, and he shifted the orientation of his fleet away from the invasion of Africa to defending against raids by a Carthaginian fleet that was of vastly inferior size and strength.² It is worth considering what a powerful Roman naval expedition to Africa might have achieved in the days before Hannibal had entered Italy. But the opportunity was lost out of fear that these raids might engender a local insurrection in Sicily, and soon afterward, Sempronius' recall rendered the invasion plan moot.

Rome controlled the western portion of Sicily, territory that had once been Carthaginian, while her longstanding ally since 263, Hiero of Syracuse, held the east of the island. Hiero supplied the Romans with food and mercenary troops in 217 or 216, but died soon thereafter, in either 216 or 215.³ The political situation took a turn for the worse from Rome's perspective. Hiero's successor, Hieronymus, opened talks with Hannibal for switching allegiance to Carthage, demanding all of Sicily as his price. After a reign of little more than a year, with no agreement made, Hieronymus was murdered by a political faction from the city of Leontini. In 214 power in Syracuse fell into the hands of two brothers, Hippocrates and Epicydes, both anti-Roman in outlook. They garrisoned Leontini with a force of 4,000 soldiers, comprised of mercenaries and Roman deserters from the army in the west of Sicily. From their base at Leontini they raided Roman territory. Syracuse alerted the Roman commander, one of the consuls for the year, Marcus Claudius Marcellus, that Leontini had turned rogue. Marcellus moved against Leontini and swiftly took it. Much of the garrison was taken prisoner, with the Romans, as deserters, being punished in accordance with Roman custom, by being first flogged and then beheaded.[4]

Hippocrates and Epicydes eluded the Romans and joined a Syracusan army of 8,000 that had been sent to join the Roman assault on Leontini. Word of the fall of the city had reached them, but in a heavily skewed manner. Livy calls the report of a massacre there 'a tissue of lies containing strands of truth'.[5] The Syracusans were convinced that the entire population of Leontini had been put to the sword. While this had not been the case, the Romans bore much responsibility for the exaggerated story that reached the Syracusans. About 2,000 Roman deserters had just been flogged and beheaded before the eyes of the Greek inhabitants. Such brutality on a massive scale may have been judged a fitting Roman punishment but its effect was to add weight to the account of a Roman massacre. Marcellus was an excellent general, having distinguished himself in battle in 222 during his first consulship by personally slaying a Gallic general in battle. This had won him the rare honour of the *spolia opima* in which he was allowed to dedicate the arms and armour of the slain enemy general to Jupiter, something that was to occur only three times in all Roman history, and never again after Marcellus obtained it.[6] On this occasion, a lighter touch, and more sensitivity to how his actions might have appeared to others, would have served Roman interests better. Instead his ruthless punishment of the deserters engendered horror and revulsion, fuelling the rumour that the inhabitants of Leontini had been slaughtered. With the distorted but still believable tale of a blood-soaked conquest filling the soldiers with outrage, Hippocrates and Epicydes led them back to Syracuse, and took over.[7] For Rome, this was a disaster. The great port city of eastern Sicily was now in hostile hands.

The turning of Syracuse away from Rome encouraged Carthage to seek to recover the territory lost to it in the First Punic War. Several Sicilian cities had already gone over to the Carthaginians, who landed an army under Himilco at Heraclea Minoa numbering 25,000 foot, 3,000 horse, and 12 elephants.[8] Agrigentum was soon captured, after a half-century in Roman possession, and the Syracusans, under siege by Marcellus, were encouraged by the arrival of a strong Carthaginian force. The Romans found that Syracuse was a difficult target. Initially they had thought to carry the city by a rapid assault, just as they had done at Leontini. They might have achieved that result, Livy writes, if not for the scientist Archimedes, who was 'a peerless observer of the sky and heavenly bodies', and 'an even greater marvel when it came to inventing and constructing artillery and war engines with which he would, with very little effort, frustrate any large-scale enemy operation'.[9]

Archimedes placed artillery all along the walls where he thought they would be most useful. Marcellus mounted a major assault by sea. Sixty of his quinqueremes attacked the Achradina section of the wall where it met the water's edge. Archers and slingers aboard the galleys kept up a steady rain of missiles so that the Syracusans could not remain on the walls without being injured. Other quinqueremes were lashed together to form a catamaran-like vessel, with a siege tower and other siege engines placed on their decks.[10] These combined ships mounted the *sambuca* bridging device, which Polybius describes in some detail. The contraption was meant to deliver a party of soldiers to the battlements of an enemy-held wall. It consisted of a 4ft wide ladder long enough to reach the top. The sides of this ladder were shielded with protective breastworks and the top was protected by a wicker covering. The device was raised and lowered by means of ropes and pulleys fixed to the tops of the masts on the ships carrying it. Men at the sterns pulled on the ropes while others at the bow used long poles to keep the ladder upright. Once the ladder was close to the wall, the crews set it against it. Four soldiers were stationed on the ladder to do battle immediately with any defenders present. After them came their fellows, and thus a section of the wall could be taken and held.[11]

If this description of the *sambuca*, so named because of its resemblance to a musical instrument bearing that name, brings to mind the corvus boarding-bridge, then we have at least another clue as to what was inspiration for the corvus - the need to deliver troops to an enemy position rapidly and safely - and perhaps how the corvus was carried when the ship was not going into battle. It is significant that the pulleys for the *sambuca* should be explicitly attached to the tops of the ships' masts. This detail lends credence to the proposition that the corvus pole may simply have been an ordinary ship's mast used to mount the boarding-bridge, suggesting that the corvus was a device that was more easily lowered and stowed when not needed as is commonly assumed. The putative and oft-repeated reason given for the disappearance of the corvus - the frightful losses of Roman ships to storms that were blamed on the top-heaviness of the corvus - must at the least be reassessed if the corvus pole was merely a mast that could be lowered easily or taken off a ship when not needed for fighting.

Outside of Syracuse, these *sambuca* ships were greeted by stones hurled by artillery set on the walls. When Roman ships attempted to close to get inside the range of the stones from swing beams held over the wall, other of Archimedes' machines dropped heavy grappling hooks down upon them. These hooks caught the Roman galleys, and lifted them into the air by means of a lead counterweight on the other end of the beam. Once the ship's prow had been drawn out of the water, it was released to crash back down with tremendous force, and the ships so treated were swamped.[12]

Marcellus now tried to take Syracuse by an attack from the land, but this too was defeated by Archimedes and his clever defences. Foiled, the Romans decided to blockade the city. Marcellus departed with a third of his army to retake the Sicilian cities that had defected to Carthage. The Syracusans were now so confident of their situation that they detached some of their troops, 10,000 infantry and 500 cavalry, and sent them with Hippocrates to join Himilco's Carthaginians for further operations against the Romans. Marcellus caught them by surprise before they could link up with Himilco, and captured the whole of the infantry force while they were busy making camp. Hippocrates and the cavalry fled, and found safety with Himilco.[13]

Marcellus went back to the siege at Syracuse, where a few days later a Carthaginian fleet of fifty-five ships under the command of Bomilcar appeared in the Great Harbour. At the same time, on the other side of the island, a Roman fleet of thirty quinqueremes landed the First Legion at Panormus. Bomilcar sought out a battle with this legion, but they approached each other along different routes, with the Carthaginians marching along an inland trail, while the Romans followed the coast with their fleet proceeding just offshore in support. Having missed the Romans, Bomilcar, now back at Syracuse, decided to leave. He refused to seek a naval fight with the Romans, who had twice as many ships as he did. His men were also eating the food that the Syracusans needed to hold out, and went back to Africa with his ships.[14]

Himilco, upon his own approach to Syracuse, saw that the Roman siege lines were too well fortified for him to make any impression on them, and turned to bringing other Sicilian cities to his side. Murgantia, a storehouse town for the Romans, defected, as did other cities in Sicily. The alacrity with which Sicilian cities threw their lot in with the Carthaginians highlights the unwelcome nature of Roman overlordship. For many Sicilians, the Romans were as alien as the Carthaginians, and paying Roman taxes was hardly pleasant. At one city in central Sicily, Henna, the citizens complained to the Roman garrison commander that he should return the keys to the city gates to them if they were not simply the slaves of the Romans but instead free men in alliance with Rome. The Hennans were already in league with Himilco and sought to rid themselves of the garrison, but its commander, Lucius Pinarius, was aware of their intentions. He played along until he called them to an assembly to discuss the matter. Once he had the irksome Hennans gathered together in a theatre, he summoned his men and slaughtered the unarmed townspeople.[15] Henna remained in Roman hands, but the massacre spurred other defections to Carthage.

The fall of Syracuse was a long time in coming. The siege was still ongoing in 212 when a Spartan named Damippus was captured by the Romans. Epicydes asked that he be ransomed. During the negotiations, which were taking place close to the walls of Syracuse, the Romans noticed that one section of the walls was lower than had been earlier thought. Marcellus put 1,000 men over it at night during a feast in honour of Artemis while the Syracusans were sleeping off the effects of their wine. They were followed soon afterward by the rest of his army. Even so, Syracuse was so large that the Romans held only a part of the city, the Epipolae, with Epicydes still in control elsewhere and a Carthaginian fleet under Bomilcar moored in the Great Harbour. Marcellus tried to convince the rest of the city to surrender, but one section, the Achradina, was held mostly by Roman deserters, and they were certain that giving up would mean their deaths and would not treat with the Roman envoys.[16]

Himilco and Hippocrates arrived outside the city and Hippocrates set up a fortified camp in the Great Harbour. Bomilcar used the cover of a storm to escape from the Great Harbour with thirty-five ships to Carthage, where he persuaded the Carthaginian government to give him additional ships to take back to Syracuse. With his fleet now increased to 100 he returned to the besieged city a few days later. There was an outbreak of plague, and both sides suffered. Marcellus brought most of his men into the city where they could be cared for indoors, and the Sicilians left the area to be away from the sickness, but the Carthaginians, who were encamped near the Great Harbour, suffered terribly and were, according to Livy, 'wiped out' by the disease.[17]

The Sicilians assembled a large army to go to the rescue of the Syracusans who were still holding out. Bomilcar made his way back to Carthage once more and was given a fleet of 130 galleys and 700 transports to resupply his allies. Unfavourable winds kept him from rounding Cape Pachynus, and Epicydes, fearing that Bomilcar would lose heart, left Syracuse by sea to join Bomilcar. The Carthaginian admiral was 'dreading a naval engagement' with the Romans, says Livy, not because of inferior numbers, since he had more ships, but because the Roman fleet had the wind in its favour. After a few days the winds that caused him so much concern lessened, and he made ready to engage the Roman fleet. Bomilcar, for whatever reason, fled as soon as enemy ships approached, and went to Tarentum, which was in Carthaginian hands at this time. The cargo ships were ordered back to Carthage, and Epicydes abandoned Syracuse entirely and went to Agrigentum.[18]

Syracuse was later was betrayed to the Romans by its mercenary garrison, and while the citizenry were spared (except for Archimedes, who is said to have been slain) the city was ransacked.[19] Livy writes that 'the quantity of booty taken was so great that more would hardly have been forthcoming if it were Carthage itself that had been captured'.[20] The paintings and statuary of the wealthy city were removed by Marcellus and sent to Rome.

The Syracusans had been deprived of their property, but were by and large left with their lives. There was more unpleasantness to come. The disruptions and displacements caused by the siege and the sack brought about a famine. Luckily for both the Romans and the miserable inhabitants of the city, the Roman naval commander at Lilybaeum, Titus Otacilius Crassus, had conducted a hugely successful naval raid on Utica in Africa, seizing 130 grain freighters and plundering the countryside. He was back at Lilybaeum in the Sicilian west only two days after setting out, and hearing of the fall of Syracuse which had just occurred, sent the grain there, relieving the food emergency.[21]

Roman control of Sicily was by no means total. Carthage still held Agrigentum on the southern coast. Here Hanno and Epicydes had their haven, and they were joined there by another Carthaginian officer, Muttines, who had served with Hannibal and been sent by him to replace Hippocrates, who was now dead. Muttines was an enterprising commander, and took his Numidian cavalry on raids deep into Roman-held lands and gave encouragement by his presence to pro-Carthaginian communities on the island. Muttines, Hanno, and Epicydes went on the offensive against the Romans, but the old bugbear of mercenary dissatisfaction made yet another appearance, at the worst possible time. While engaged with Marcellus in battle near the Himera River, and with the Carthaginians getting the better of the Romans, some 300 Numidians mutinied and stood down at Heraclea Minoa. Muttines went off to calm them, and get them back into the fight. Before departing he warned Hanno and Epicydes not to do anything without him.

This upset Hanno, who considered the low-born Muttines to be an upstart. The problems with the Numidians were not limited to those who had gone to Heraclea Minoa. While Marcellus was arraying his troops for battle he was approached by ten of them. Their discontent seems to have originated in the dismissal of a native officer. Though the circumstances are not given, one can imagine that Carthaginian high-handedness and insensitivity to the feelings of their foreign troops were to blame for the predicament. These Numidians told Marcellus that they sympathized with the 300 men who had gone to Heraclea Minoa. When battle was joined, before Muttines had returned, the Numidians did not engage the Romans but fled from the field with the rest of the Carthaginian army, hiding away in surrounding towns and avoiding Agrigentum which they expected to come under siege.

Muttines would remain a thorn in the side of the Romans long afterward, raiding aggressively out of his fortified base at Agrigentum. When the end came for Carthage in Sicily, Muttines was at the centre of the action. Hanno was with him in the city, full of jealousy for his more talented underling. Having learned nothing from the earlier disaster at the Himera, in 210 Hanno transferred

Muttines' command to his own son. He thought that doing this would break the bond that Muttines had with his Numidian horsemen. Muttines, incensed, chose to hand the city over to the Romans. The Roman commander in Sicily was Marcus Valerius Laevinus and to him Muttines sent several agents to work out a plan. Muttines' Numidians opened the gates to the Romans on the appointed day, and Roman troops surged into the town. Hanno and Epicydes barely escaped back to Carthage. The Sicilian cities that had allied themselves with Carthage were reclaimed by the Romans, and Sicily was as a whole made into a Roman province. From now on Sicilian grain would be used to feed the hungry masses of Rome and Italy.[22] Rome's legions would also make use of it too. The agricultural produce from Sicily enabled her to raise and sustain her numerous legions over the course of the war.[23] Rome routinely had twenty or more such formations in the field in any given year.

Sardinia

In 217, a fleet of seventy Punic warships operating out of Sardinia struck at Italy near Pisae. Their intention was to make contact with Hannibal's army, which had just recently won at Lake Trasimene. The Romans reacted by putting to sea a much larger fleet of 120 quinqueremes, and the Carthaginian fleet fled back to Sardinia.[24] Seventy war galleys was not an inconsiderable force, but it could do little when the Romans possessed such an overwhelming advantage in numbers.

Heavy Roman taxation (made necessary to pay for the war) caused enormous discontent among the Sardinians. In 215, a rebellion erupted under the leadership of a local nobleman named Hampsicora. The job of crushing the revolt was given to Titus Manlius Torquatus, a former consul and an old 'Sardinia hand' who had previously put down the Sardinians after the island had been taken from Carthage. Manlius landed his expeditionary force at Caralis, and short of legionaries, drafted crewmen from his ships to serve in his army. In this way he scraped together a force of 1,200 cavalry and 22,000 infantry.[25] A Carthaginian force commanded by Hasdrubal the Bald sailed for Sardinia to aid the rebels but it ran into a storm and had to put into the Balearic Islands. This reduced the problems that Manlius would be immediately forced to confront. Manlius invaded rebel-held territory, and brought the Sardinians to battle. Three thousand were killed and 800 captured by the Romans. The rest fled to the city of Cornus. The revolt might have been stamped out then and there, but the Carthaginian fleet arrived in the nick of time to keep it going, and Manlius pulled back to Caralis, thereby allowing Hampsicora to link up with the Carthaginian army that had just landed.

Hasdrubal began his campaign by looting the farmland of Rome's allies. Manlius confronted him outside of Caralis. In the four-hour battle that ensued, the Sardinians proved to be no match for the Romans, and were defeated. The Carthaginian troops had more staying power, and held their own for some time, but they too turned and ran once they saw that the Sardinians on the other end of the line were fleeing. These men were trapped by the Romans who had just driven off the Sardinians, with the Romans executing a turning manoeuvre that cut off the Carthaginian's avenue of retreat. Livy calls the conclusion of the engagement 'more a bloodbath than a battle' and gives Sardinian/Carthaginian losses as 12,000 killed and 3,700 captured.[26] Hasdrubal the Bald was taken captive and Hampsicora died by his own hand. The revolt smashed, Sardinia would be the target of a handful of Carthaginian naval raids in subsequent years, but was now firmly back in Roman control.

At roughly the same time, a Roman fleet under Titus Otacilius Crassus sailed out of Lilybaeum in Sicily when word came that Hasdrubal's fleet had gone from the Balearics to Sardinia. It ran into the Carthaginians as they sailed back from Sardinia to Africa. A brief fight took place, with the Romans capturing seven ships and the rest of the Carthaginian fleet escaping the encounter.[27]

Chapter Twenty-Five

Carthage's Spanish Ulcer

Publius Cornelius Scipio's decision to send his army on to Spain even when Hannibal was known to have gotten past him on his way to Italy had been a sound strategic decision. Roman troops in Spain contested Carthage's prime recruiting grounds and source of revenue. Hannibal was well-aware that the enemy might try to take the fight to Spain while he was away in Italy, and had left his brother with substantial forces to defend the country. Here Rome's edge in manpower enhanced the strategic superiority that it derived from control of the sea. We have already seen that Hannibal lost many thousands of hard-to-replace troops on the march to Italy, a route that was forced on him because sea transit was denied to his army. His campaign would have benefited greatly from an open overland line of communication through northern Italy across Gaul back to Spain. This was never to be, because Rome's military presence in the north of Spain prevented it. Scipio had sent his brother Gnaeus to Spain with his sixty ships and army while he returned to Italy. In 218, Gnaeus Cornelius Scipio made landfall at Emporion, a Massilian (Greek) colony on Spain's eastern coast. This became the naval base from which he mounted raids up and down the coast as far as the Ebro, receiving the surrender of a number of seaside cities. Once they had been secured, he marched his troops inland and brought over several other cities to his side. A victorious battle was fought against the Carthaginians under Hanno near Cissa. Hanno was taken captive, and the region of Spain north of the Ebro came over to Rome.[1]

Hasdrubal Barca was based further south, and moved north of the Ebro when he learned of Roman successes. He surprised the Roman fleet's crews, who had grown complacent as their army had been continually triumphant. The Roman sailors were wandering across the Spanish countryside careless of their own security when Hasdrubal's troops attacked. Those men who were not slain ran for the safety of their ships. Hasdrubal withdrew and established his winter quarters at New Carthage. Scipio returned in the meanwhile and found that disaster had befallen his fleet. He punished those he found responsible for the losses and went into winter quarters at Tarraco.[2]

Over the winter at New Carthage Hasdrubal Barca reconditioned the thirty quinqueremes that had been left to him by his brother Hannibal. He found the crews for another ten such ships, and at the start of the summer of 217 he had a fleet of forty ready for combat. These ships were placed under the command of Hamilcar, while Hasdrubal led his army northward to the Ebro, with the fleet travelling with it along the shore. Gnaeus Scipio rejected fighting on land, and instead responded by putting some of his best soldiers aboard thirty-five of his own quinqueremes. Two days out of Tarraco he landed near the Ebro. Two Massilian reconnaissance ships were sent to search for the enemy fleet, which was found at anchor off the mouth of the Ebro. Scipio moved quickly to attack, but the Carthaginians were warned of his approach by their own scouts.[3] The Carthaginians fought with determination, but only for a little while, thereby conforming to the old pattern of Roman-Carthaginian naval battles. In the early part of the engagement, two Punic ships were captured outright; four more were disabled, and the others disengaged and sought the safety of the shore. The crews of these vessels disembarked and found protection with their soldiers, allowing the Romans to come right in and tow away many of their galleys. Polybius gives the total haul taken by the Romans as twenty-five ships.[4]

The Roman Senate was delighted by the achievement, and fitted out twenty additional ships to go to Spain with Gnaeus' brother Publius Cornelius Scipio in command. Both brothers were to undertake the direction of the Iberian campaign together, which the Roman government considered of paramount importance. Should the Carthaginians ever secure Spain for themselves it would have meant that the troops and supplies of that country would have been fed straight into the Carthaginian war machine, fuelling its bid for control of the sea while also making more soldiers and money available for Hannibal in Italy.[5] Far from being a needless distraction from what might have superficially been regarded as the principal battlefield in Italy, Spain was in fact a central arena where Carthaginian power could be broken. It was of vital importance that the Carthaginian forces that were in Spain remained pinned down, unable to march to the aid of Hannibal, who could have used reinforcements. Once Publius Cornelius Scipio arrived in theatre he and his brother moved south of the Ebro to contest the Carthaginians for the southern regions where their hold was strongest. The Scipio brothers marched to Saguntum, but could not take it. Their opponent Hasdrubal had already retired to the primary Punic base at New Carthage, and the campaigning for 217 came to an end.[6]

In the year 215 the Romans won a battle at Ibera against Hasdrubal Barca that prevented him from going to Italy with his army. In subsequent years the command of Carthaginian troops in Spain was divided between Hasdrubal Barca, his brother Mago Barca, and Hasdrubal Gisgo. The division of Punic forces in Iberia, as opposed to their concentration under one commander, would be a longstanding feature of the Carthaginian effort there. This resulted in a spreading out of Carthaginian armies when they might have been stronger if massed together. This may have been done because supplying the troops was easier if they could live off of the produce of more widely spaced territories. It may also have been the result of the three generals' unwillingness to agree on a common strategy.[7] This may have been particularly difficult to achieve now that the firm hand of Hannibal, with his unparalleled prestige and charisma, was absent.

The Scipio brothers extended their control over a portion of Spain south of the Ebro, but these years, which are inadequately described by Livy, seem to have been something of a stalemate in which neither side could strike a decisive blow. In 211, the Carthaginian armies were reinforced and were now more powerful than they had been in years. Facing the Scipios were the two brothers of Hannibal, Hasdrubal and Mago, and Hasdrubal Gisgo. Unwisely, the Scipios divided their army between them. Both divisions were defeated, and each brother was slain.[8] It was a victory of a sort for the Romans that the survivors were able to escape to the north-east. The Romans were fortunate that they had not been ejected from the peninsula altogether, but held a position north of the Ebro.

By far the most consequential change to the tenor of the Spanish campaign after the demise of the Scipio brothers was the appointment of Publius Cornelius Scipio (the son of Publius) to the command of Roman army there. In 210 the 25-year-old took up the command of the demoralized Roman troops. One of his most valuable moves came very early on. He made his base at Tarraco, where he wintered. He had good intelligence about Carthaginian forces, which had now spread out across the peninsula. Mago Barca was far off in what is now southern Portugal. Hasdrubal Gisgo was in Lusitania, also now modern Portugal, while Hasdrubal Barca was in the region of Toledo. Scipio began a muster of his fleet and legions at the mouth of the Ebro. The target of this expedition was to be New Carthage, Carthage's principal base in Spain. Inside this city was a massive amount of supplies, as well as the Carthaginian arsenal and treasury.[9] It also possessed a magnificent harbour and sat at the end of a direct crossing from the African continent. This important city had been left with a tiny garrison of just one thousand, while the three armies of Carthage had dispersed around the peninsula to campaign. This was to prove to be a ghastly error of judgment, one that could only have been made possible by the tripartite division of the Iberian command. While there can be no doubt that the Carthaginians believed themselves to be safe from Roman attack at least for the time being, and so embarked upon various other activities of secondary consequence, the defence of New Carthage should have been deemed to be of supreme importance. Instead, it was left almost undefended. Scipio's army crossed the Ebro in the spring of 209 with 25,000 infantry and 2,500 cavalry, a force that would have been easily outnumbered by the combined strength of the Punic armies in Spain.

That there was dissension among the Carthaginian generals is confirmed by Livy, who has Scipio, in a speech to his troops in preparation for the attack, encourage them on the grounds that the divided enemy armies would not join together because of their 'internal conflicts'.[10] Polybius also notes that there had been difficulties between the Punic commanders. The result of this unhappy arrangement was to leave the principal Punic base extremely vulnerable to a Roman assault. Scipio wisely kept his plan secret, since if word had leaked to the enemy of his designs on the city then one of the armies would surely have moved to protect it. Each of the Punic armies was at least ten days' march from New Carthage, and the maintenance of surprise would give Scipio additional time in which to make his attack and complete the capture of the city. The assault was two-pronged, with both a land and a sea element. While Scipio advanced southward, the fleet under Gaius Laelius sailed at a prescribed pace so that it would arrive outside of New Carthage at the same time, six days after they had both set out, just as Scipio appeared outside its walls.

Polybius writes that New Carthage had been left so drastically underdefended because 'so long as the Carthaginians controlled almost the whole of Spain, the possibility that anyone would think of besieging the city had never been foreseen'.[11] Apart from the small garrison, there was no one in the city, despite its large population, who had real military training. They were 'artisans, tradesmen, and sailors', but none had experience of soldiering.[12] In this regard New Carthage was very much similar to old Carthage. The bulk of the inhabitants were commercially-minded and productive, but incapable of fighting. That task was given to mercenaries. In the aftermath of her great defeats in the dark years of 218–216, Rome had been able to raise tens of thousands of additional men to carry on the fight. Carthage, though it had reinforced its armies in Spain, could not call up the same numbers of men, and the demand for troops to fill out its field armies resulted in a scantily-protected base of operations.

Scipio discovered from native fishermen that the lagoon outside New Carthage was shallow and could be crossed without much problem when the evening tide receded. Scipio's troops assaulted the walls, and the garrison commander, also named Mago, perhaps seeing that his position was nearly hopeless, put weapons in the hands of 2,000 of the sturdiest civilians that he could find and led them in a charge against the Roman camp, thinking that this might derail the Roman attack. The plan was more daring than worthwhile. These men were not soldiers and Scipio's legionaries drove them off without much trouble. The Romans followed them back to the city, and through the gate. They threw up their scaling ladders unopposed, and as soon as the tide went out, Scipio's men moved up to the wall on that side, which had been left undefended because the lagoon was not considered crossable.[13] New Carthage was soon in Roman control.

The haul of booty taken (the Romans were extremely diligent in their pillaging of the place) was gathered in a heap in the middle of the market square where it was shared out among the legions. The loot and whatever other military gear taken were nothing, however, compared to the hurt that had been done to Carthage's position in Spain. The most important Punic stronghold on the peninsula, one that might have withstood a prolonged siege indefinitely just as Lilybaeum had done in the First Punic War, was in Roman hands. The 300 Spanish hostages whom the Carthaginians had confined there to ensure their peoples' loyalty were now in Scipio's custody, and their physical well-being could not be threatened any longer. Scipio also returned the native Spanish soldiers whom he had captured to their tribes, building a reputation for fairness and clemency that might sway them to the Roman side in the future.[14] The bulk of his other captives, some 10,000 and mostly civilians, were used to further the Roman war effort. Two thousand were made public slaves. These were the highly skilled blacksmiths who could make and mend Roman weaponry. It was probably at this time that, at Scipio's prompting, the Romans adopted the famed *gladius hispaniensis* sword as their primary sidearm.

The rest were sent to the fleet for service as rowers. Scipio had captured eighteen ships but lacked the spare rowers to crew them all. A larger fleet would have great value in patrolling the coast for Carthaginian ships and for supporting his own land operations. Scipio had to improvise, and his solution was to impress his captives as oarsmen. The use of unfree men as crewmen in a war galley in the ancient world was not at all common practice.[15] Their incorporation into the Roman navy can only have been allowable because of the heavy losses suffered by the Romans during the war up till then and by the severe demands on Roman manpower by other theatres.

If anything should be clear by now, calling this conflict 'the war with Hannibal', as it is often called, is deeply inaccurate. Rome was at war on several fronts at once, and each had their own claim to Rome's soldiers. Placement of these captives aboard the vessels of his fleet in the proportion of two Romans for every one captive enabled Scipio to increase his fleet from thirty to forty-eight manned quinqueremes.[16] The strategic benefit of the seizure of New Carthage was vast. The Romans' line of communications along the eastern coast of the peninsula was made immeasurably safer with New Carthage in their possession. Scipio would next need to penetrate deeper into Spain, into lands that had been held by Carthage for years, to eject them from the country. He could never have done this with the threat of a Punic-controlled New Carthage to his rear.[17]

In subsequent campaigning, Scipio would go on to inflict several defeats on the Carthaginian forces that were still at large, principally at the Battle of the Baecula and at the Battle of Ilipa. Perhaps the most significant victory that Scipio won was his delay of any major attempt at reinforcing Hannibal with troops pulled from Spain until 208, when Hasdrubal Barca marched to Italy to find his brother. Hasdrubal would enter Italy in 207, and fight and lose at the Battle of the Metaurus, while his brother Hannibal, stuck in southern Italy on the other side of the Roman armies, was impotent to help him.

By 206, Mago Barca had just about given up on Spain and was intent upon returning to Africa. He had fresh orders from Carthage. He was to go to Liguria and there open up a new front against the Romans in the north. The Carthaginian government expected that the Romans would soon be invading Africa, and moved to create a threat to Rome that would forestall such a move. With this new operational direction, Mago set about plundering the treasury, temples, and ordinary citizens of Gades, Carthage's last major holding in Spain.[18] He sailed his fleet against New Carthage, thinking to take the city back from Rome. He deployed his soldiers against the same section of the walls that Scipio had attacked and surmounted when he had captured it in 209. The city was better defended than Mago had anticipated, or perhaps hoped, and his attack was a catastrophe. When he sailed back to Gades he left behind 800 dead.[19]

Gades had had enough with Carthage and her high-handed ways. War weariness, the looting of the temples, and disgust at the behaviour of Mago's soldiers, who even now were plundering the area, had caused the Phoenician people of Gades to shut their gates against the Carthaginians. Mago persuaded the city's officials to discuss their difficulties with him, and when they came, he had them flogged and crucified.[20] Finished with Spain, he next took his fleet to Minorca, where he and his men resided over the winter of 206–5.

Chapter Twenty-Six

Africa

Africa would now be the target of Roman operations. The continent had never been entirely forgotten. There had been several Roman naval raids on Africa or the islands between it and Sicily in the years 218–215.[1] In 218, a Carthaginian flotilla of twenty galleys was sent to raid the Italian coast. This force had been caught by a squadron sent by King Hiero of Syracuse. From the prisoners taken it was discovered that another fleet was now bound for Sicily with the intention of capturing Lilybaeum. That city was placed on alert for the approach of the Punic ships, which arrived not long afterward, just before sunrise. The watchful Romans had been waiting with their crews at the ready, and once they had spotted the Carthaginians they took to their ships.[2]

Though the engagement that ensued was far smaller than the titanic clashes of the First Punic War, the general course of the battle was very similar. The Romans desired to make it a fight of boarding actions while the Carthaginians sought to manoeuvre and ram. The Romans outnumbered their enemy, and most importantly, their galleys carried many more marines. Seven Carthaginian ships were taken in short order, while the others fled. Only one Roman ship is reported as having suffered any battle damage, and this ship though holed by Punic ram, was nonetheless brought back safely to Lilybaeum.[3] One further Roman operation was undertaken in 218, and this resulted in the seizure of Melita (Malta).[4]

In 217 the Romans mounted a disastrous raid on Africa. The mission went awry when the Romans became overconfident and rashly plundered the countryside without caution. The natives turned the tables on them and drove them back to their ships, with the Romans losing approximately 1,000 men.[5]

The year 216 was not much better. A Roman fleet again raided Africa but the praetor leading the operation was badly wounded. Fiscal and supply troubles plagued the Sicilian command. Titus Otacilius Crassus, in charge of the Roman fleet at Lilybaeum, complained to the Senate that his soldiers and sailors were neither being paid nor issued their grain rations on time. There was no way for him to make up the deficit with the resources to hand in Sicily. This was in the dark period just after Cannae, and the senators told him firmly that he would have to fend for himself since they had nothing to give. The unhappy situation was not limited to Sicily; the Romans in Sardinia were experiencing the same shortages. Otacilius was able to find some relief by requesting aid from King Hiero of Syracuse, who obligingly stepped forward, just as he had in 263, to relieve Rome of its supply problems. Livy calls Hiero 'a man without peer in his support for the Roman people', and his assessment was correct. The king provided Otacilius with six months' worth of grain and enough money to pay his soldiers' wages too.[6]

No naval raids by Rome are recorded for the years 214–211, and this was certainly due to the far more pressing need to keep her ships at the ready in Sicily while she fought tooth and nail for control of the island.[7] In 210, with that control finally established, Marcus Valerius Messala led a raid on Africa in which he plundered in the vicinity of Utica.

Rumours abounded that Carthage was preparing a massive fleet with which to take back Sicily. In 208, Marcus Valerius Laevinus was placed in command of the 100-ship Sicilian fleet at Lilybaeum. Fears that Carthage was engaged in preparations for a renewal of the Sicilian War prompted the Roman Senate to put additional ships into service, reaching a total of 281 among all theatres. This figure was the highest to be seen during the Second Punic War.[8]

Laevinus took his fleet to Africa that year (208) and made a landing near Clupea. He sent his troops to plunder the lands about, but these were quickly recalled when news arrived of the approach of a Carthaginian fleet of eighty-three warships. Just off Clupea, Laevinus fought a battle with them, in which he took eighteen ships and dispersed the others.[9]

Laevinus' victory at Clupea was no fluke. In 207 he undertook another raid against Africa, where he plundered the lands around Utica and Carthage. The Roman ships were intercepted by a Carthaginian fleet of seventy ships as it made its way back to Lilybaeum. The Romans again got the better the Carthaginians, taking seventeen galleys as prizes and sinking four others. The remainder of the Punic fleet fled from the encounter. Significantly, this battle seems to have been a decisive blow against Carthaginian seapower, as Livy says concerning the outcome that the sea had 'now been made safe by this defeat of the enemy fleet', enabling large quantities of grain to be shipped to Rome without worries of Carthaginian interference.[10]

The Romans made another raid against Carthage in 205. This was done at the direction of Publius Cornelius Scipio, back from Spain and now consul himself. He sent Caius Laelius with thirty newly-built ships south to Sicily, but the timbers of these hastily constructed galleys were so green that they had to be beached at Panormus to be dried out. So the raiding force was much smaller in size than had been planned. With the decline of the Carthaginian navy, the Romans had reduced their own naval presence in Sicily, with Laevinus being ordered to return to Rome with all but thirty of the ships he had at Lilybaeum.

Laelius duly took the thirty warships left behind for him against Africa, where he made a landing at Hippo Regius. This attack, despite its unremarkable size, caused panic at Carthage, where rumour spread that it was Scipio who had arrived with an invasion army. In the emergency that beset them, the Carthaginians reacted in their usual manner by hiring more mercenaries. But they also recruited from among their own citizens, such was the feeling of danger in the city. Livy writes that they were disappointed with the numbers of men whom they could recruit, finding 'no military strength in their own urban, or agrarian, proletariat, whereas Rome, they noted sourly, could draw from their own people and those of Latium to fill the ranks of their legions'.[11] Such was the sorry state of Carthage's defences that opposition to Laelius was practically non-existent as he looted the farms of Africa, and he returned to Lilybaeum with his ships filled with booty.[12]

In 205, internal Roman political conflict hampered Scipio's desired expedition to Africa. The root of the disagreement was over the future course of the Roman state. One faction in Rome wanted an expansive empire, and it backed Scipio and his attack on Africa. The other party was reluctant to press Rome's dominion any further. Money was scarce, the war had dragged on long enough, and an invasion of Africa promised many risks. This latter group was led by the estimable Fabius, the cautious man who had prevented Rome from succumbing to Hannibal in the early years of the war. He preferred to see the struggle ended rather than expanded. This faction's main preoccupation was the colonization of northern Italy, which was still predominately Gallic in character. They were not enthusiastic about Scipio's African mission, especially because Hannibal was still in Bruttium and had not yet been defeated.

Scipio was given command of the province of Sicily, but this did not come with the right to levy any new troops or ships. He was not explicitly tasked with going to Africa either, but was given the power to determine when to launch such an attack when he judged it in the interests of the Roman state. He would have use of the soldiers already in Sicily; these were the 'Cannae legions', disgraced survivors of the disaster at Cannae who had served in quasi-exile in Sicily for the past decade. There was also a small fleet of thirty ships at Lilybaeum. He was, however, given permission to enlist volunteers.[13] He enrolled 7,000 volunteers, and had 30 new warships built. From the felling of the trees to the launch of these twenty quinqueremes and ten quadriremes, just forty-four days elapsed.[14] The Romans were still proficient in constructing ships rapidly in large batches. The kit-building methods used in 260 and 242 were just as effective in producing seaworthy quinqueremes and quadriremes in 205. The ancestry of Scipio's quinqueremes could probably be traced back to the fine ship taken from Hannibal the Rhodian off Lilybaeum in 250.

Scipio had pledged not to use public funds to pay for his African expedition as a means to persuade the Senate to give him the Sicilian command. This was just as well, since the treasury was depleted. The outpouring of aid from communities in Italy for their national hero was extraordinary, and made up for the lack of official financial support. They paid for his thirty ships; they promised soldiers for the campaign; provided silk and caulking; grain was delivered to feed the men; 40,000 javelins were supplied for the troops, and money was donated to pay for the upkeep of the crews.[15]

Pay for the crews, as well as simply finding enough men to man the ships, had been recurring problems for the Romans over the course of the war. In 214 the Senate had resorted to ordering private citizens to come forward with men for the fleet and money to pay for them. Those Romans with property assessed at between 50,000 to 100,000 asses (the as was a small copper coin) had to provide one crewman and six months of his pay. Those with property valued at 100,000 to 300,000 asses were required to provide three crewmen and a year's pay for each. If the value of the citizen's property lay between 300,000 to 1,000,000 asses, he was to supply 5 crewmen to the fleet along with their annual pay. For Romans with property in excess of a million asses, the requirement was seven men and their yearly pay. Senators had to find eight such men and contribute their annual salaries too.[16] Livy implies that most of the men so provided under this system were slaves.[17]

A similar measure was taken in 210. In that year, Marcus Valerius Laevinus, co-consul along with Marcus Claudius Marcellus, had ordered that private citizens should again provide oarsmen for the fleet. These were scarce once enrolment of most other able-bodied men in the legions had been finished. They were also to provide money to pay these men, and thirty days' worth of rations. Livy writes that the 'announcement met with such a howl of protest, and such indignation, that what was lacking for a riot was not so much the conditions as a leader'.[18] The citizens complained that their wealth had already been taken to pay for rowers. All they had left now was their land, and they could not pay what they did not possess.

With a tax revolt brewing, Laevinus hit upon a solution. He convinced the senators to donate their own gold, silver, and bronze coins to pay for the fleet's crews.[19] So the noble senators provided a fine example for their lessers to imitate if they so chose. Yet they did not forget to be repaid. Six years later, in 204, at Laevinus' prompting, it was judged high time that the senators should get their money back, which they did. This was occurring while Scipio in Sicily was outfitting his African expeditionary force out of the aforesaid voluntary contributions, not from the Roman treasury directly. The Roman treasury it would seem, was not so empty as to make such repayment impossible. The

Senate's parsimony toward Scipio was therefore prompted as much by factional opposition to him as it was by hesitation at the cost of equipping the expeditionary force itself.

Scipio's fleet was meticulously organized. Forty-five days of rations were put aboard each ship, including fifteen days' supply of cooked food. Scipio also ensured that every ship carried as many days' worth of water as it did of grain. With his muster completed, Scipio readied his fleet to sail for Africa. The size of his army is subject to dispute, and even the ancient sources that Livy had on hand disagreed with each other. But it was certainly large, as Scipio culled transports from all over the Sicilian coasts to find sufficient shipping to move it. His invasion fleet numbered 40 war galleys and 400 transports. The forty war galleys were divided into two squadrons, with twenty placed on each side of the 400 transports as escorts.

The day of departure in 204 was something of a holiday for the people of Lilybaeum and elsewhere in Sicily. They stood by the docks to watch Scipio's fleet go. Soldiers being left behind to guard the province came to wish their fellows shipping out well. Lilybaeum had been the origin of many naval raids in the past, but this expedition was different. It would not be returning within days or weeks, but was a bid to win the war. 'Scipio had made it known', Livy writes, 'that the purpose of his voyage was to draw Hannibal away from Italy, carry the war over to Africa, and finish it there.'[20]

Scipio's ships sailed out and made for Africa. A dense fog rolled in by noon, and the ships were hardly able to see one another, and came close to colliding in the gloom. The Romans made it across despite the difficulty in navigating, and landed at the 'Headland of the Beautiful One', modern Cape Farina, on which was situated the important city of Utica. The ensuing land campaign went poorly for Carthage. The Romans plundered where they would, and there were repeated calls to bring Hannibal back to defend the homeland.

In 203, Scipio was laying siege to the city of Utica, with his siegeworks pressing closer to the city's walls. He was drawn away by the report of a massing of 30,000 Carthaginian troops under Hasdrubal Gisgo, Scipio's one-time opponent in Spain, and Syphax, the Numidian king. He defeated this army in battle, but then learned that the Carthaginian fleet, or what remained of it at any rate, had sortied and was heading for Utica. Scipio had left his camp woefully undermanned when he had marched out to fight. His army was sluggish in movement too, being weighed down by loot that his soldiers had collected. Such were the perils of victory. The Romans halted at Tunis on the coast and looked on in horror as the Carthaginian ships sailed by on their way to Utica. The legionaries stopped what they were doing and hurried on as quickly as they could to Utica. The fleet had remained behind there, helping in the siege, but its vessels had been converted into siege units, and were utterly unprepared to fight in a conventional ship-to-ship battle. If the Carthaginians should arrive first, the result would be a massacre.[21]

Fortunately for Scipio, the Punic fleet took its time in getting to Utica. Had the Carthaginians moved swiftly, they would have fallen upon a surprised and defenceless Roman fleet and destroyed it. The siege would have been ended, Scipio's army would have been trapped in Africa, and the threat to Carthage removed at a stroke. But the Carthaginians were disoriented by their recent defeats, and had no confidence in their naval power, even though it was stronger here in African waters than that of the Romans. They appear to have wasted one entire day puttering around at sea, though this may have been a period of crash training for the crews of their ships. It is probable that the hastily recruited men were inexperienced and needed practice in rowing and manoeuvring before they sailed to meet the Romans. The Romans had won each of the previous large-scale encounters, and the Carthaginians could not have been wholly optimistic about their chances. Only on their second day at sea did the Punic fleet reach Utica and array their ships in battle formation.[22]

This delay gave Scipio the time to make his way back to prepare a defence. The Romans, contrary to their usual aggressiveness, refused to come out and fight. Scipio was probably outnumbered, and a sea battle with his ships set up for a siege would have been impossible. He placed his war galleys, which would ordinarily have been tasked with protecting his transports, behind those ships instead. He set four rows of these freighters in front of his galleys, and lashed them together with ropes. He ran gangplanks between the ships to connect them so that his legionaries could cross from one to another. Gaps were left open between each freighter so that Scipio's smaller and lighter scout ships could dart out to strike at the enemy and then retreat behind shelter. One thousand hand-selected marines were placed aboard the transports, and they were supplied with large quantities of missile weapons.[23]

The Carthaginians attacked once it had become clear that the Romans would not budge. The Romans on the transports had a height advantage over the sleeker but lower Punic galleys. The Carthaginians had trouble reaching the Romans above them with their missiles, while the Romans' weapons dropping down from on high, hit harder.

Not all went well for the Romans. The little scout boats that were running in and out of the shelter of the transports were easily sunk by the larger Carthaginian galleys, or they became so mixed up with the enemy that the Romans on the transports could not throw their own weapons for fear of hitting their own men should they miss.

The Carthaginians employed devices that Livy calls 'harpagones' against the Roman transport ships. These were grappling irons – poles which had large iron hooks on one end. They hurled them at the transports, and the harpagones became stuck fast. The Romans could not sever them or the chains that connected them to the Carthaginian ships. The Punic galleys then backed water and began to pull the transports along with them. Under the strain, the ropes that bound the transports together began to snap. If they held, several ships in a row were hauled away. The Roman marines were able to retreat to the second line of ships only just before the last of the gangplanks connecting the ships were shorn. Some sixty transports were captured and brought back to Carthage in this way. The victory, such as it was, did much to hearten the despondent Carthaginians after so many losses.[24]

Carthage soon sued for peace and sent an embassy of their thirty men, the Council of Elders, to treat with Scipio. His peace terms were the evacuation of Carthaginian forces from Italy and Gaul; prisoners of war, deserters, and runaway slaves were to be turned over; the Carthaginians would not return to Spain; they were to depart the islands between Italy and Africa; they would supply 500,000 measures of wheat and 300,000 of barley; they would pay a war indemnity of 5,000 talents; and all of their war galleys save for 20 would be surrendered.[25]

Livy claims that the Carthaginians were merely stalling until Hannibal and his brother Mago could be recalled and had returned to Africa. The temporary truce that prevailed during the peace talks was intended to allow each man to return home safely with his army. It is difficult to come down one way or the other on this. Italy and Gaul would have had to be evacuated under a peace treaty anyway, so the recalls could well have been made in good faith. On the other hand having the protection of these two large armies with their experienced commanders would be of more benefit to Carthage whether the peace talks succeeded or failed, and so it may simply have been a bid for time. They sent a delegation to Rome to negotiate a treaty, and during this period both Hannibal and his brother Mago received their recall orders. Mago in the meantime was wounded in battle in northern Italy. He boarded his men for Africa, and set sail, but died while still at sea. Hannibal received the order in an ill-mood. He had expected the recall, and had prepared ships for the voyage home. This did not make it any easier for him to accept. He gnashed his teeth and groaned, Livy says, and was 'barely able to hold back his tears'.[26] This is preposterous, of course; Hannibal was made of sterner stuff than that. But he was certainly anguished by the failure of sixteen years of campaigning in Italy. He blamed the Carthaginian government for not assisting him. 'Those men who were long trying to bring me back from here by blocking the shipment of reinforcements and cash are no longer using devious means to recall me, but are doing it openly', he complained bitterly. He had not been defeated by the Romans 'but by the Carthaginian senate with its carping jealousy'.[27]

Hannibal sent his unfit men to garrison other towns. He would have no use for them in Africa and would not waste space in his transports on them. 'Rarely, they say, has anyone departing from his own country displayed such distress as Hannibal did then as he left the country of an enemy.'[28] He turned to look back at the retreating coast of Italy, cursing the gods, and reproaching himself for not having marched on Rome right after he had won at Cannae. Livy states that the Senate had ordered Roman commanders to prevent Hannibal from leaving. Once he had returned to Africa he would be greatly strengthening Carthage's hand against Scipio. But there seems to have been no attempt whatsoever to hinder his departure, which was orderly and unhurried. Mago's departure from the north was similarly untroubled. A strong presumption must be made that the Romans on the ground judged it preferable to see Hannibal gone from Italy, a goal they had sought for sixteen years, than to try to keep him in place while the peace was negotiated.

At the same time, the truce between Scipio and Carthage became less certain. A convoy of 200 Roman cargo ships escorted by 30 war galleys became scattered by a strong wind. Most of these cargo ships were blown to the island of Aegimurus while others were taken to Aquae Calidae, just across from Carthage. The Carthaginians seized the ships and their supplies in violation of the truce. Scipio sent a delegation in a quinquereme to make a formal complaint about the seizure. On their way back this ship was attacked by three smaller Carthaginian quadriremes, but its crew put up a heroic defence. It was a larger vessel, and the Carthaginians could not board from their lower ships. Having run out of missile weapons, her oarsmen rowed as fast as they could, and ran their ship aground not far from the Roman camp. The spectacle brought the soldiers rushing out, and though the ship was lost, the crew made it ashore safely.[29]

Scipio considered the truce to be over, and soon was engaged in combat with Hannibal and his army. They collided at last in the titanic Battle of Zama in 202, which Scipio won. The initial brilliance of Hannibal and his dramatic victories over the Romans in the opening years of the war had not been enough to secure the defeat of Rome. While he stayed in Italy, the Romans defeated the Carthaginians in all other theatres, and in the person of Scipio, developed a general equal to himself. The Roman army had improved too, becoming tactically more adroit and capable of sophisticated battlefield manoeuvres.

Carthage asked for peace, again. Scipio briefly contemplated placing Carthage under siege but thought the effort too great with a negotiated peace on offer. The terms that the Carthaginians agreed to were again, that deserters, prisoners of war, and runaway slaves be handed over; that their war elephants be turned over, and that they would train no others; that their warships be surrendered except for a mere ten triremes – some 500 were transferred and these were taken out to sea and set afire; the seized transport ships were to be returned, along with their contents; 100 hostages were given up to the Romans; the Carthaginians were forbidden to make war either outside Africa or in it without Roman permission; and a colossal indemnity of 10,000 talents of silver was to be paid in annual instalments over 50 years. For his great victory over Hannibal, Scipio would be given the agnomen, something akin to an additional surname, of 'Africanus.' This was well deserved. In the years of his campaigning in Spain, Scipio Africanus had matured as a general, and had honed his tactical skills until he was a match for Hannibal and could defeat him at Zama.

Hannibal went to Carthage, a city in whose name he had fought for decades but had not visited for some thirty-five years since he had departed for Spain in the company of his father in 237. After having lived his entire life in a military camp, Carthage's resolutely civilian ways troubled him. The people of the city had not lived as he and his soldiers had for the decades of war that he had experienced in Spain and Italy. It was difficult for Carthage to raise the necessary money to make the first payment to the Romans. He was asked why he smiled while the rest of the people wept at their misfortune. Hannibal replied that he did not smile out of happiness, but because he was 'insane with suffering'. The time for tears, he told them, 'was when our weapons were taken from us, our ships burned; and an interdiction placed on foreign wars – that was the blow that finished us off'.[30] He chided their tightfistedness. 'It is so true that we feel public misfortunes only to the extent that they impinge on our private interests, and in them there is no sting more painful than the loss of money. And so there was no groaning when the spoils were being hauled away from defeated Carthage ... But now, because tribute must be gathered from private sources, you are in mourning.'[31]

Chapter Twenty-Seven

Seapower in the Second Punic War

As for the lack of support that Carthage showed for Hannibal's military mission in Italy, it cannot be supposed that the Carthaginian government was ignorant of the broad outlines of Hannibal's activities and predicament there. Communications may have been at times spotty, but there seems to have been no realistic means to keep reports of the war from filtering out of Italy. Carthage's refusal to send more aid to Hannibal was almost certainly the result of deliberate war policy choices made by its government. A determined effort to reinforce Hannibal could have been made. Carthage conducted several such efforts to send troops to other theatres, such as one that saw 4,000 infantry and 500 cavalry go to Spain in 216.[1] A further 1,500 cavalry, 12,000 infantry, 20 elephants, and 20 silver talents were sent to Spain in 215. Sardinia saw 1,200 cavalry and 22,000 cavalry dispatched to it in 215 also. A major Carthaginian army of 3,000 horse, 25,000 foot, and 12 elephants landed in Sicily in 213 while Syracuse was besieged by Roman legions.[2]

In 212 there was the naval expedition of Bomilcar to rescue Syracuse comprising 130 war galleys and 700 transport ships. There were other successful reinforcement efforts. The Carthaginian presence in Sicily was again supplemented later in 212 by 8,000 infantry and 3,000 cavalry delivered by ship.[3] Even when the war had noticeably turned against her, Carthage was still able to supply her armies in various theatres with large numbers of troops that she never made available to Hannibal. She sent 10,000 soldiers to Spain in 207, and in 205 Mago Barca's force of 12,000 infantry, 2,000 infantry, and 30 ships was conveyed to Liguria in northern Italy. In 204, Mago was sent a further 6,000 infantry, 800 cavalry, 7 elephants, and 25 ships.[4] Had Carthage genuinely desired to augment the army that Hannibal had at his disposal, she could have done so. Though Rome, as we have established, maintained some measure of control of the sea just about everywhere with the exception of waters between Africa and Sicily, it cannot be alleged that Carthage was incapable of mounting a reinforcement expedition if it had so chosen. In 215 Bomilcar was able to sail to Locri to deposit a small group of reinforcements with Hannibal. He was able to do this by avoiding the Straits of Messina which were under constant Roman guard. We should not suppose that a similar run could not have been made in the absence of Hannibal holding a major port, such as Tarentum. Locri itself would remain in Carthaginian possession for many years after Cannae, until 205 when it was captured by the Romans. The notion that Carthage could never maintain control of the sea for long enough to make a serious crossing from Africa, similar to one that Napoleon had hoped for when contemplating an invasion of Britain, is inapposite.[5] Though we may use terms such as 'control of the sea' to describe situations in which one side is noticeably dominant over another, Roman naval patrols were never restrictive enough to prevent the movement of men and material to southern Italy or Sicily. It would certainly have been dangerous for a Carthaginian fleet to run a Roman gauntlet to Italy, but it would not have been completely out of the question.

The Carthaginians fully intended to make another reinforcement expedition to Hannibal under the command of his brother Mago in 215. This mission was ready to depart for Italy when word arrived of Hasdrubal Barca's defeat at Ibera by the Scipio brothers. With the Spanish theatre now in dire need of additional support, these troops (12,000 infantry and 1,500 cavalry) were diverted there instead.[6] For many years after Cannae, the Carthaginians would have had a better chance of making a reinforcement mission to Hannibal, as exemplified by their successes in doing so elsewhere, than they had when they sent Hanno to the rescue of Hamilcar at Eryx in 241.

The successful reinforcements listed above should not be taken to mean that Roman dominance at sea was of no benefit of any kind. There is always the possibility that, notwithstanding the evidence cited above, Roman naval power in and around Italy was forbidding enough to dissuade Carthage from making the kind of reinforcement expedition on behalf of Hannibal akin to the ones that she mounted to other, less well-defended theatres. The risk that a Punic fleet laden with precious soldiers and supplies might run into a Roman fleet in Italian waters and be massacred may have been one judged too great to run. At this distance of time it is impossible to say with precision just what calculations were made in Carthage regarding the feasibility of putting more troops at the disposal of Hannibal. It is certainly noteworthy that during the siege of Syracuse in 212, Bomilcar turned away from the Roman fleet at Cape Pachynus while leading an expedition of similar size to one that would have been needed to make a difference to Hannibal. But we lack the kind of reliable fleet strengths that would make clear just what Carthage's admirals foresaw and feared when contemplating a significant movement of ships and troops to Italy.

The Roman navy was powerful enough to deter both Hannibal and his brother Hasdrubal from making the seaborne crossing from Spain to Italy, choosing in both cases to instead go by land. In the early years of the war, the land route through Gaul was the safer option. The large-scale reinforcements by sea of various theatres did not begin until after Cannae, when Rome's manpower situation had worsened considerably and the legions were given priority in the allocation of available men. Why Hasdrubal should have chosen to go by land in 208, when presumably sea travel was a viable and faster option, may have had something to do with Hasdrubal's own lack of a good port close to hand, such as the much-missed New Carthage, where he could embark his men and supplies without interference from Scipio.

It should also be added that Hannibal had paved the way for Hasdrubal's crossing of southern Gaul, not least by making the Gallic tribes friendlier to Carthage. Hasdrubal's passage through Gaul enabled him to recruit soldiers from among the tribes, something he could not have done so easily had he gone directly to Italy from Spain. It must also be considered that the Carthaginian government saw the land route through Gaul to Italy as being the more prudent means of sending additional troops there when all the risks of a seaborne mission were taken into account. Hasdrubal had been previously ordered by his government to go by land to Italy in 216, and his exit from Spain was only prevented by his defeat at the Battle of Ibera in 215.

Mago Barca was able to move from Minorca to Liguria in 205 with 12,000 infantry, about 2,000 cavalry, and 30 war galleys.[7] A thirty-ship flotilla was hardly an extensive protective escort, indicating that Mago can't have expected to encounter much opposition at sea. The major war efforts were being made by both sides on land. With this force he quickly seized Genua (modern Genoa), and was in the next year reinforced by his government with 6,000 infantry, 800 cavalry, 7 elephants, and 25 warships. He was also provided with funds sufficient to recruit mercenaries to augment his troops.[8]

These two missions must be taken as evidence that a seaborne reinforcement mission to Hannibal was at least possible, though this does not mean that the seas held no peril for the Carthaginian navy. Livy reports that a convoy of eighty freighters was intercepted by Gnaeus Octavius off Sardinia at this time. He further writes, intriguingly, that they were either bringing grain supplies to Hannibal or that they were going back to Carthage bearing plunder accumulated from Etruria as well as prisoners of war.[9] It seems more probable that this convoy was bringing supplies to Hannibal, though why a supply mission would have been attempted now after so many years of neglect is open to question.

In addition to her failure to adequately reinforce and resupply Hannibal during the war, there is also the matter of why Carthage did not undertake a sustained effort at sea to wrest control of it from Rome. The Second Punic War was a land war, and the naval engagements fought during it do not compare for the most part in size or importance to those of the First. Carthage had lost the struggle for naval dominance at the Battle of the Aegates Islands in 241, and did not attempt to reverse the verdict of that encounter. She was not without the ability to build another great fleet to challenge Rome for naval mastery. Carthage had the means to sustain land operations in several theatres at once; Italy, Spain, and Sicily. There should have been sufficient resources to construct a fleet large enough to mount a serious challenge to Roman naval dominance. As we have seen, Bomilcar ran from a Roman fleet off Cape Pachynus in 212 despite having 130 warships at his command.[10] The size of this fleet bespeaks an empire still possessing considerable wealth.

Roman command of the sea in the second war was never suffocating, as the various resupply expeditions indicate, but it was still very real. Had Carthage fought for and won control of the sea then it would have been the Romans who had to make long marches to distant battle fronts. Philip's Macedonians would have mercilessly harried the Adriatic coasts of Italy, and Sicily and Sardinia could have been retaken in the absence of sizeable Roman reinforcements. The younger Scipio would have had to brave the perils of the march westward through Gaul to Spain rather than quietly sailing his troops to Emporion as he did. Africa would have been safe from Roman naval raids. The course of the war would have been very different.

The Carthaginians may have been reluctant to stake so much of their war effort on fighting the Romans at sea, since it had been just a generation ago that they had suffered so many defeats at their hands. It is worth recalling that Carthage's only naval victory in the First Punic War came at Drepana in 249, and was due largely to Pulcher's poor command and control of his fleet. The corvus may have gone from Roman ships, but this absence was probably not due to Carthaginian efforts, and the Romans may have been seen as nearly invincible in naval engagements. The Carthaginians had not hesitated to run from the Romans in 215 when their fleet met that of Otacilius on its way home from Sardinia. Ironically, the Carthaginians may have believed that they had better chances in land battles against the Romans than in naval engagements, despite their long history of seafaring excellence when compared to that of the enemy.

Apart from the reluctance to fight against the Romans at sea, there is also the question of Carthaginian war aims, and how her troop dispositions may have shown what she was really after. Hannibal, it cannot be doubted, was seeking to strike a mortal blow at Rome. But the government in Carthage appears to have been less interested in a death match in Italy with its Italian rival and more desirous of regaining what she had lost to Rome in the First Punic War or shortly thereafter, Sardinia and Sicily, or holding onto Spain. It is not surprising then that the greater part of the troops that Carthage sent into the war were not directed to Italy but to Spain, Sicily, and Sardinia.[11] The thinking of the Carthaginian authorities was that by placing the greater weight of their efforts there, they would control these lands when a tired Rome came to negotiate a peace with them. Hannibal's campaign in Italy promised no tangible benefits, since his prospects for defeating the Romans decisively receded with each passing year. His main use to Carthage in the years after Cannae, when it became clear that Rome and its confederation would survive, was to keep the Roman legions occupied in Italy while the wars for what Carthage really wanted, Spain, Sardinia, and Sicily, could be waged without the full might of Rome brought to bear in any one of them.

Livy writes of a conversation before the Carthaginian senate between Hanno, an opponent of Hannibal's Italian war, with Hannibal's brother Mago, that is said to have taken place in 216, shortly after Cannae. Hanno, reluctant to send more troops to Italy, reminds Mago of the see-saw nature of the prior conflict with Rome. 'There are a large number of us still alive who remember how victory shifted back and forth in the earlier Punic war', Hanno said. 'Prior to the consulship [of Gaius Lutatius Catulus, Roman victor at the Aegates Islands] we seemed successful as never before in land and sea operations.' But they were still defeated at the Battle of the Aegates Islands, Hanno noted. 'Suppose on this occasion', Hanno asked Mago, 'fortune should shift. When we go down in defeat do you expect peace-terms such as no one offers now when we are winning?'[12] Though Hannibal on this occasion did get his troops, it was only after much delay, and they took until the next year, 215, to arrive in Italy.

The attitude displayed by Hanno highlights the unhappiness that many in the Carthaginian government felt towards Hannibal's Italian campaign. If the victory at Cannae had been the destruction of Roman power, Hanno had snidely asked Mago during the same conversation, which of the peoples of the Latin league had since then come over to the Carthaginian side? For that matter, had any Roman switched his allegiance to Hannibal? Mago acknowledged that neither had occurred. Hanno smelled blood. 'Have the Romans sent Hannibal ambassadors to sue for peace?', Hanno asked. 'Have you in fact received any report of peace being talked about in Rome?' The answers to both of those questions were also no. 'So', Hanno concluded, 'we have a war in which we are no further forward than the day Hannibal crossed into Italy'.[13] Hannibal's campaigning in Italy in the post-Cannae period resembles nothing so much as his father Hamilcar's stalemate in Sicily in the 240s at Hiercte and Eryx. This ambivalence towards Hannibal's endless war in southern Italy, which was allowed to continue without much support while Carthaginian authorities turned their attention elsewhere, replicated his father's experience during the First Punic War. The Romans could dislodge neither man from their bases until defeat elsewhere forced them to evacuate. Despite both father and son's unparalleled military acumen, neither fought campaigns that were decisive to the wars in which they took part.

A counterfactual comes to mind when considering the conflicting war aims of Hannibal and the government of Carthage. Hannibal had forced his government to go to war when he had attacked Saguntum, and he had won incredible victories in Italy. His departure from Spain and the dispatch of Roman forces there had also put Spain at risk, and now Carthage had to fight them for the possession of the valuable country. Despite the damage done by Hannibal, Carthage was strategically less well off with Spain threatened by Rome's armies than it had been when she was busy subduing the Spanish tribes before the war. Hannibal's gamble had failed to win a decisive victory in Italy, and had also left the Carthaginian position in Spain vulnerable to Roman arms. What if Hannibal had backed down at Saguntum and not forced Rome to declare war in 218? What if he and Carthage had pursued a longer-term strategy of bringing Iberia fully within Carthaginian control, and built up the wealth of the province? When he left Spain in 218, the country was far from quiescent. Carthaginian rule was resented by many Spanish tribes, and these became allies of Rome in later years. Had Carthage taken the time over several decades to solidify its hold over Spain with its rich silver mines and capable fighting men, her empire would have been wealthier and more powerful. Hamilcar Barca had made outstanding progress in moulding Spain into a Carthaginian province. This work was continued by his son-in-law Hasdrubal. The wealth that Spain produced, and which would only have increased with further development, could have been the basis of a renewed Punic Empire comprising Africa and Spain. A showdown with Rome may still have arrived at some point, but it is hard to believe that Carthage would not have been in a better position both economically and militarily to fight Rome under such circumstances than the ones that existed as of 218. Instead, she was dragged by Hannibal into a war that came too soon after the injuries suffered during the First Punic War and the Mercenary War. If the Carthaginian senate decided that its main interests lay in Spain, and that the greater weight of its war effort should be concentrated there, or perhaps in Sicily, where it seemed for a while that she might regain what she had lost after 241, this was only because, by any rational calculation, they were. Hannibal was deprived of additional soldiers and resources because his chosen theatre of Italy promised little gain to Carthage.

It may be fairly asserted then that while Roman seapower was not the decisive factor in Rome's eventual defeat of Carthage in the Second Punic War, it was inarguably of great importance to her. Seapower may not have conferred victory, but had Rome lacked control of the sea, or had the balance of power at sea been more weighted in Carthage's favour at the outset of the war, she certainly might have lost it. Hannibal would perhaps not have taken his long and injurious route across Gaul in 218 that saw him lose more than half of his original force.

Similarly, had a sea voyage been practical and reasonably safe, it stands to reason that his brother Hasdrubal would have gone to Italy by ship in 208 rather than by the same hazardous route through southern Gaul and the Alps that he had traversed a decade earlier.

The impact of Roman seapower was not equivocal in the contest with Philip V of Macedonia. It is only right to conclude that Roman control of Adriatic waters prevented the Macedonians from intervening in Italy during the fraught years after Trasimene and Cannae. Rome regained her balance soon enough, while the alliance agreement between Philip and Hannibal was still being ironed out, to solidify its hold on the waters of Italy's eastern coast. Rome's fleet in the Adriatic was also made up of heavier ships, quinqueremes, for which Philip's lighter warships were no match, and he was never able to supply the aid that might have altered the situation in Italy in favour of Hannibal. The Macedonian front soon became a sideshow in which Rome showed little interest once diplomacy had secured her Greek allies to tie down Philip, but the rapid recession of the Macedonian threat was nevertheless made possible by Roman naval strength in the region.

Part V

Destroying Carthage

Chapter Twenty-Eight

Roman Naval Operations in the East

Rome as a nation had rarely known peace. She had too many enemies on her frontiers for that. Each victorious war with a tribe or rival polity brought her within range of a new set of opponents. She quickly transitioned into a state of conflict with these. The advance of Roman power and political interests in the south, especially with regard to Italian Greek states such as Tarentum, had brought about her wars with Pyrrhus. The control that Rome obtained over the communities of southern Italy made her sensitive to the doings of Sicilian cities. When Messana, and possibly the rest of Sicily, seemed poised to become a Carthaginian protectorate, she had intervened, thereby bringing about the First Punic War. Rome battled Gauls and Illyrians in the subsequent period, and then went to war with Carthage again over a boundary dispute in Spain that threatened the friendly city of Saguntum. The Second Punic War had ended in victory, but as soon as peace had been made the Senate sought to go to war against Philip V of Macedonia. In 200, the matter was set before the people in the *Comitia Centuriata* for a vote. Not surprisingly, the people, physically, mentally, and emotionally exhausted by years of war with Carthage, said no.[1]

Discerning that the Roman people had not chosen correctly, the Senate, which desired to punish Philip for various infractions, put the vote before them again. The consul, Publius Sulpicius Galba, spoke, reminding all that Philip had desired to strike at them when Hannibal had been despoiling Italy after Cannae, and had entered into an alliance with the Carthaginian general. He might strike again with the large fleet that he possessed. The fall of Saguntum, unaided by Rome, had encouraged Hannibal to make war against her. Rome should make war now in Greece, Sulpicius Galba argued, and not allow Philip to think that Rome would fail again to go to the aid of an ally, Athens, which had been recently assailed by Macedonia. It had taken Hannibal four months to march to Italy from Spain; it would take Philip only four days to make his way to Italy. Galba raised the spectre of another detachment of the southern regions of Italy should a Greek army land on the peninsula. Pyrrhus had invaded Italy, as master of just Epirus, a small part of the Macedonian kingdom. Philip had the resources of all Macedonia and the Peloponnesus too at his command and was thus a far more potent monarch than Pyrrhus.[2] This was on the whole, nonsense. Philip was not so strong in military power, naval or otherwise, to present a genuine threat to Rome. But the speech worked, and the *Comitia Centuriata*, when it reconvened and revoted, approved the war.[3]

The First Macedonian War (215–205), fought as part of the larger Second Punic War, had sputtered along once the Romans had lost interest in it. Having assured themselves that Philip was no major threat to Italy, they turned their attentions elsewhere. Their move against Philip now, in 200, at the appeal of Athens, was a chance to settle scores for the stab in the back that Philip had tried to administer by allying himself with Hannibal in 216. The Romans had no difficulty with the Macedonian fleet, belying the putative threat to Italy that Sulpicius Galba had conjured, and landed an army under Galba's command at Apollonia in 200. The Aetolian League, an independent confederation of Greek states, came over to Rome. Over the next years, the Romans pressured Philip. In 198, with Titus Quinctius Flamininus as consul, peace talks were held, but these collapsed when Philip came to understand that the Romans meant to drive him out of Greece entirely.[4] The Romans were soon joined by another Greek confederation, the Achaean League. Further negotiations took place, but these too came to nothing. The war was brought to a conclusion in 197 when the two sides met among the hills of Cynoscephalae in Thessaly. Philip's army was mostly inexperienced, with Macedonia said to have been denuded of men of military age.[5] In contrast, with the Second Punic War only recently concluded, Rome was awash with experienced soldiers. Flamininus had wisely recruited mainly Scipio's long service, professionalized veterans, 'men of proven courage who had served in Spain and Africa', Livy writes.[6]

The Macedonian phalanx was well-nigh irresistible on level ground, but became disorganized on rough terrain. The right wings of both armies drove the other's left wings back. The decisive blow came when an anonymous Roman tribune spotted an opportunity to strike the Macedonians in the rear. He took twenty maniples from the pursuing Roman right and led them back to the other side of the field, where they hit the Macedonian right from behind. The attack in the rear was terrible enough, but the unwieldy phalanx could not even turn about to absorb the assault from an unexpected quarter.[7]

The Roman victory at Cynoscephalae ended the Second Macedonian War. Hostilities with Philip ceased while the peace terms were referred to Rome for ratification. In 196, as part of the peace settlement, Macedonia was forbidden to make war without Roman permission and agreed to pay an indemnity of 1,000 talents. She was to withdraw her garrisons from all of Greece, and the Greek states of Europe and Asia were now free and to be governed by their own laws. Philip was also made to surrender his warships, with the exception of five ships and a massive 'royal war galley', said to be a 'sixteen', that was judged to be of 'almost unmanoeuvrable proportions'.⁸ This ship was a legacy of the era of monster galley building that the Hellenistic monarchs had indulged in during the third century BC. Whether they had been constructed in a bid for the prestige of having the biggest ships, or perhaps to serve as siege units against fortified ports, these super-large warships were not much use in a conventional naval battle.

The conclusion of the Second Macedonian War did not resolve all of the problems in Greece, which was far too fractious. The Aetolians were disappointed by their share of the spoils as part of the peace settlement. They were convinced that they had been the most responsible for the victory at Cynoscephalae. This made them ripe for alliance with another power when the Romans took their time in evacuating Greece themselves.

The Roman presence in Greece had aroused the interest of the nearby monarch of the Seleucid Empire, Antiochus III. Antiochus had done much to reconstitute the early Seleucid state by campaigning from 212 to 205 in the distant eastern satrapies that had fallen outside of effective control for some years. Once back in the west, he had made an alliance with Philip V to carve up the outlying possessions of the wobbly empire of Ptolemaic Egypt. Philip desired Egypt's Aegean possessions, while Seleucus sought to take Egyptian holdings in Palestine and Syria. Defeat at Cynoscephalae had ended Philip's adventurism, but Antiochus, surnamed 'the Great', was still hungry, and had the resources of a massive empire not very much smaller than that originally conquered by Alexander to sustain his ambitions. Once he had finished collecting the Ptolemaic holdings in the Levant, he moved his headquarters to the Ionian city of Ephesus on the western coast of Asia Minor. At Ephesus, Antiochus established his primary naval base, a clear sign that he was interested in expanding across the Aegean into Greece.

He was encouraged in this by Hannibal Barca, who had arrived at his court after being expelled from Carthage by his political enemies there and had become an adviser to the king. He was still ferociously anti-Roman in outlook. Hannibal had been a suffete, or magistrate, in Carthage in 196. Carthage was straining under the heavy burden of the crushing indemnity that the Romans had laid on them as part of the peace agreement. Hannibal had quickly come to understand that Carthage was losing out on fees and taxes because of corruption and lax enforcement of harbour dues. If these were paid, he argued, Carthage would be able to pay the indemnity. He reorganized the city's finances with such success that Carthage had the wherewithal to offer to repay the remainder of the fifty-year indemnity in a lump sum payment. But Hannibal's actions infuriated his aristocratic enemies, and, in league with the Romans who also loathed the man, they drove him out of the city in 195.⁹

Livy relates a story in which Hannibal is said to have urged Antiochus to take the offensive and bring the war to Italy where he would find both men and sufficient supplies. He asked the king to give him a fleet of 100 war galleys, 10,000 infantry, and 1,000 cavalry. With this force he would sail first to Carthage to incite a rebellion against Rome. If he had no success there he would then go to Italy where he would start a war somewhere on the peninsula. The king, he counselled, should in the meanwhile himself cross to Europe with an army, ready to cross the Adriatic to Italy.[10]

Hannibal no doubt harboured a bottomless ire toward Rome, and would have wished it nothing but ill. The ship and troop numbers were easily within the capability of Antiochus to field. On the other hand, the plan seems fanciful at best, and it is difficult to see why Hannibal would have believed that he could spark a successful war anywhere in Italy against Rome after he had spent sixteen fruitless years there. It is most probable that this story, however much it may have been believed in Rome, was in truth a symptom of the terror that the name of Hannibal could still inspire in Roman minds rather than his actual intent. A trumped up fear of a landing in Italy by Philip V's forces in conjunction with a rising of hostile Italic peoples had been used to gain the support of the Roman people for a declaration of war with Macedonia. Livy's scenario of a Seleucid attack on Italy led by Hannibal seems to have been a similarly feverish and less than believable war scare.

It was not that the Romans were without real enemies. In Greece itself the king found allies among those frustrated with Rome. The Aetolians were still smarting from what they perceived to be the unfavourable settlement in the wake of the Second Macedonian War. They blamed the Romans for not giving them their due, and looked to Antiochus for help in driving out the Romans. In 192, Antiochus landed in Greece with 100 warships, 200 transports, and a small army.[11] But his foray into Greece was a disappointment. The Greeks did not respond with an uprising against the Romans, and the Aetolians were unsatisfactory allies, perhaps proving that the Romans had assessed them correctly. The Romans defeated the king in battle at the famed pass at Thermopylae in 191, and he fled back across the Aegean to Ephesus. The strategic focus of the war then turned to the Aegean, where the Romans hoped to gain naval superiority to secure the Hellespont and assure a safe crossing of their army to Asia Minor.

In Ephesus, Hannibal warned the king that the Romans were seeking dominion over the whole world and that his kingdom would never be safe from them unless he took action to stop them.[12] Antiochus had his chief admiral, Polyxenidas, a Rhodian exile, prepare his fleet for battle. The Romans themselves had amassed a powerful fleet in the Aegean under the command of Gaius Livius Salinator, comprising 155 war galleys, including 3 from Carthage that were now fighting with the Romans as allies. The Seleucids had a fleet of approximately the same size, seventy warships, and they considered their ships to be faster. Also to their advantage, in Polyxenidas' reckoning, was their knowledge of the local waters and winds in the region, and their larger number of smaller support ships.

The two fleets met off Corycus in Asia Minor in 191, and the Romans won handily. The narrative of the battle supplied by Livy leaves much to be desired, in that its seems startlingly improbable that the experienced admiral Polyxenidas should seek to tackle a Roman fleet of 155 big, quinquereme-sized galleys with just his 70 ships plus an unknown number of smaller craft in the *lembos* (bireme) category. Ten Seleucid ships were sunk by Roman rams, and thirteen others were captured. The only ship lost to the Roman-allied fleet was a single Carthaginian galley.[13] Interestingly, Carthage was clearly building at least a few new warships just a decade after the peace of 201, which had seen hundreds of her warships consigned to the flames. She contributed six galleys to the Roman naval force in the Aegean. Though these were clearly made in contravention of the treaty that had ended the Second Punic War, the Romans did not seem to have minded the violation.[14] The assistance that Carthage provided was presumably worth more to Rome than maintaining the technical inviolability of the peace terms, and the ships may also have been sent to persuade the Romans that Carthage was a solid ally and not in league with Antiochus, with whom Hannibal Barca now served, in any way.

Antiochus understood that he would require more and larger ships to fight the Romans, seeking 'to equal the enemy fleet in strength and size'.[15] Over the winter he dispatched Hannibal to Syria to collect a fleet of Phoenician ships, and Polyxenidas was tasked with refitting the remains of the Corycus fleet and building new ships to supplement it.

In the next year, 190, the Seleucids were ready for a rematch with the Romans. Hannibal's new fleet was being completed in Syria, and Polyxenidas had regrouped at Ephesus with his own rebuilt fleet. The consuls for Rome in this year were Gaius Laelius, a friend of Scipio Africanus, and Lucius Cornelius Scipio, Africanus' brother. Though not in command, Africanus went with Lucius to Greece to cross with the army to Asia. Before that crossing could be made, however, the Seleucid navy had to be neutralized so that it could not wreak havoc on Roman transports as they moved across the Hellespont.

The new Roman fleet commander for 190 was Lucius Aemillius Regillus, who replaced Salinator. His Rhodian ally had been severely wounded when its fleet of thirty-six war galleys had been ambushed and destroyed at Panhormus on Samos. Polyxenidas had fooled the Rhodian admiral, Pausistratus, into believing that he was interested in defecting in exchange for a reinstatement in Rhodes, from which he was exiled. Polyxenidas pretended to lay up his fleet and keep it unready for battle, but all the while he was actually preparing it for war. When Pausistratus uncautiously arrived in the harbour at Panhormus expecting a parley with his enemy counterpart, Polyxenidas swooped in with his ships and bottled up the whole Rhodian fleet. The result was a disaster in which Pausistratus perished when his galley was overwhelmed by three Seleucid quinqueremes and only seven of his ships managed to escape. Though the Rhodians had been devastated, their anger at the deception caused them to redouble their efforts in the naval war with Antiochus, and twenty further ships were dispatched to join their Roman allies.[16]

The Rhodians would meet and defeat Hannibal at the Battle of Sidê in 190 when they intercepted him moving his fleet of forty-seven ships westward along the coast of southern Asia Minor. This fleet, which he had finished forming over the winter, contained many large ships, including three heptaremes, or sevens, and four hexaremes, or sixes. The rest were quinqueremes and quadriremes, of which there were thirty, and ten triremes. The heptaremes and hexaremes were substantially larger than the standard Roman ship, which was still the quinquereme. It cannot be doubted that Antiochus had drawn the conclusion that Rome's advantage in bigger galleys, as witnessed at Corycus, had to be nullified. The Rhodian fleet of thirty-six galleys that it encountered off Sidê was composed of ships even lighter than those of the Romans. The standard Rhodian ship was the quadrireme, of which the Rhodian admiral Eudamus had thirty-two, and four triremes.

The heavyweight ships did little to benefit the Seleucids. Superior Rhodian seamanship was more than enough to overcome Hannibal's edge in the size and weight of his galleys. An initial disruption of the Rhodian battle line was quickly overcome, and one of Hannibal's massive sevens was rammed and sunk by a lighter Rhodian ship, causing the Seleucid right wing to flee.[17] The Rhodians pursued, but these ships were recalled by the hard-pressed Eudamus by means of a signal flag, an order which was obediently followed. The outnumbered Eudamus was locked in combat with the left wing of the Seleucid fleet, and once the Rhodian reinforcements arrived Hannibal extricated his ships from the battle, having lost twenty-seven of his original forty-seven.

The Scipios were still with their army at the Hellespont preparing for a crossing. Antiochus saw little merit in fighting a land battle with the Romans and thought that the best way to stop it from coming over to Asia was to smash the Roman fleet which it would need to protect it. Polyxenidas encountered the Roman fleet of eighty ships under Regillus at Myonessus later that year. The Seleucid fleet of eighty-nine ships outnumbered the Roman-allied force, but the Rhodians, in particular, were highly motivated, and still smarting over

Polyxenidas' treachery at Panhormus. Eudamus, who had joined the Romans with his twenty-two ships, spotted Polyxenidas' flagship and rowed straight for it. The allied fleet smashed its way through the centre and left divisions of the Seleucid battle line. Polyxenidas took the opportunity to flee, and the sight of him retreating caused the Seleucid right, which had not yet engaged, to turn about and flee too. The Romans lost just two ships, with some others damaged, while Polyxenidas had seen forty-two of his ships lost, including thirteen captured.[18]

With its defeat at Myonessus, the Seleucid navy had been rendered impotent to prevent a Roman crossing of the Hellespont by the Scipio brothers. The final showdown with Antiochus came on land at Magnesia in 190. The Roman army commanded by Lucius Cornelius Scipio was still filled with battle-tested veterans who had served with Scipio Africanus in Spain and Africa. The result of the battle was much in favour of the Romans, with Livy having the king fleeing from the field after losing over 50,000 men. Roman losses are said to have been light, with them and their allies losing just 349 men.[19]

Antiochus sought peace. The terms that he received were neither light nor excessive. The king agreed to pay an indemnity of 15,000 talents of silver, an awesome amount but one that was not beyond his royal resources. He was also made to 'surrender' Hannibal, which actually meant that Hannibal had to leave Seleucid territory, which the Carthaginian did. Antiochus had to withdraw his forces back beyond the Taurus Mountains, leaving the Aegean and western Asia Minor outside of his control. Importantly, he was to give up his fleet except for just ten ships which were forbidden to sail further west than Cape Sarpedonium. He was further forbidden to go to war in either Europe or the Aegean, and Rome was to be the arbitrator of any disputes with states in those regions.[20]

Within little more than a decade since the end of its all-consuming war with Carthage, Rome had met and defeated two of the great powers of the Hellenistic East. In the conflict with Antiochus, Roman naval power had been the key to allowing Roman armies to cross to the enemy's Asian territories and decisively defeat him in battle. Though the victories of Flamininus at Cynoscephalae and Lucius Cornelius Scipio at Magnesia loom larger in memory, the naval victories won by Rome at Corycus and Myonessus were equally important in bringing the war against the Seleucid Empire to a successful conclusion. The Hellespont crossing was safe and untroubled by enemy warships because the Seleucid fleet had been comprehensively defeated at sea.

Hannibal, for his part, made his way out of Antiochus' realm, but the Romans pursued him over the following years. He came at last to the court of Prusias, king of Bithynia. The Romans pressured Prusias to extradite the Carthaginian, such was their hatred and dread of the man. Prusias gave in, and in 183 BC encircled Hannibal's house with soldiers. Hannibal imbibed poison and died.[21] It was hardly a fitting end for one of history's great captains. Yet one wonders how the fate of Hannibal and the hundreds of thousands who perished in the Second Punic War might have been different had he been less obsessed with defeating Rome no matter the cost to him, his soldiers, or his people.

Dynastic infighting brought about a renewal of conflict with Macedonia. Relations between it and Rome had been good for the most part, but the Romans nevertheless had suspicions, which were justified, concerning Philip V's expansionist intent. Philip's son Demetrius was a hostage in Rome during the 190s where he had won over many with his charm, but upon his return to Macedonia his older brother Perseus accused him of seeking to obtain the succession in league with Rome. Philip rashly put his son to death and then became heartsick when he realized that he had made a mistake. Philip died soon after in 179, and the anti-Roman Perseus took the throne. War erupted by 171. In this Third Macedonian War the Romans were initially hampered by their legions being commanded by less than ideal generals. Matters changed when the consul for 168, Lucius Aemilius Paullus, the son of the consul who had been killed at Cannae in 216, assumed command of the war. Perseus was brought to battle at Pydna that same year. The Romans were able to use the greater flexibility of their legion formation to insert small units of men in the gaps that opened up in the powerful but much less manoeuvrable Macedonian phalanx. Employing their *gladius* short swords to deadly effect, the Romans forced their way past the long pikes of the Macedonians and butchered the near-defenceless phalangites.[22] Perseus would soon be taken captive, and Macedonia's centuries-long role as a major power was ended forever.

Chapter Twenty-Nine

A Third War with Carthage

Carthage had spent the half-century since the peace of 201 conscientiously paying the indemnity it owed to Rome. Hannibal's financial reforms had been of enormous benefit to the city's coffers, and made the burden of payment bearable. Carthage had also flourished economically in the decades since the war. Ironically, defeat in the Second Punic War had been good for business. Now that there was no overseas empire to administer or defend, Carthage was able to concentrate upon that her people did best, which was make money.

While Rome busied itself in the task of building an empire in Spain and Greece, Carthage focused upon commercial profit. Her trade expanded after the war, and her merchant ships busied themselves ferrying goods from one Mediterranean port to another. Trade with Italy had grown tremendously.[1] Also, the loss of Sicily and Sardinia in the First Punic War had made the Carthaginians develop their nearby African agricultural lands more heavily. These had been spared destruction, and their productivity was extraordinary. In 200, for example, the Carthaginians had enough on hand to deliver 400,000 bushels of grain to the Romans for their war with Macedonia. Twenty years later the Carthaginians would send 1,000,000 bushels of grain and 500,000 bushels of barley to feed Roman troops fighting there.[2] This reflected an agricultural strength that was remarkable for a nation that had not long ago lost a major war. This dynamism would cause the Romans no little consternation when they considered Carthage's prosperity as they themselves fought war after war for dominion over the Mediterranean.

Carthage had enough money to pay for the renovation of its harbour complex, which comprised a commercial harbour for merchant ships, which was enlarged, and a circular military harbour just behind it. Notably, the military harbour, lying as it did to the rear of the merchant harbour, and protected by walls, could not be seen from outside the city. In its centre was an island with a circular boathouse atop it. There were enough shipsheds in the military harbour to berth at least 170 galleys. Some 30 ships could be stored within sheds radiating from the island, while the remaining 140 would have been housed along the circumference of the harbour.[3]

One Roman who was alarmed at the soaring economic might of Carthage was the elderly Marcus Porcius Cato. He was a stoic Roman of the old school, a staunch traditionalist, and a longtime political opponent of Scipio Africanus. He had long mistrusted Rome's foremost general on account of his Hellenophile propensities. In the Senate during the 150s he would relentlessly call for eliminating Carthage. *Carthago delenda est*, (Carthage must be destroyed), he would repeat again and again. In one instance he is said to have held up a ripe fig before the assembled senators and revealed that it had been picked at Carthage just three days beforehand.[4] For Cato, Carthage was just too close for comfort. In the 260s it had been the fearful prospect of a Carthaginian-controlled Sicily that had impelled Rome to go to war over Messana. Now, after two long and brutal wars had been fought between the two states, it was the proximity not of Sicily but of Carthage that was worrisome.

Cato's logic was sound, even if the immediate threat from Carthage was nil. There was no chance that Carthage's ships would soon be landing on Italian shores to do anything except trade. But the potential for harm was there, should Carthaginian policy ever change. In the near future Carthage would also be emerging from the half-century of indemnity payments that she had made to Rome every year. Rome would no longer be obtaining this annual subsidy, and her continued existence would not be of much use to Rome. There was also the likelihood that Carthage's growth would gather speed now that the indemnity payments were finished and the money saved could be released into the local economy. Some Romans were against war. The two-time consul, Publius Cornelius Scipio Nasica, is said to have been for peace because he believed that a rival state would keep the Romans alert and thus strong.[5] This meant nothing to Cato and the party favouring the destruction of Carthage, who were waiting for an excuse to go to war.

Unfortunately, the Carthaginians were to provide the war party in Rome with the *casus belli* that would ensure her annihilation. Carthage had been troubled for many years by the rival North African kingdom of Numidia. Its monarch, Massinissa, was now very old, but in his younger days he had been a key ally of Scipio Africanus in the final years of the Second Punic War. His contribution of excellent Numidian light horsemen had been crucial in enabling the Romans to overcome the edge that the Carthaginians had traditionally enjoyed in cavalry. Massinissa had been boldly encroaching on Carthaginian holdings, aided by the indistinctness of the border between the two states that Scipio had laid down in the peace of 201, as well as the favouritism of the Roman Senate when it was called upon to adjudicate Massinissa's claims when Numidia and Carthage were at loggerheads.

At some point before 162, Massinissa took the region of Emporia from Carthage, land that had been considered to lie outside of Carthaginian territory proper but which had nevertheless been under its control for an extended period of time. Massinissa had even previously asked Carthage for permission to move through it, thus demonstrating that even he considered it to be Carthaginian territory. The cities of the area, however, remained under Carthaginian dominion after Massinissa's acquisition. The Romans were called upon to arbitrate, as was their right under the treaty of 201. They naturally sided with their old ally Massinissa, and made Carthage not only give up the cities and the land of Emporia but pay an indemnity to him of 500 talents too.[6] Polybius was under no illusions about Roman aims, and labelled as bad faith their failure to act as an impartial judge. Massinissa's claims on Emporia were not valid, but Rome sided with him anyway because she felt it in her own interests to do so.[7]

Encouraged by Roman support, Massinissa's ambition and grandiose claims on Carthage increased. He took more territory, and was soon laying claim to all of the lands of Carthage except for the city itself. When he placed the town of Oroscopa under siege in 151 the Carthaginians had had enough of his provocations. Seeing that they would never receive justice before any Roman tribunal, they decided to fight back, and formed an army of 25,000 infantry and 400 cavalry under their general, Hasdrubal, to do battle with the Numidians.[8] They had no choice in the matter. Massinissa's repeated land-grabs had been rewarded by his Roman ally, which only emboldened him to make further demands. Significantly, the year 151 saw Carthage make the final instalment payment of its fifty-year indemnity to Rome. One of the last compelling reasons for Roman restraint against Carthage, the money that it received annually from her, was gone. Also, with Rome having defeated its major rivals in the Mediterranean world, Carthage's value as an ally that could supply vast amounts of food for Rome's campaigning armies was much reduced.

Appian relates that the Carthaginian army was lured by Massinissa into 'a great desert that was surrounded by hills and crags, and destitute of provisions'. The Carthaginians took refuge atop a hill and Massinissa, echoing Roman practice, encircled it with a wall and waited them out.[9] Starvation and sickness forced them to surrender, though Hasdrubal managed to escape back to the city.[10]

Upon Carthage's undeniable transgression against the prohibition of going to war in Africa without Roman approval, the Roman war machine swung into action. Appian says that the Senate had only been looking for 'some petty excuse' for war, and now had it.[11] In 149, the Romans sent an army of 80,000 infantry and 4,000 cavalry under the consul, Manius Manilius, and a fleet of fifty quinqueremes and one hundred smaller galleys commanded by his co-consul,

Lucius Marcius Censorinus, to Utica. That city, seeing that Carthage was doomed, had given itself up to Rome before the fleet had sailed, and thereafter acted as a base of operations against Carthage.

Carthage had no mercenaries or supplies with which to resist and surrendered. The terms that they received from the consuls were that they should give over to them 300 children from noble families as hostages and crucially, they agreed to 'obey their orders in other respects'. In exchange, the Romans promised that the freedom and lands of Carthage would be preserved.[12] This promise was a flat-out falsehood. Once the Carthaginians had handed over their weapons and artillery, the Romans made their final demand. The population of Carthage was to be evacuated and relocated to a distance of no less than ten miles from the sea. The city itself was to be destroyed completely. The existences of both Carthage as a maritime city and its people as a nation of seafaring traders were to be ended forever.

Consul Censorinus said to them that they would be better off if they forgot their nautical heritage. It had only brought them trouble. 'The sea reminds you of the dominion and power you once acquired by means of it', he said. 'It prompts you to wrongdoing and brings you to grief. By this means you invaded Sicily and lost it again. Then you invaded Spain and were driven out of it.'[13] Seapower for the Carthaginians, said the consul, was not worth the misfortune that it brought. He provided them with a remarkable landlubber's survey of antique political science. '[T]he Athenians', the consul noted, 'when they became a maritime people, grew mightily, but they fell as suddenly. Naval prowess is like merchants' gains – a good profit today and a total loss tomorrow.'[14]

Censorinus told them that the Athenians had brought ruin on themselves by seeking command of the sea. They 'could not restrain their greed until they had lost everything, and were compelled to surrender their harbour and their ships to their enemies, to receive a garrison in their city, to demolish their own long walls, and to become almost exclusively an inland people'. He advised the Carthaginians to do the same. A 'maritime city seems to me to be more like a ship than like solid ground', he said, 'being so tossed about on the waves of trouble and so much exposed to the vicissitudes of life, whereas an inland city enjoys all the security of terra firma. For this reason the ancient seats of empire were generally inland, and in this way those of the Medes, the Assyrians, the Persians, and others became very powerful.'[15]

Find a suitable spot inland at which to make a new home, Censorinus urged the Carthaginians, where they would 'no longer be in the presence of the thing that excites you, so that you may lose the memory of the ills that now vex you whenever you cast your eyes upon the sea empty of ships, and call to mind the great fleets you once possessed and the spoils you captured and proudly brought into your harbour, and gorged your dockyards and arsenals'.[16]

The Carthaginians had been pressed to the wall, after having made concession after concession, and now learned that they were to be ruined anyway. They disregarded the consul's advice to quit their home. They chose to fight.

With its excellent location on a peninsula connected to the mainland by a three-mile wide isthmus, Carthage was a difficult prospect for a siege. The city was large and well-protected. Her fortifications had once given Africanus pause, and this spared the city from a siege in 202 following Zama. It had walls 45ft high running some 20 miles in length. The civilian population eagerly joined in to help man the ramparts. The city's workshops produced new weapons to replace the ones that had been given up to the Romans. Each day 100 shields, 300 swords, 1,000 missiles for artillery, and 500 darts and javelins were made.[17]

Hasdrubal was tasked with organizing Carthaginian defences and supplies outside of the city in the African hinterland. Appian says he had an army of 30,000 with him. Within Carthage itself yet another Hasdrubal was given command of the city's defence.

Roman discipline in the siege lines outside of the city left much to be desired. The anticipation of an easy victory had given way to the realization that the capture of a great city would be difficult. Illness spread in the Roman camp as thousands of men waited in unsanitary conditions. Then a surprise Carthaginian attack with fireships came close to destroying the Roman fleet.[18] Censorinus went back to Rome to preside over the election for the next year's magistrates, leaving Manilius in command of the siege. Manilius put up a wall around his camp to prevent a recurrence of the fireship attack and built a fort outside the city where his supply ships could dock. The consul also began pillaging the surrounding countryside but many of his foragers were slain by lurking Carthaginians.

About the only positive of this early period was the emergence of Scipio Aemilianus. He was the biological son of Lucius Aemilius Paullus, the victor of Pydna, and grandson by adoption of Scipio Africanus, as Rome's foremost soldier. In one instance, his perspicacity had prevented a massacre of Roman troops who had entered Carthage through a breach in the wall. These men had found themselves surrounded by the Carthaginians but Aemilianus had intelligently kept his own men from going further than the wall, and when the advance party of legionaries was repulsed, his troops were ready to keep them from being slaughtered.[19] Aemilianus would show himself to be a careful and resourceful commander. When a battle against Carthaginian forces outside of the city at Nepheris went badly, Scipio was there to rescue four cohorts of legionaries who had been surrounded atop a hill. For these and other exploits,

Appian writes, 'he was proclaimed as the only worthy successor' of Paullus, his father, and the august family of his adoptive grandfather Scipio Africanus.[20]

The new Roman consul for 148 was Lucius Calpurnius Piso. The siege fared little better with him in charge. He attacked the city of Hippagreta, which was serving as a base for privateering against the Roman supply ships sailing for Africa, and spent the summer besieging the place to no effect. The Carthaginians came to the aid of the Hippagretans, and two sallies launched from the city resulted in the destruction of Piso's siege engines. With the end of campaigning season, Piso went into winter quarters.[21]

Having shown himself to be a superior soldier, Aemilianus was elected to the consulship for 147. The Roman people were fully behind his election, and granted him the authority to conscript replacements for those who had fallen in the war and enlist as many volunteers as he could find among Rome's allies. He then sailed to Utica, where he found Piso and Lucius Hostilius Mancinus, the admiral of the fleet, still making a hash of the siege of nearby Carthage. Piso was away from the city laying siege to an inland town. Mancinus, still at Carthage and left to his own devices, had brought his ships close to a section of the wall which had been previously ignored because it was defended by forbidding cliffs. Perhaps dreaming that he might steal the glory of taking the city while his colleague was elsewhere, he mounted an ill-advised attempt to surmount them by means of ladders. The Carthaginians emerged from one of their gates but were driven back by the Romans, who rushed through the still-open gate. Mancinus followed after them with the men of his ships, but found himself unable to go much further than the wall, where he encamped for the night. He was without food, and sent messengers to request help from Piso and other magistrates at Utica to come to his aid before his ships, lying close to the shore, were smashed on the rocks.[22]

Scipio, in Utica, received these requests, and hurriedly sailed to Carthage. As he approached he had his men stand upon the decks of their ships to give the appearance of greater numbers. These ships rowed in quickly and extracted the Roman troops. Mancinus was packed up and sent back to Rome without hesitation. Scipio found that discipline among the Roman army was almost nil, with the soldiers doing little to advance the siege but instead embarking on unapproved plundering expeditions into the surrounding territory.[23]

With his new command little better than an armed mob, his first move was to restore some measure of discipline to the army. He then began to construct siegeworks to cut off the landward approaches to the metropolis, recognizing that the city was being sustained by the trickle of supplies that was able to get through by sea because the Roman naval blockade was not wholly effective. Galleys were as limited as ever in preventing blockade runners from slipping past them, and they were also hindered by the nature of the coastline around Carthage.[24] He would have to sever this last avenue of supply to the city's defenders if the siege was to bite.

The Carthaginians could have used a better commander in this dark time. Hasdrubal was hoarding what little provisions flowed into the city and distributed some of it to the army, but used much of the remainder to throw lavish banquets for his friends and supporters while the general populace went hungry. He executed Roman prisoners in full view of the Roman troops standing outside in their siege lines, ensuring that the ordinary civilians could expect no mercy from the enemy and would have no choice but to resist to the bitter end.[25]

To deny the enemy use of the sea, Scipio constructed a mole to wall off Carthage's two harbours, to which entrance was gained via a single narrow mouth. The Carthaginians saw that this mole would close their only lifeline, and they embarked on a frenzied effort to dig a channel from the rearward naval harbour to the sea beyond the confines of the Roman mole. Their excavation was hidden from Roman eyes by the secluded nature of the military harbour, which lay behind the outer commercial harbour. While the channel was being dug, inside the naval harbour they built fifty complete triremes plus a number of auxiliary vessels out of stockpiled timber. This was an astonishing project given the restrictions of the siege. In late 147, when the channel had reached the sea, this fleet sailed out and showed itself to the Romans, who had remained entirely unaware of this new construction.[26]

The Romans were caught completely off guard, and had the Carthaginians been ready to act aggressively that day they might have descended upon the unprepared Roman fleet and destroyed it. Instead, the Carthaginians merely sailed in front of the Romans in a frightening but ultimately useless show of strength. They were not themselves capable of doing any real fighting, having had no chance to train on the open sea. When they emerged three days later they found the Romans waiting. The Roman fleet rowed ahead to meet them, in this final sea battle between Rome and Carthage. The Carthaginians used their small boats to good effect, ramming the larger Roman galleys and breaking their oars. But this was not enough to secure victory. They retreated, with the outcome still in doubt, thinking that they would resume the fighting the next day.[27]

When the small boats reached the entrance to the newly-dug channel they clogged up the passage, making it impossible for the bigger galleys behind them to get through to the harbour. The galleys put in at a nearby quay that had been used by merchant ships to unload cargo outside of the merchant harbour proper. To protect themselves they turned about, facing the Romans with their bow-mounted rams pointing outward. The Romans attacked, but found themselves vulnerable to counterattack when they tried to turn their galleys around in the confined space. Five ships from the allied city of Sidê in Asia Minor hit upon the idea of dropping anchors and then rowing ahead to strike at the penned Punic galleys. The Sidetans then pulled themselves straight back out of reach by means of these ropes, safeguarding themselves from attack. This procedure was effective, and the rest of the fleet began to do the same. Appian gives no precise losses for the Carthaginians, but says their fleet was severely damaged.[28] This battle had followed the trajectory of nearly all of the naval engagements between Rome and Carthage. The Carthaginians fought well enough, but the Romans won.

The fall of Carthage was not long in coming. The forces that Carthage had operating outside of the Roman siege lines were destroyed by Aemilianus at Nepheris, removing the threat to the Roman army from the rear. With no supplies entering the city, hunger began to further weaken the people, already hurting from the limited food they were receiving. In the spring of 146, Aemilianus' troops found their way into the city, first at the inner harbour. He fed more soldiers into the breach, and vicious street fighting ensued. For six days the Romans fought in relays as exhausted men were replaced by fresh troops. The Carthaginians fought desperately but the starvation-weakened people had no chance.

Hasdrubal approached Aemilianus in secret and cravenly begged for mercy. Elswehere, Roman deserters made their final stand with Hasdrubal's wife and two sons at the Temple of Aesculapius. Scipio brought forward Hasdrubal, and the soldiers standing on the roof of the temple hurled insults at the man. They set fire to the temple, not wanting to be taken captive. Hasdrubal's wife appeared beside them with her boys as the flames engulfed the structure. Wearing the best clothing that remained to her after three years of siege, she poured scorn onto her unworthy husband. She first killed her children and pushed their bodies into the flames. She then threw herself into the fire. 'Such, they say', Appian writes, 'was the death of the wife of Hasdrubal, which would have been more becoming to himself.'[29]

Carthage was sacked with a frightening thoroughness. The loot to be had in such a grand city, even one in such reduced circumstances, was astonishing. The life of Carthage had ended. The empire of Rome was in the ascendant. Aemilianus watched the once proud city burn, with his friend, the Greek historian Polybius, at his side. He mused on the transitory nature of greatness, and the fickleness of human affairs. Carthage had once been the mistress of a mighty empire, and now it was in ruins. Presciently, he feared that one day it would be Rome that succumbed to an enemy.

Conclusion

Victory at Sea and the Rise of the Roman Empire

The economic consequences of the First Punic War were enormous for Rome. She captured tens of thousands (at least) of slaves, most of whom were taken back to Italy to work the farms that had been stripped of men to provide recruits for the legions. It is difficult to see how the Romans could have kept so many men stationed overseas for so long if it had not been able to rely upon the captive labour that it had seized to supplement its pared-down workforce. The mass infusion of slaves transformed Rome into a slave society, at least for the wealthier Roman citizens who could afford them.[1] Rome had begun the slow and inexorable process of changing from a polity centred upon yeoman farmers into one where inequality among the citizenry was far greater.

The many wars of the third century BC began the dire revolution that altered the character of the Roman state. Free farmers were the backbone of the legions. In time, many of these men would find their livelihoods taken away because of the influx of unfree labour. Slaves became the permanent agricultural labour force on the farms of the big landowners during this period, when Rome's armies won many victories and brought home a multitude of slaves. Such was the number of enslaved people now available in the third century BC to tend the large estates (*latifundia*) that alternative forms of agricultural production, such as sharecropping and tenancy, which were hardly equitable arrangements themselves, were disdained in favour of outright worker bondage. Slaves came to be favoured because they were not liable to conscription for the legions, and thus would not be drawn away to serve and leave the wealthy landlords' estates bereft of workers.[2]

This revolution was a long one, and would in time be especially marked in the south of Italy where the *latifundia* became an extensive feature of the agricultural economy.[3] The losses incurred by Rome's Italian allies must have been enormous, though a hard figure will never be had. It is certainly likely that Rome's allies sent more men to serve in the fleets than Rome herself did. Their losses in fleet battles and especially the great storms would have been horrific. It is probable too that their people experienced the same kind of economic misfortune as Rome's own citizens had.[4] The decline of the free peasant farmer was an Italian story, not just a Roman one.

Apart from the increasing poverty of the class from which Rome drew its soldiers, there was a change during the wars with Carthage concerning the relationship between the soldiers and their generals. The first traces of the patron–client relationship that would come to define (and sour) the Roman military of the late Republic appeared during the war with Hannibal. The principal reasons for this were the 'proletarianization' of the army, still a citizen militia, but one which now enrolled larger numbers of poorer citizens, and the extended deployments which Roman soldiers served.[5] These men would become ever more attached to their generals, seeing in them not only successful war leaders but as patrons to look out for their solders' interests when their military service finally ended. They became the soldiers of the ultra-wealthy politicians who dominated Roman politics, not of 'Rome' as they had once been. The ties that bound them were more formalized than those which had previously connected patrons and clients in civilian life to one another. Roman client-legionaries would swear an oath of allegiance directly to their patron-general.[6] Over time, the interests of the soldiers and the good of the Republic diverged. In the 40s BC, the Republic would meet its end after five centuries of existence when tens of thousands of legionaries chose to follow their commander, Julius Caesar, against the legitimate government of Rome.

Rome became ever more harsh in its extraction of resources from the provinces of its empire. The *equites*, or knights, comprised the class just below the senatorial aristocrats. Though they did not partake in the political life of the Republic, they did help themselves to the spoils of the empire. Knights formed tax-farming companies of *publicani* that purchased at great cost the right to collect taxes from the provinces. Once they had paid their money up front to the Roman government, they had every incentive to go out and take as much as they could lay their hands on to make back their money and earn a profit. It made them hateful figures abroad but it was a lucrative business. Their wealth was so great that they were able to cripple politicians who sought to put the Italian peasant farmer back on the land or to obtain better treatment of the provincial populace groaning under the weight of Roman taxation.[7]

The Carthaginians mishandled their struggles with Rome. Better choices might have preserved their remarkable civilization from extinction. Some of their failures were at root social in origin. The Carthaginians as a people did not take to the military life, apart from a tiny group of officers, and they relied upon hired soldiers and subject levies to do their fighting. They also had severe difficulties in opening up citizenship to outsiders which would have had the effect of binding other peoples in the empire more tightly to them. This failure is especially difficult to countenance when so many nearby peoples shared their Phoenician language and ancestry.

There was also the matter of Carthage's self-defeating treatment of unsuccessful generals. Sometimes commanders would lose through little or no fault of their own, and crucifixion seems to have been a bit excessive a punishment. Fear of failure may have caused Carthaginian generals to be less than zealous about prosecuting their wars, especially in the First Punic War as it dragged on its final decade after Drepana.

If the regained prosperity of Carthage in the half-century after Zama tells us anything, it is that the commercial genius of the Carthaginian people when combined with the fecundity of her African farmland made a potent combination. Had Carthage from the outset made Africa the basis of her wealth, and focused upon developing the resources of that continent instead of bidding for dominion over Spain, history might have been very different and better for her in the long run.

The protectorate that she acquired in Spain through the efforts of Hamilcar Barca in the aftermath of the First Punic War brought huge quantities of precious metals to Carthage but also embroiled it in wars with the fierce native peoples there. The Barcid project also caused friction with Rome, a powerful state that need not have been antagonized over lands that were not Carthaginian in a fundamental sense. When Hannibal took Saguntum in 219 he had personally involved his entire nation in a war with a power that had defeated it before. A clear-eyed appraisal of the events in Spain shows that Carthage had largely lost control of her foreign policy to Hannibal. There can be no doubt that the Barcids had been aided back in the mother city by a sizeable and prominent faction that approved of overseas expansion. But such a direction was bound to bring on conflict with Rome, whose ally Massilia had its own trading interests to protect. An African-centred empire of the kind that was preferred by Hanno the Great and the faction that collected around him during the latter stages of the First Punic War would not have entailed such risks.

Even if one grants that Carthaginian expansion in Spain rather than in Africa was the better move, the colonization of the peninsula might have been undertaken differently. When Hannibal departed Spain for Italy in 218 he left behind him a province that was not pacified. Many regions of Spain had not been touched by Carthage, and the generals that remained would have difficulty controlling it. It was also vulnerable to a Roman counteroffensive, which was readily anticipated. Hannibal marched to Italy, smashed army after army, but this did not bring about the defeat of Rome as he had so clearly expected. Instead, he remained confined to Italy for almost the entire duration of the war while the Spanish possessions that he, his father, and brother-in-law had laboured so long to establish and enlarge were subdued by the Romans. If Carthage had been given perhaps another generation in which to solidify its hold on the Iberian Peninsula, twenty-five years or so, then its military and economic power would have been greater than it was when war came in 218. Instead of Spain being a liability, it might have been the engine that fuelled further Carthaginian expansion.

The Romans were honest enough to admit to themselves that they were at a deep disadvantage in nautical skill, and would remain so for the foreseeable future when they decided to challenge Carthage for control of the sea. Their shipbuilding policy was intelligent. They had no compunction about using a captured enemy vessel as a model for their standard quinquereme. Settling upon this particular ship made adopting their preferred tactics of prow-to-prow ramming followed by boarding simpler. The Romans needed only to have ships as large as those that they expected to face in the enemy fleet for such tactics to work. Having more or less identical galleys, instead of a hodgepodge of varied craft, meant that a Roman admiral took to sea with a fleet of ships with the same characteristics. The mounting of the corvus boarding-bridge and its effect on handling would have been the same for each.

Logistically, adhering to a single design meant that mass production of such galleys was faster, as each ship was made of identical parts. The Romans could search their forests for timber, cut it to the necessary length, shape the parts, and then stockpile them for use as galleys were built at the shipyard. Both Roman and Carthaginian ships were constructed as kits, making assembly out of ready to hand parts quicker than if made in a more labour-intensive craft production method. Through the First Punic War, the Romans constructed just two distinct models of quinquereme. The first was based upon the Carthaginian war galley that had run aground in 264, while the second was based upon the wonderful ship of Hannibal the Rhodian captured in 250, and used as the template for the ships of the new fleet that won at the Aegates Islands. This was a conservative approach, made possible at least in part by the glacial slowness of technological improvement, but the Romans showed that they could recognize a good design and stick with it until something clearly superior came along. This second design seems to have been the model for Roman quinqueremes, for many decades after the end of the First Punic War.

The Romans were successful in their first encounters with the enemy navy, despite their lack of experience or any affinity for seafaring. The Romans may have inhabited a peninsula but they were landlubbers at heart, and would remain so. They were probably shocked by the degree of their success. They did not settle for draws but pressed on to win lopsided victories. Roman naval setbacks during the First Punic War were occasioned not by Carthaginian fighting skill but by the arrogance of Roman admirals (Pulcher at Drepana); grave misjudgment (the destruction of Pullus' convoys); and storms.

Despite a long headstart in naval matters, the Carthaginians were unable to translate their edge in skill into victories at sea. The precariousness of maritime supremacy in the ancient world was such that it could be overturned by a nation of farmers with almost no experience. At root, the reliance of Carthage upon manoeuvre tactics was ill-advised. The war galleys of antiquity were simply not put to best use by emphasizing rowing skill. The ability to row well was of course not a bad thing. It was just that it was not always sufficient to bring victory in battle. In unrestricted waters where ships could manoeuvre without hindrance a fleet that was superior in shiphandling skill would probably defeat a clumsier foe, all else being equal. The inherent limitations of galley warfare made these kinds of confrontations difficult to achieve. Fleets typically hugged the coast, with only one flank exposed to the open sea. Admirals in command of a less skilled fleet knew their own limitations and would not make things easy for a more proficient opponent. The great insight of the Corinthians, to avoid manoeuvring fights in which they would be at a disadvantage and instead go straight at their Athenian enemy, highlighted the underlying weakness of manoeuvre-and-ram tactics. The Corinthians did not chase the Athenians across the open sea but chose to drive right at them. The Syracusans utilized the same tactic in their battles with the Athenians in their city's constricted Great Harbour. Similar tactics would be employed by the Romans and deliver victory at sea. The foundation of the empire was owed as much to Rome's navy as her legions.

Notes and References

Introduction
1. Polybius, 1.20.
2. Thiel, *A History of Roman Sea-Power before the Second Punic War*, p. 9.
3. Livy, 9.30.
4. Goldsworthy, *The Punic Wars*, p. 96.
5. Thiel, *A History of Roman Sea-Power before the Second Punic War*, pp. 9–10.
6. Thiel, *A History of Roman Sea-Power before the Second Punic War*, p. 32.
7. Scullard, *A History of the Roman World*, p. 148.
8. Goldsworthy, *The Punic Wars*, pp. 69–70.
9. Scullard, *A History of the Roman World*, p. 89.
10. Picard, *The Life and Death of Carthage*, p. 183.
11. Polybius, 1.11.
12. Picard, *The Life and Death of Carthage*, p. 187–88.
13. Polybius, 1.13.

Chapter 1
1. Goldsworthy, *The Punic Wars*, p. 23.
2. Polybius, 3.48.
3. Polybius, 3.59.
4. McGing, *Polybius's Histories*, p. 92.
5. Polybius, 1.14.
6. Walbank, *Polybius*, p. 5.
7. Walbank, *Polybius*, p. 21.
8. Polybius, 1.13.
9. Polybius, 1.13.
10. Polybius, 1.14.
11. McGing, *Polybius's Histories*, p. 92.
12. Polybius, 3.9.
13. McGing, *Polybius's Histories*, p. 211.
14. Lazenby, *Hannibal's War*, p. 260.

Chapter 2
1. Cunliffe, *Greeks, Romans, & Barbarians*, p. 63.
2. Grant, *History of Rome*, p. 10.
3. Plutarch, *Pyrrhus*, §21.
4. Goldsworthy, *Roman Warfare*, p. 43–4.
5. Polybius, 6.52.
6. Goldsworthy, *The Complete Roman Army*, p. 29.
7. McNeill, *Plagues and Peoples*, p. 118–9.

8. Rosenstein, *Rome and the Mediterranean*, p. 80.
9. Woolf, *Rome: An Empire's Story*, p. 42.
10. Holland, *Rubicon*, p. 29.
11. Boatwright, *The Romans*, p. 100.
12. Luttwak, *The Grand Strategy of the Roman Empire*, p. 41.
13. Bagnall, *The Punic Wars*, p. 41.
14. Plutarch, *Antony*, Book LXIV.2.
15. Flower, *The Cambridge Companion to the Roman Republic*, p. 77.
16. Kennedy, *Rise and Fall of the Great Powers*, p. 181.
17. Polybius, 1.6.
18. Turchin, *War & Peace & War*, p. 152.
19. Head, *Armies of the Macedonian and Punic Wars*, pp. 71–73.
20. Rodgers, *Greek and Roman Naval Warfare*, p. 266.
21. Caven, *The Punic Wars*, p. 1.
22. Boatwright, *The Romans*, p. 104.
23. Dorey and Dudley, *Rome and Carthage*, p. 27.
24. Rodgers, *Greek and Roman Naval Warfare*, p. 266.
25. Rodgers, *Greek and Roman Naval Warfare*, p. 267.
26. Picard, *The Life and Death of Carthage*, pp. 165–6.
27. Miles, *Carthage Must Be Destroyed*, p. 60.
28. Miles, *Carthage Must Be Destroyed*, p. 62.
29. Miles, *Carthage Must Be Destroyed*, p. 140.
30. Diodorus, 17.41.
31. Arrian, 2.24–25.
32. Curtius Rufus, 4.4.18.
33. Miles, *Carthage Must Be Destroyed*, p. 73.
34. Caven, *The Punic Wars*, p. 1.
35. Bagnall, *The Punic Wars*, p. 13.
36. Goldsworthy, *The Punic Wars*, p. 30.
37. Bagnall, *The Punic Wars*, p. 13; Miles, *Carthage Must Be Destroyed*, p. 130.
38. Fields, *Carthaginian Warrior 264–146 BC*, p. 12
39. Goldsworthy, *The Punic Wars*, p. 33.
40. Goldsworthy, *The Punic Wars*, p. 32.
41. Fields, *Carthaginian Warrior 264–146 BC*, p. 12
42. Scullard, *A History of the Roman World*, p. 146.
43. Goldsworthy, *The Punic Wars*, p. 118.

Chapter 3
1. Diodorus, 23.1.
2. Finley, *Ancient Sicily*, p. 3.
3. Drews, *The End of the Bronze Age*, p. 72.
4. Finley, *Ancient Sicily*, p. 18.
5. Finley, *Ancient Sicily*, pp. 19–21.
6. Finley, *Ancient Sicily*, p. 52.
7. Scullard, *A History of the Roman World*, p. 31.
8. Finley, *Ancient Sicily*, p. 53.
9. Finley, *Ancient Sicily*, p. 69.

10. Finley, *Ancient Sicily*, p. 70.
11. Diodorus, 13.80.
12. Miles, *Carthage Must Be Destroyed*, p. 124.
13. Diodorus, 13.114.
14. Miles, *Carthage Must Be Destroyed*, p. 126.
15. Miles, *Carthage Must Be Destroyed*, p. 126.
16. Finley, *Ancient Sicily*, p. 81.
17. Diodorus, 16.80.
18. Diodorus, 19.5–9; Miles, *Carthage Must Be Destroyed*, p. 145.
19. Diodorus, 20.3–7.
20. Diodorus, 20.10.
21. Diodorus, 20.10.
22. Diodorus, 20.10.
23. Diodorus, 20.43.
24. Miles, *Carthage Must Be Destroyed*, pp. 152–153.
25. Miles, *Carthage Must Be Destroyed*, pp. 153–154.

Chapter 4
1. Casson, *Ships and Seamanship in the Ancient World*, p. 235–6.
2. Hanson, p. 237.
3. Casson, *Ships and Seamanship in the Ancient World*, p. 281ff.
4. Morrison, *The Athenian Trireme*, pp. 258–9.
5. Hanson, *A War Like No Other*, pp. 261–2.
6. Polybius, 1.25.
7. Morrison, Coates, and Rankov, *The Athenian Trireme*, p. 277.
8. Hale, *Lords of the Sea*, p. 24.
9. Hale, *Lords of the Sea*, pp. 24–5.
10. Hale, *Lords of the Sea*, p. 25.
11. Roth, *The Logistics of the Roman Army at War*, p. 191.
12. Wallinga, *The Boarding-Bridge of the Romans*, pp. 49–50.
13. Delgado, *Encyclopedia of Underwater and Maritime Archaeology*, p. 43.
14. Polybius, 1.51.
15. Van Creveld, *Technology and War*, p. 53.
16. Jones, *The Art of War in the Western World*, p. 88.
17. Murray, *The Age of Titans*, p. 30.
18. Murray, *The Age of Titans*, p. 127.
19. Murray, *The Age of Titans*, p. 30.
20. Casson, *The Ancient Mariners*, pp. 132–3.
21. Murray, *The Age of Titans*, p. 224.
22. Herodotus, 8.16–17.
23. Green, *The Greco-Persian Wars*, pp. 144–145.

Chapter 5
1. Thucydides, 2.83–84.
2. Thucydides, 2.90–92.
3. Thucydides, 7.36.
4. Thucydides, 7.34.

5. Kagan, *The Sicilian Expedition and the Peace of Nicias*, pp. 302–303.
6. Thucydides, 6.6.
7. Kagan, *The Sicilian Expedition and the Peace of Nicias*, pp. 303–4.
8. Thucydides, 7.12.
9. Thucydides, 7.52.
10. Thucydides, 7.70.
11. Thucydides, 7.72.
12. Kagan, *The Peloponnesian War*, p. 320.
13. Kagan, *The Peloponnesian War*, p. 61.
14. Kagan, *The Peloponnesian War*, p. 60.
15. Thucydides, 1.49.
16. Thucydides, 1.49.

Chapter 6
1. Polybius, 1.7.
2. Lazenby, *The First Punic War*, p. 36.
3. Polybius, 1.9.
4. Scullard, *A History of the Roman World*, p. 148.
5. Polybius, 1.10.
6. Polybius 1.10.
7. Polybius, 1.11.
8. Diodorus, 23.1.
9. Thiel, *A History of Roman Sea-Power before the Second Punic War*, p. 157.
10. Lazenby, *The First Punic War*, p. 49.
11. Zonaras, 8.9; Lazenby, *The First Punic War*, p. 49.
12. Diodorus, 23.2.
13. Diodorus, 23.2.
14. Lazenby, *The First Punic War*, pp. 43–6.
15. Polybius, 1.11.
16. Diodorus, 23.4.
17. Polybius, 1.16.
18. Diodorus, 23.4.
19. Diodorus, 23.4.
20. Keppie, *The Making of the Roman Army: From Republic to Empire*, pp. 21–22.
21. Polybius, 1.18.
22. Polybius, 1.19.
23. Scullard, *A History of the Roman World*, p. 149.
24. Polybius, 1.20.
25. Connolly, *Greece and Rome at War*, p. 271.
26. Polybius, 1.38.
27. Ackroyd, *Venice: Pure City*, p. 178.
28. Hackett, ed., *Warfare in the Ancient World*, Connolly, Peter, *The Early Roman Army*, p. 142.
29. Suetonius, *Tiberius*, 2; Lazenby, *The First Punic War*, pp. 65–6.
30. Morrison, ed., *The Age of the Galley*, p. 71.
31. For a reconstruction of the oaring systems of ancient war galleys, see Warry, *Warfare in the Classical World*, pp. 98–99.

32. Morrison, *The Athenian Trireme*, p. 155.
33. Casson, *Ships and Seamanship in the Ancient World*, p. xxii; illustration no. 124.
34. Morrison, ed., *The Age of the Galley*, p. 68.
35. Morrison, ed., *The Age of the Galley*, p. 69.
36. Polybius, 1.26.
37. Casson, *The Ancient Mariners*, p. 145.
38. Polybius, 1.20.
39. Warry, *Warfare in the Classical World*, p. 119.
40. Connolly, *Greece and Rome at War*, p. 271.
41. Delgado, *Encyclopedia of Underwater and Maritime Archaeology*, pp. 260–2.
42. Delgado, *Encyclopedia of Underwater and Maritime Archaeology*, p. 262.

Chapter 7
1. Rodgers, *Greek and Roman Naval Warfare*, footnote 3, p. 274.
2. Polybius, 1.21.
3. Polybius, 1.21.
4. Goldsworthy, *The Punic Wars*, p. 106.
5. Matyszak, *Chronicle of the Roman Republic*, p. 84.
6. Polybius, 1.22.
7. Thiel, *A History of Roman Sea-Power before the Second Punic War*, 182–3.
8. Thiel, *A History of Roman Sea-Power before the Second Punic War*, p. 43.
9. Tarn, *Hellenistic Military and Naval Developments*, p. 107.
10. Arrian, 2.23.
11. Thucydides, 7.41.
12. Polybius, 1.22.
13. Polybius, 1.21.
14. Polybius, 1.22.
15. Casson, *The Ancient Mariners*, p. 146.
16. For detailed discussion of several ideas on how the corvus was built and operated, see Wallinga, *The Boarding-Bridge of the Romans*, p. 5, and Thiel, *A History of Roman Sea-Power before the Second Punic War*, p. 101.
17. Polybius, 1.22.
18. Livy, 36.43.
19. Polybius, 1.22.
20. Rodgers, *Greek and Roman Naval Warfare*, p. 271.
21. Thiel, *A History of Roman Sea-Power before the Second Punic War*, p. 177.
22. Tarn, *Hellenistic Military and Naval Developments*, p. 149.

Chapter 8
1. Polybius, 1.23.
2. Penrose, ed., *Rome and Her Enemies: An Empire Created and Destroyed by War*, p. 55.
3. Polybius, 1.23.
4. Polybius, 1.23.
5. Lazenby, *The First Punic War*, p. 70.
6. Diodorus, 23.10.
7. Thucydides, 7.70.
8. Thucydides, 7.36; Kagan, *The Peace of Nicias and the Sicilian Expedition*, pp. 302–303.

9. Rodgers, *Greek and Roman Naval Warfare*, p. 275.
10. Polybius, 1.23.
11. Lazenby, *The First Punic War*, p. 67; Thiel, *A History of Roman Sea-Power before the Second Punic War*, p. 124.
12. Goldworthy, Adrian, *The Punic Wars*, pp. 108–9.

Chapter 9
1. Goldsworthy, *The Punic Wars*, p. 105.
2. Zonaras, 8.11.
3. Diodorus, 23.9.
4. Miles, *Carthage Must Be Destroyed*, p. 184.
5. Lazenby, *The First Punic War*, p. 73.
6. Rodgers, *Greek and Roman Naval Warfare*, p. 278.
7. Polybius, 1.24.
8. Zonaras, 8.11.
9. Polybius, 1.24.
10. Polybius, 1.24.
11. Zonaras, 8.12.
12. Polybius, 1.24.
13. Polybius, 1.25.
14. Polybius, 1.25.
15. Polybius, 1.25.

Chapter 10
1. Polybius, 1.25.
2. Polybius, 2.24.
3. Polybius, 1.26.
4. Polybius, 1.26.
5. Polybius, 1.26.
6. Polybius, 1.26.
7. Lazenby, *The First Punic War*, p. 86.
8. Polybius, 1.27.
9. Polybius, 1.28.
10. Polybius, 1.29.
11. Polybius, 1.29.
12. Polybius, 1.29.
13. Diodorus, 23.11.
14. Polybius, 1.30.
15. Polybius, 1.31.
16. Diodorus, 23.12.
17. Diodorus, 23.13.
18. Diodorus, 23.13.
19. Polybius, 1.32.
20. Polybius, 1.35.
21. Diodorus, 23.15.
22. Diodorus, 23.12.
23. Payne, *The Roman Triumph*, p. 53.

Chapter 11
1. Polybius, 1.36.
2. Polybius, 1.36.
3. Thiel, *A History of Roman Sea-Power before the Second Punic War*, p. 233.
4. Thiel, *A History of Roman Sea-Power before the Second Punic War*, p. 233.
5. Lazenby, *The First Punic War*, p. 111.
6. Polybius, 1.37.
7. Lazenby, *The First Punic War*, p. 112.
8. Polybius, 1.37.
9. Polybius, 1.38.
10. Diodorus, 20.55.
11. Polybius, 1.72.

Chapter 12
1. Polybius, 1.38.
2. Thiel, *A History of Roman Sea-Power before the Second Punic War*, p. 248–9.
3. Polybius, 1.39.
4. Polybius, 1.39.
5. Diodorus, 24.1.
6. Polybius, 1.42.
7. Diodorus, 24.1.
8. Polybius, 1.49.
9. Polybius, 1.44.
10. Polybius, 1.46.
11. Polybius, 1.47.
12. Polybius, 1.47.

Chapter 13
1. Diodorus, 24.3.
2. Holland, *Rubicon*, pp. 153–5.
3. Diodorus, 24.3.
4. Diodorus, 24.3.
5. Diodorus, 24.3
6. Polybius, 1.51.
7. Diodorus, 24.4
8. Polybius, 1.50.
9. Polybius, 1.52.
10. Suetonius, *Tiberius*, §3.
11. Lehoux, *What Did the Romans Know?*, p. 28.
12. Diodorus, 24.1.
13. Thiel, *A History of Roman Sea-Power before the Second Punic War*, p. 286.
14. Polybius, 1.53.
15. Diodorus, 24.1.
16. Thiel, *A History of Roman Sea-Power before the Second Punic War*, p. 287.
17. Polybius, 1.55.

Chapter 14
1. Polybius, 1.55.
2. Zonaras, 8.16.
3. Diodorus, 24.5.
4. Gabriel, *Hannibal*, p. 5; Lazenby, *The First Punic War*, pp. 145–6.
5. Thiel, *A History of Roman Sea-Power before the Second Punic War*, p. 299.
6. Thiel, *A History of Roman Sea-Power before the Second Punic War*, p. 300.
7. Polybius, 1.57.
8. Polybius, 1.57.
9. Polybius, 1.57.
10. Diodorus, 24.8.
11. Diodorus, 24.7.

Chapter 15
1. Birley, p. 160.
2. Hanson, *A War Like No Other*, p. 251.
3. Zonaras, 8.16.
4. Zonaras, 8.16.
5. Polybius, 1.59.
6. Thiel, *A History of Roman Sea-Power before the Second Punic War*, p. 304.
7. Goldsworthy, *The Punic Wars*, p. 123.
8. Lazenby, *The First Punic War*, p. 152.
9. Polybius, 1.60.
10. Polybius, 1.61.
11. Diodorus, 24.11.
12. Polybius, 1.61.
13. Lazenby, *The First Punic War*, p. 169.
14. Lazenby, *The First Punic War*, p. 165.
15. Polybius, 1.73; Lazenby, *The First Punic War*, p. 164.
16. Miles, *Carthage Must Be Destroyed*, p. 197.
17. Dorey and Dudley, *Rome against Carthage*, pp. 29–30.
18. Lazenby, *The First Punic War*, p. 164.
19. Thiel, *A History of Roman Sea-Power before the Second Punic War*, p. 308.
20. Zonaras, 8.17.

Chapter 16
1. Zonaras, 8.17.
2. Polybius, 1.62; 3.27.
3. Diodorus, 24.13.
4. Appian, *Sic*. Fragment I.
5. Finley, *Ancient Sicily*, p. 122.

Chapter 17
1. Grainger, *Hellenistic & Roman Naval Wars, 336–31 BC*, p. 98.
2. Polybius, 1.20.
3. Scullard, *A History of the Roman World*, p. 149.
4. Polybius 1.56.

5. Paine, *The Sea & Civilization: A Maritime History of the World*, p. 122.
6. Thiel, *A History of Roman Sea-Power before the Second Punic War*, p. 128.

Chapter 18
1. Polybius, 2.8.
2. Polybius, 2.8.
3. Polybius, 2.8.
4. Polybius, 2.10.
5. Polybius, 2.11.
6. Polybius, 2.11.
7. Polybius, 2.12.
8. Polybius, 2.23.
9. Polybius, 2.24.
10. Polybius, 2.27.
11. Polybius, 2.31.

Chapter 19
1. Goldsworthy, *The Punic Wars*, p. 133.
2. Polybius, 2.7.
3. Polybius, 1.66.
4. Polybius, 1.67.
5. Polybius, 1.67.
6. Polybius, 1.67.
7. Polybius, 1.68.
8. Polybius, 1.69.
9. Polybius, 1.72.
10. Polybius, 1.74.
11. Polybius, 1.78.
12. Polybius, 1.81.
13. Polybius, 1.85.
14. Polybius, 1.87–8.
15. Polybius, 1.88.
16. Polybius, 3.28.
17. Bagnall, *The Punic Wars*, pp. 123–124.

Chapter 20
1. Charlton, *The Military Quotation Book*, p. 61.
2. Polybius, 3.11.
3. Everitt, *The Rise of Rome*, p. 446, n. 247.
4. Dorey and Dudley, *Rome and Carthage*, p. 30.
5. Polybius, 3.10.
6. Scullard, *A History of the Roman World*, p. 176.
7. Boak, *A History of Rome to A.D. 565*, p. 114.
8. Polybius, 3.10.
9. Dorey and Dudley, *Rome and Carthage*, p. 31.
10. Zonaras, 8.17.
11. Scullard, *A History of the Roman World*, p. 176.

12. Gabriel, *Hannibal*, p. 70.
13. Diodorus, 25.10; Gabriel, *Hannibal*, p. 71.
14. Miles, *Carthage Must Be Destroyed*, p. 219.
15. Dorey and Dudley, *Rome and Carthage*, p. 31.
16. Miles, *Carthage Must Be Destroyed*, p. 220.
17. Miles, *Carthage Must Be Destroyed*, pp. 220–221.
18. Appian, *Iber.* 2.
19. Soren, et al., *Carthage: Uncovering the Mysteries and Splendors of Ancient Tunisia*, p. 103.
20. Bagnall, *The Punic Wars*, p. 146.
21. Gabriel, *Hannibal*, p. 9–10.
22. Diodorus, 25.12.

Chapter 21
1. Polybius, 2.13.
2. Polybius, 2.13.
3. Polybius, 2.36.
4. Polybius, 3.16.
5. Polybius, 5.101.
6. Polybius, 3.33.
7. Polybius, 3.35.
8. Polybius, 3.35.
9. Polybius, 3.60.
10. Polybius, 3.56.
11. Mahan, *The Influence of Seapower upon History*, p. 17.
12. Polybius, 3.40.
13. Livy, 21.51.
14. Polybius, 3.90.

Chapter 22
1. Livy, 22.49.
2. Dorey and Dudley, *Rome and Carthage*, p. 68.
3. Livy, 25.11.
4. Livy, 26.20
5. Livy, 26.20.
6. Livy, 26.39.
7. Livy, 26.39.
8. Livy, 26.39.
9. Livy, 26.39.
10. Livy, 26.39.

Chapter 23
1. Dorey and Dudley, *Rome and Carthage*, p. 120.
2. Polybius, 5.109.
3. Livy, 23.33.
4. Dorey and Dudley, *Rome and Carthage*, p. 120–1.
5. Livy, 23.38.
6. Livy, 24.40.

7. Goldsworthy, *The Punic Wars*, p. 257–8.
8. Caven, *The Punic Wars*, p. 185.
9. Livy, 26.24.
10. Livy, 26.28.
11. Livy, 27.32.
12. Lazenby, *Hannibal's War*, pp. 167–168
13. Caven, *The Punic Wars*, p. 219.
14. Rodgers, *Greek and Roman Naval Warfare*, p. 345.

Chapter 24
1. Mahan, *The Influence of Seapower upon History*, p. 17.
2. Rodgers, *Greek and Roman Naval Warfare*, pp. 319–20.
3. Goldsworthy, *The Punic Wars*, p. 260.
4. Goldsworthy, *The Punic Wars*, p. 261.
5. Livy, 24.30.
6. Dorey and Dudley, *Rome and Carthage*, p. 123.
7. Goldsworthy, *The Punic Wars*, p. 262.
8. Livy, 24.35.
9. Livy, 24.34.
10. Livy, 24.34.
11. Polybius, 8.4.
12. Livy, 24.34.
13. Livy, 24.36.
14. Livy, 24.36.
15. Livy, 24.39.
16. Dorey and Dudley, *Rome and Carthage*, p. 129.
17. Livy, 25.27.
18. Livy, 25.27.
19. Dorey and Dudley, *Rome and Carthage*, pp. 131–2.
20. Livy, 25.31.
21. Livy, 25.31.
22. Livy, 26.40.
23. Goldsworthy, *The Punic Wars*, p. 267.
24. Polybius, p. 3.96.
25. Livy, 23.40.
26. Livy, 23.40.
27. Livy, 23.41.

Chapter 25
1. Polybius, 3.76.
2. Polybius, 3.76.
3. Polybius, 3.95–96.
4. Polybius, 3.96.
5. Polybius, 3.97.
6. Bagnall, *The Punic Wars*, p. 197.
7. Bagnall, *The Punic Wars*, p. 204.
8. Lazenby, *Hannibal's War*, pp. 130–131.

9. Livy, 26.42.
10. Livy, 26.41.
11. Polybius, 10.8.
12. Polybius, 10.8.
13. Polybius, 10.14.
14. Gabriel, *Scipio*, p. 99.
15. Gabriel, *Scipio*, p. 99.
16. Gabriel, *Scipio*, p. 99.
17. Lazenby, *Hannibal's War*, p. 140.
18. Livy, 28.36.
19. Livy, 28.36.
20. Livy, 28.37.

Chapter 26
1. Lazenby, *Hannibal's War*, p. 197.
2. Livy, 21.49.
3. Livy, 21.50.
4. Livy, 21.51.
5. Livy, 22.31.
6. Livy, 23.21.
7. Lazenby, *Hannibal's War*, p. 197.
8. Lazenby, *Hannibal's War*, p. 197.
9. Livy, 27.29.
10. Livy, 28.4.
11. Livy, 29.3.
12. Livy, 29.4–5.
13. Rodgers, *Greek and Roman Naval Warfare*, pp. 364–5.
14. Livy, 28.45.
15. Livy, 28.45.
16. Livy, 24.11.
17. Lazenby, *Hannibal's War*, p. 101.
18. Livy, 26.35.
19. Livy, 26.35–36.
20. Livy, 29.26.
21. Livy, 30.10.
22. Livy, 30.10.
23. Livy, 30.10.
24. Livy, 30.10.
25. Livy; 30.16.
26. Livy, 30.20.
27. Livy, 30.20.
28. Livy, 30.20.
29. Livy, 30.25.
30. Livy, 30.44.
31. Livy, 30.44.

Chapter 27
1. Livy, 23.26.
2. Gabriel, *Hannibal*, p. 216.
3. Livy, 26.21.
4. Gabriel, *Hannibal*, p. 216.
5. Rodgers, *Greek and Roman Naval Warfare*, p. 350.
6. Dorey and Dudley, *Rome against Carthage*, p. 98.
7. Lazenby, *Hannibal's War*, p. 196.
8. Livy, 29.4.
9. Livy, 28.46.
10. Gabriel, *Hannibal*, p. 216.
11. Rodgers, *Greek and Roman Naval Warfare*, p. 329.
12. Livy, 23.13.
13. Livy, 23.13.

Chapter 28
1. Livy, 31.6.
2. Livy, 31.7.
3. Livy, 31.8.
4. Scullard, *A History of the Roman World*, p. 228.
5. Pietrykowski, *Great Battles of the Hellenistic World*, p. 199.
6. Livy, 32.9.
7. Livy, 33.9.
8. Livy, 33.30.
9. Caven, *The Punic Wars*, p. 264.
10. Livy, 34.60.
11. Livy, 35.43.
12. Livy, 36.41.
13. Livy, 36.45.
14. Grainger, *Hellenistic & Roman Naval Wars, 336–31 BC*, p. 140.
15. Livy, 37.8.
16. Livy, 37.12.
17. Livy, 37.24.
18. Livy, 37.30.
19. Livy, 37.44.
20. Scullard, *A History of the Roman World*, p. 243.
21. Goldsworthy, *The Punic Wars*, p. 327.
22. Pietrykowski, *Great Battles of the Hellenistic World*, p. 233.

Chapter 29
1. Miles, *Carthage Must Be Destroyed*, p. 325.
2. Miles, *Carthage Must Be Destroyed*, p. 324.
3. Miles, *Carthage Must Be Destroyed*, p. 326.
4. Scullard, *A History of the Roman World*, p. 278.
5. Scullard, *A History of the Roman World*, p. 278.
6. Baronowski, *Polybius and Roman Imperialism*, p. 84.
7. Eckstein, *Moral Vision in the Histories of Polybius*, p. 103.

8. Goldsworthy, *The Punic Wars*, p. 336.
9. Appian, *Pun.* 72.
10. Appian, *Pun.* 73.
11. Appian, *Pun.* 74.
12. Appian, *Pun.* 76.
13. Appian, *Pun.* 87.
14. Appian, *Pun.* 87.
15. Appian, *Pun.* 87.
16. Appian, *Pun.* 88.
17. Appian, *Pun.* 93.
18. Appian, *Pun.* 99.
19. Appian, *Pun.* 98.
20. Appian, *Pun.* 101.
21. Appian, *Pun.* 110.
22. Appian, *Pun.* 113.
23. Appian, *Pun.* 115.
24. Caven, *The Punic Wars*, p. 285.
25. Appian, *Pun.* 118.
26. Goldsworthy, *The Punic Wars*, p. 350.
27. Appian, *Pun.* 122.
28. Appian, *Pun.* 123.
29. Appian, *Pun.* 131.

Conclusion
1. Fox, *The Classical World*, p. 300.
2. Rosenstein, *Rome at War*, p. 76–77.
3. Brunt, *Italian Manpower 225 B.C. - A.D. 14*, p. 86.
4. Brunt, *Italian Manpower 225 B.C. - A.D. 14*, p. 88.
5. Gabba, *Republican Rome, the Army and the Allies*, p. 26.
6. Gabba, *Republican Rome, the Army and the Allies*, p. 27.
7. Syme, *The Roman Revolution*, p. 14.

Bibliography

Ancient Sources

Appian, *Roman History*, Books 1–8.1 (Loeb Classical Library, Harvard University Press, Cambridge, Massachusetts, 1912).
Arrian, *The Landmark Arrian: The Campaigns of Alexander* (Random House, New York, 2010).
Diodorus Siculus, *The Historical Library of Diodorus the Sicilian in Forty Books*, Volume One (Sophron, 2014).
Diodorus Siculus, *The Historical Library of Diodorus the Sicilian in Forty Books*, Volume Two (Sophron, 2014).
Herodotus, *The Histories*, Aubrey de Sélincourt translation (Penguin Books, New York London, 1954).
Livy, *The Dawn of the Roman Empire*, J.C. Yardley translation (Oxford University Press, Oxford, 2000).
Livy, *The War with Hannibal*, Aubrey de Selincourt translation (Penguin Books, New York, 1965).
Livy, *Hannibal's War*, J.C. Yardley translation (Oxford University Press, Oxford, 2006).
Livy, *Rome's Mediterranean Empire*, Jane D. Chaplin translation (Oxford University Press, Oxford, 2007).
Plutarch, *Lives* IX, (Loeb Classical Library, Harvard University Press, Cambridge, Massachusetts; London, England, 1996).
Plutarch, *The Age of Alexander* (Penguin Books, New York, 2011).
Polybius, *The Histories*, Robin Waterfield translation (Oxford University Press, Oxford, 2010).
Polybius, *The Rise of the Roman Empire*, Ian Scott-Kilvert translation (Penguin Books, New York, 1979).
Suetonius, *The Twelve Caesars* (Penguin Books, London, 1957).
Thucydides, *History of the Peloponnesian War*, Rex Warner translation (Penguin Books, London, 1954).
Thucydides, *The Landmark Thucydides*, Robert B. Strassler, ed., Richard Crawley Translation (Simon & Schuster, New York, 1998).
Zonaras, (epitome of Dio) vol. 1, Pafraets Book Company, Troy (New York, 1905).

Modern Sources

Ackroyd, Peter, *Venice: Pure City*, Nan A. Talese/Doubleday (New York, 2009).
Baronowski, Donald Walter, *Polybius and Roman Imperialism* (Bloomsbury, London, 2011).
Bagnall, Nigel, *The Punic Wars* (St. Martin's Press, New York, 2005).
Birley, Anthony R, *Marcus Aurelius: A Biography* (Routledge, London, 2000).
Boatwright, Mary T, Gargola, Daniel J, Talbert, Richard J.A, *The Romans: From Village to Empire* (Oxford University Press, Oxford, 2004).

Brown, Peter, *Augustine of Hippo* (University of California Press, Berkeley, 1967).
Brunt, P.A, *Italian Manpower 225 B.C. - A.D. 14* (Oxford, Clarendon Press, 1971).
Casson, Lionel, *Ships and Seamanship in the Ancient World* (The Johns Hopkins University Press, Baltimore, 1971).
Casson, Lionel, *The Ancient Mariners*, Second Edition (Princeton University Press, Princeton, 1991).
Crowley, Roger, *City of Fortune: How Venice Ruled the Seas* (Random House, New York, 2011).
Caven, Brian, *The Punic Wars* (Barnes & Noble Books, 1992).
Charlton, James, ed., *The Military Quotation Book* (St. Martin's Press, New York, 2013).
Cunliffe, Barry, *Greeks, Romans, & Barbarians: Spheres of Interaction* (Methuen, New York, 1988).
Delgado, James F, ed., *Encyclopedia of Underwater and Maritime Archaeology* (Yale University Press, New Haven, 1997).
De Souza, Philip, *The Ancient World at War* (Thames & Hudson, Ltd, London, 2008).
Dorey, T.A, and Dudley, D.R, *Rome against Carthage: A History of the Punic Wars* (Doubleday & Company, Inc., Garden City, New York, 1972).
Drews, Robert, *The End of the Bronze Age: Changes in Warfare and the Catastrophe CA. 1200 B.C.* (Princeton University Press, Princeton, 1993).
Eckstein, Arthur M, *Moral Vision in the Histories of Polybius* (University of California Press, Berkeley, 1995).
Fields, Nic, *Carthaginian Warrior 264–146 BC* (Osprey Publishing Ltd, Oxford, 2010).
Finley, M.I, *A History of Sicily: Ancient Sicily to the Arab Conquest* (The Viking Press, New York, 1968).
Flower, Harriet I., ed., *The Cambridge Companion to the Roman Republic*, Cambridge University Press, Cambridge, 2004.
Fox, Robin Lane, *The Classical World* (Basic Books, New York, 2006).
Gabba, Emilio, *Republican Rome, the Army and the Allies* (University of California Press, Berkeley and Los Angeles, 1976).
Gabriel, Richard A, *Hannibal: The Military Biography of Rome's Greatest Enemy* (Potomac Books, Washington, D.C, 2011).
Gabriel, Richard, *Scipio Africanus: Rome's Greatest General* (Potomac Books, Washington, D.C, 2008).
Goldsworthy, Adrian, *The Complete Roman Army* (Thames & Hudson Ltd, London, 2003).
Goldsworthy, Adrian, *Roman Warfare* (Cassel & Co., London, 2000).
Goldsworthy, Adrian, *The Punic Wars* (Cassel & Co., London, 2000).
Grant, Michael, *A Guide to the Ancient World: A Dictionary of Classical Place Names* (Barnes & Noble Books, New York, 1997).
Grant, Michael, *History of Rome* (Charles Scribner's Sons, New York, 1978).
Green, Peter, *Alexander of Macedon, 356–323 B.C.: A Historical Biography* (University of California Press, Berkeley, 1991).
Hackett, John, ed., *Warfare in the Ancient World* (Sedgwick & Jackson Limited, New York, Facts on File, 1989).
Hale, John R, *Lords of the Sea* (Penguin, New York, 2010).
Hanson, Victor Davis, *A War Like No Other* (Random House, New York, 2005).
Head, Duncan, *Armies of the Macedonian and Punic Wars, 359 BC to 146 BC* (Wargames Research Group, 1982).

Hodgkin, Thomas, *Italy and Her Invaders*, Vol. 4 (Clarendon Press, Oxford, 1896).
Holland, Tom, *Rubicon* (Doubleday, New York, 2003).
Jones, Archer, *The Art of War in the Western World*.
Kagan, Donald, *The Sicilian Expedition and the Peace of Nicias* (Cornell University Press, Ithaca, 1981).
Kagan, *The Peloponnesian War* (Viking, New York, 2003).
Kennedy, Paul, *Rise and Fall of the Great Powers* (Vintage Books, New York, 1989).
Keppie, Lawrence, *The Making of the Roman Army: From Republic to Empire* (Barnes & Noble Books, 1994).
Lazenby, J.F, *Hannibal's War: A Military History of the Second Punic War* (University of Oklahoma Press, Norman, 1998).
Lazenby, J.F, *The First Punic War* (Routledge, London, 1996).
Lehoux, Daryn, What Did the Romans Know? (The University of Chicago Press, Chicago, 2012).
Luttwak, Edward N, *The Grand Strategy of the Roman Empire* (The John Hopkins University Press, Baltimore, 1976).
Mahan, Alfred Thayer, *The Influence of Seapower upon History* (Dover Publications, Inc., New York, 1987).
Matyszak, Philip, *Chronicle of the Roman Republic: The Rulers of Ancient Rome from Romulus to Augustus* (Thames & Hudson, Ltd, London, 2003).
Matyszak, Philip, *Expedition to Disaster* (Pen & Sword Ltd, Barnsley, 2012).
McGing, Brian, *Polybius' Histories* (Oxford University Press, Oxford, 2010).
McNeill, William H, *Plagues and Peoples* (Random House, New York, 1976).
Morrison, J.S, Coates, J.F, Rankov, N.B, *The Athenian Trireme: The History and Reconstruction of an Ancient Greek Warship*, Second Edition (Cambridge University Press, Cambridge, 2000).
Paine, Lincoln, *The Sea & Civilization: A Maritime History of the World* (Alfred A. Knopf, New York, 2013).
Payne, Robert, *The Roman Triumph* (Abelard-Schuman, London, 1962).
Picard, Gilbert Charles, Picard, Colette, *The Life and Death of Carthage* (Taplinger Publishing Co., New York, 1968).
Pietrykowski, Joseph, *Great Battles of the Hellenistic World* (Pen & Sword Books, Barnsley, 2009).
Rosenstein, Nathan, *Rome and the Mediterranean 290 to 146 BC: The Imperial Republic* (Edinburgh University Press, Edinburgh, 2012).
Rosenstein, Nathan, *Rome at War: Farms, Families, and Death in the Middle Republic* (The University of North Carolina Press, Chapel Hill, 2004).
Roth, Jonathan P, *The Logistics of the Roman Army at War (264 B.C. – A.D. 235)* (Brill, Leiden, 1999).
Scullard, H.H, *A History of the Roman World* (Routledge, London, 2013).
Salimbeti, Andrea, and D'Amato, Raffaele, *The Carthaginians 6th-2nd Century BC* (Osprey Publishing Ltd, Oxford, 2014).
Soren, David, Ben Abed Ben Khader, Aicha, Slim, Hedi, *Carthage: Uncovering the Mysteries and Splendors of Ancient Tunisia*, Simon and Schuster, New York, 1990.
Syme, Ronald, *The Roman Revolution* (Oxford University Press, London, 1968).

Bibliography 245

Tarn, William Woodthorpe, *Hellenistic Military and Naval Developments* (Cambridge University Press, Cambridge, 1930).
Tarn, W.W, *The Journal of Hellenic Studies*, Vol. XXVII, (1907).
Thiel, J.H, *A History of Roman Sea-Power before the Second Punic War* (North-Holland Publishing Company, Amsterdam, 1954).
Turchin, Peter, *War & Peace & War: The Life Cycles of Imperial Nations* (Pi Press, 2006).
Van Creveld, Martin, *Technology and War* (The Free Press, New York, 1991).
Wallinga, H.T, *The Boarding-Bridge of the Romans* (J.B. Wolters, Groningen, 1956).
Warry, John, *Warfare in the Classical World* (Salamander Books Ltd, London, 1980).
Woolf, Greg, *Rome: An Empire's Story* (Oxford University Press, Oxford, 2012).

Index

Ab Urbe Condita, 12
Acarnanians, 142
Achaean League, 208
Achaeans, 9, 142
Achradina, 177, 179
Acrae, 56
Actian Naval Monument, 36
Actium, Battle of, 20, 36
Adherbal, 107, 110–12, 118, 136–7
Adriatic, 14, 141, 143, 172, 201, 204, 210
Aegates Islands, 107, 124
Aegates Islands, Battle of, 62, 124–5, 128, 130, 132, 136, 200, 202, 226
Aegean, 209–10, 213
Aegimurus, 196
Aegusa, 124
Aemilianus, Publius Cornelius Scipio, 9, 219–22
Aeolian Islands, 84–5
Aerenosii, 164
Aesculapius, Temple of, 222
Aetolian League, 173, 208
Aetolia/Aetolians, 173, 209–10
Africa, 104, 165, 174–5, 180, 182, 189–91, 193, 198, 201, 203
Africanus, *agnomen*, 197
Agathocles, 28, 30–2, 51, 136
agnomen, 63
Agrigentum, 5, 11, 30, 56–8, 63, 134, 147, 176, 179–80
Akra Leuke, 160
Alalia, Battle of, 29
Aleria, 83
Alexander the Great, 22–4, 31, 61, 66
Algeria, 22
Alicante, 161
Allia, Battle of the, 15
Alps, 164-6, 204
American Civil War, 21

Ampurias *see* Emporion
Andosini, 164
Antigonus Doson, 163
Antiochus III 'the Great' 70, 157, 209–13
Antipater, Lucius Coelius, 12
Antony, Mark, 20
Apollonia, 143, 172–3, 208
Appian, 13, 51, 131, 160, 217, 219–20, 222
Aquae Calidae, 196
Archimedes, 176–7, 179
Archimedes, machines, 177
Ariminium, 166
Artemis, 179
Artemisium, Battle of, 40–1
Asculum, Battle of, 15, 21
Asia, 211
Asia Minor, 210–12, 221
Asina *see* Scipio, Gnaeus Cornelius, 63
Aspis, 93, 99
Athens, 44
Athlit ram, 36
Atilius, Gaius, 145
Autaritus, 151

Babylonia, 24
Baecula, Battle of the, 188
Baetis River, 159
Balearic Islands, 182
Barca, meaning, 120
Barcids, 161
Barcids, coins, 160
Bargusii, 164
beaching, 34
Beneventum, Battle of, 21, 32
Bithynia, 213
Blaesus, Gaius Sempronius, 104
blockade, 45
blockade runners, 108
boarding-bridge, 6

Index

boarding-bridge *see* corvus
Bomilcar, Carthaginian admiral, 168, 179
Bomilcar, Carthaginian general in 310 BC, 30
Boödes, 63
Bostar, 94
Britain, 23
bronze, 23
Bronze Age, 23
Brundisium, 143, 172
Bruttium, 167, 170–1, 191
Byblos, 23

Cadiz *see* Gades, 158
Caepio, Gnaeus Servilius, 104
Caiatinus, Aulus Atilius, 84, 104
Camarina, 51, 84, 101, 104
Cannabis sativa, 62
Cannae, 12, 22, 166, 196, 199, 202, 204, 207, 214
Cape Bon, 30
Cape Farina, 193
Cape Hermaeum, 93, 99, 115
Cape Licinium, 164
Cape of Italy, 77–8
Cape of Italy, Battle of, 63
Cape Pachynus, 87, 117, 179, 199–200
Cape Passero *see* Cape Pachynus
Cape Sarpedonium, 213
Cape Tyndaris, 84–5
Capitoline Hill, 19
Capua, 167–8, 171
Caralis, 181–2
Cartagena *see* New Carthage, 162
Carthage, 22, 88, 102
Carthaginians, 22–7, 82, 87, 106
   Africa, 5, 22–4, 126–8, 158–9, 197, 203, 215, 225
   Council of Thirty Elders, 24, 63, 195
   crucifixion, 25, 31, 55, 82, 84, 125, 131, 151, 153, 160, 188, 225
   fleet, 84, 89, 102, 114, 117
   generals, 25
   harbours, 215
   indemnity, 216
   marines, 26, 74, 89, 100, 124–6
   mercenaries, 17, 25–6, 29–30, 56–7, 74, 82, 89, 94, 97, 106, 124–5, 127–8, 132, 146–53, 161, 186, 191, 200
   names, 27
   navy, 26, 58
   peace, 102
   seapower, 4–6, 89, 194, 198–204, 218
   Second Punic War reinforcements, 198–9
   'senate', 24–5, 76, 196, 202–203
   ship construction, 102, 201, 211, 226
   Spain, 158–61
   suffetes, 24
   territory, 22
   trade, 24
   war galley, 58
Carthalo, 117–18, 120, 136–7
Cassius Dio, 13
Cato, Marcus, Porcius, 216
Catulus, Gaius Lutatius, 123–4, 202
Caudex, Appius Claudius, 53–5
Celtiberians, 158
Censorinus, Lucius Marcius, 218–19
Chalcis, Battle of, 42
Cicero, 113, 132
Cisalpine Gaul, 21, 145
Cissa, 183
Clupea, 190
columna rostrata, 76, 79–80
Comitia Centuriata, 207–208
Corcyra, 142–3, 173
Corcyraeans, 48, 142
Corinth/Corinthians, 173
   tactics, 5–6, 44–5, 47–8, 64, 76, 85, 114, 170, 227
Cornus, 181
Corsica, 23, 83
corvus, 6, 64–80, 85, 91–3, 99, 105, 114–16, 121, 136–7, 177, 201, 226, 232
   at Mylae, 73–80
   disappearance of, 114–17
   meaning, 66
   operation of, 66–70
   origins of, 64–6
   similarities with *sambuca*, 177
Corycus, 211–13
Crassus, Manius Otacilius, 56
Crassus, Titus Otacilius, 58, 180, 182, 189
Crista, Quintus Naevius, 172
Croton, 169
crucifixion, 25, 125, 131, 225
Cumae, 120, 135

cursus honorum, 19
Cyamosorus River, Battle of, 52
Cyclades, 163
Cyllene, 173
Cynoscephalae, Battle of, 208–209, 213
Cyprus, 37

Damippus, 178
Darius, 28
Decius, 51
Demetrius of Pharos, 143, 163
Demetrius, son of Philip V, 214
Democrates, 169
deserters, 84, 121, 130, 150, 175–6, 179, 195–6, 222
diekplous, 38–9, 45, 47–8
Diodorus Siculus, 12, 28, 30–1, 53, 55–6, 76, 94–7, 102, 106, 110, 112, 117–18, 120–1, 125, 130, 159, 161
Dionysius I, 28, 39, 61
'dolphins', 66
Drepana, 83, 107, 118, 120, 123, 125, 130
Drepana, Battle of, 110–17, 121, 126–7, 131–2, 136–8, 201
Duilius, Gaius, 64–5, 73, 79–80, 82, 97
duoviri navales, 5

Ebro River, 160, 162, 183–5
Echetla, 56
Ecnomus, Battle of, 61, 86–93
Ecnomus, Carthaginian losses, 91
Ecnomus, Roman losses, 91
Ecnomus, *triarii*, 88, 90–1
Egypt/Egyptians, 40–1, 131, 209
Elche *see* Helice
elephants, 57, 94, 96–7, 105, 150, 161
Elis, 173
Elissa, 23
Elymians, 28
Emporia, 217
Emporion, 160, 183, 201
Enna, 84
Ephesus, 209–11
Epicydes, 175–6, 178–81
Epidamnus, 142–3
Epipolae Heights, 29
Epirus, 8, 31, 36, 141, 207

Epitome Historiarum, 13
equites, 224
Erineus, Battle of, 44–5, 76
Eryx, 120–2, 124–6, 128, 130–1, 137, 157, 159, 199, 202
Etruria, 200
Etruscans, 7, 15, 113
Eudamus, 212–13

Fabius Pictor, Quintus, 11–12
Fabius *see* Maximus, Marcus Fabius
Faesulae, Battle of, 144
Falto, Quintus Valerius, 123
fasti triumphales, 19
feigned flight, 93
First Punic War, peace treaty, 130
Flaccus, Lucius Valerius, 58
Flaccus, Publius Valerius, 171–2
flamen martialis, 123
Flamininus, Titus Quinctius, 208, 213
Frontinus, Sextus Julius, 54
Fuller, J.F.C., 157
Fulvius, Gnaeus, 143

Gades, 22, 158–9, 188
Galba, Publius Sulpicius, 173, 207–208
galley tactics, 35–6
galleys, construction, 59
galleys, masts, 115
Gaul/Gauls, 26, 87, 141, 144–5, 151, 157, 160, 162–4, 199–200, 204, 207
Gela, 28, 30, 53
Gelon, 28–9
Gisgo, Carthaginian officer in Sicily, 130, 146, 149–52
gladius, 16, 214
gladius hispaniensis, 16
Gracchus, Tiberius, 113
grappling hooks, 46
Great Harbour, 29, 37, 45–6, 64, 66, 76, 92, 176, 227
Greece/Greeks, 172, 174, 208–10
Gulf of Corinth, 173

Hadranum, 56
Hamilcar Barca, 10, 120–2, 124–8, 130, 135, 146, 149, 150–3, 157–61, 203

Hamilcar, Carthaginian commander at Ecnomus, 90–3
Hamilcar, Carthaginian fleet commander in Spain, 184
Hamilcar, Carthaginian general at Himera, 29
Hamilcar, Carthaginian general at Panormus, 83
Hamilcar, Carthagininan general in 406 BC, 30
Hampsicora, 181–2
Hannibal Barca, 157, 161–3, 165–6, 170–2, 174–5, 180, 183–5, 188, 191, 195–7, 200–204, 207–13, 225
   death, 214
   finances, 209, 215
Hannibal the Rhodian, 70, 107–108, 123, 191, 226
Hannibal, Carthaginian commander at Cape of Italy and Agrigentum, 57, 63
Hannibal, Carthaginian commander at Mylae, 73, 84
Hannibal, Carthaginian fleet commander at Lilybaeum, 107
Hannibal, Carthaginian fleet commander at Xiphonia, 56
Hanno the Great, 126–7, 158, 225
Hanno, Carthaginian commander at Aegates Islands, 124, 128
Hanno, Carthaginian commander at Ecnomus, 90–1
Hanno, Carthaginian commander at Messana, 55
Hanno, Carthaginian general at Agrigentum, 180–1
Hanno, Carthaginian general at Cissa, 183
Hanno, Carthaginian general at Heraclea Minoa, 57
Hanno, Carthaginian general during Mercenary War, 148, 150–3
Hanno, Carthaginian general in 310 BC, 30–1
Hanno, Carthaginian general in Sardinia, 152
Hanno, member of Carthaginian senate, 202
harpagones, 195
Hasdrubal Barca, 161, 163–4, 183–5, 188, 198, 200

Hasdrubal Gisgo, 184–5, 193
Hasdrubal the Bald, 181–2
Hasdrubal, Carthaginian commander inside Carthage, 219, 221–2
Hasdrubal, Carthaginian general at Lilybaeum and Panormus, 250 BC, 105–106
Hasdrubal, Carthaginian general, 216, 219
Hasdrubal, son of Hanno, 94
Hasdrubal, son-in-law of Hamilcar Barca, 10, 161–2
Hecatontapylus, 126–7, 150
Helice, 161
Hellespont, 210–13
Helorum, 56
Henna, 178
Heraclea Minoa, 57, 83, 94, 176, 180
Heraclea, Battle of, 21
Heracles-Melqart, 160
Herbesus, 57
Herodotus, 40
hexareme, 90, 212
Hiercte, 120, 125, 137, 159, 202
Hiero, 28, 51–3, 55–7, 130, 135, 147, 152, 172, 175, 189–90
Hieronymus, 175
Himera, 29–30, 83
Himera River, 180
Himilco, Carthaginian general at Heraclea Minoa, 176, 178–9
Himilco, Carthaginian general at Lilybaeum, 106–108, 117
Hippagreta/Hippagretans, 220
Hippana, 84
Hippo Acra, 150, 152
Hippo Regius, 191
Hippocrates, 175–6 , 178–80
Hispania, 158
Historia Romana, 13
Histories, 5, 9–10

Ibera, 184
Ibera, Battle of, 199–200
Iberia (Spain), 22, 158–60, 184, 203
Ilipa, Battle of, 188
Illyria/Illyrians, 141–3, 163, 171–3, 207
Ilourgetes, 164

Indo-European, 14
Indortes, 159
Italian manpower, 87

Jupiter Capitolinus, Temple of, 7, 19

Krimisos River, battle, 30
kyklos, 42

Laelius, Gaius, 186, 190–1, 211
Laevinus, Marcus Valerius, 171–3, 181, 190, 192
Lake Trasimene, Battle of, 166–7, 171, 181, 204
latifundia, 223
lembos/lemboi, 37, 163, 171, 211
Leontini, 56, 175–6
Levant, 209
Library of History, 12
Libya/Libyans, 22, 24, 88, 102, 122–3, 126, 149–50, 153, 163–4
Liguria, 188, 198, 200
Lilybaeum (Marsala) wreck, 59
Lilybaeum, 30, 32, 82–3, 87, 106–10, 113, 117–20, 123–4, 130, 165, 175, 180, 182, 189–91, 193
Lipara, 63, 84, 105
Lissus, 163
Livy (Titus Livius), 12, 167–9, 176, 179, 182, 185–6, 190–3, 195–6, 200, 202, 208, 210–13,
Locri, 198
Longanus River, Battle of, 52
Longus, Tiberius Sempronius, 165–6, 175
Lucania, 167
Luceria, 171
Lusitania, 185
Lycortas, 9

Macedonia/Macedonians, 163, 171–4, 201, 204, 207–208, 214
Macedonian alliance with Hannibal, 171, 174
Magnesia, Battle of, 213
Mago Barca, 184–5, 188, 195–6, 198, 200, 202
Mago, Carthaginian commander at New Carthage, 186

Malta *see* Melita
Mamertines, 51–3, 55
Mancinus, Lucius Hostilius, 220
Manilius, Manius, 217, 219
Manlius *see* Torquatus, Titus Manlius, 181–2
Marcellus, Marcus Claudius, 176–80, 192
Marcus Aurelius, 122
Marettino, 124
Marsala *see* Lilybaeum
Marseilles *see* Massilia
Massilia/Massilians, 160, 165, 183–4, 225
Massinissa, 216–17
Mathos, 149–53
Maximus, Manius Valerius, 56
Maximus, Marcus Fabius, 166, 191
Megara, 56
Megellus, Lucius Postumius, 56
Melita (Malta), 189
mercenaries, 25, 30, 51–3, 56, 106–107, 125, 141, 146–51, 153, 159, 161, 180
Messala, Marcus Valerius, 190
Messana, 8, 51–2, 54–6, 58, 63–4, 73, 86–7, 104, 117, 141, 146–7, 175, 207, 216
Messene, 163
Messina *see* Messana
Messina, Straits of, 51, 198
Metapontum, 170
Metaurus, Battle of the, 188
Metellus, Lucius Caecilius, 105–106
Milazzo *see* Mylae
Minorca, 188, 200
Mount Eryx, 120–1
Mount Hiercte, 120
Murgantia, 178
mutiny, 81, 148
Muttines, 180–1
Mylae, 64,
Mylae, Battle of, 72–3, 75–86, 92, 116, 136
Myonesssus, 212–13
Myttistratum, 82, 84

Nasica, Publius Cornelius Scipio, 216
Nassus, 173
Naupactus, 42–3, 173
Naxos, 28
Neapolis, 5

Neetum, 56
Nepheris, 219, 222
New Carthage, 162, 183–8, 200
Nico, 169
Nicopolis, 36
Nobilior, Servius Fulvius Paetinus, 100
Numidia/Numidians, 20, 22, 26, 57, 95, 126–7, 151, 180–1, 193, 216–17
Nutria, 143

Octavian's Campsite Memorial *see* Actian Naval Monument
Oenidae, 173
Olbia, 83
Olympias, 33
Oretani, 161
Oricum, 172–3
Oroscopa, 216
Otacilius *see* Crassus, Titus Otacilius

Pacilius, Gaius Furius, 105
paean, 43
Paestum, 169
Palermo *see* Panormus
Panhormus, 211–13
Panormitis, 106
Panormus, 29, 63, 83–4, 104–106, 120, 133, 178, 190
Parallel Lives, 13
Paropus, 83
Paterculus, Gaius Sulpicius, 84
Paullus, Lucius Aemilius, 9, 145, 163, 214, 219, 220
Paullus, Marcus Aemilius, 100
Pausistratus, 211–12
Paxi Islands, 142
Peloponnesian War, 5, 29, 39, 42, 47
Peloponnesus, 207
periplous, 38–9, 45, 47–8, 90
Perseus, king of Macedonia, 214
phalanx, 15, 96–7, 208, 214
Pharos, 143, 163
Philinus 11, 78
Philip V, 163, 168, 171–4, 201, 204, 207–10, 214
Phintias, 117
Phocaea, 29, 36

Phoenice, 141, 146–7
Phoenicia/Phoenicians, 22–4, 61, 159, 188, 211, 225
Phormio, 42
Pillars of Hercules, 23
Pinarius, Lucius, 178
Pisa *see* Pisae
Pisae (Pisa), 145, 165, 181
Piso, Lucius Calpurnius, 220
pitch, 34
Plutarch, 13, 20
Po Valley, 165
Poggio Di Sant'Angelo *see* Ecnomus
Polybius, xiii, 5, 7–13, 16, 21, 37, 53–4, 56–8, 61–9, 71, 73, 75, 77–80, 83–9, 91, 93, 97, 99–102, 108, 112, 115–17, 121, 123, 125–6, 130, 132, 134, 141–5, 147–50, 152–3, 157–8, 162–4, 167, 177, 184, 186, 217, 222
Polybius as source, 9–12
polyreme, 39
Polyxenidas, 210–13
pomerium, 113
Postumius, Aulus, 123, 143
privateers, privateering, 122–3
Prusias, 213
Ptolemy, 131
publicani, 224
Pulcher, Publius Claudius, 60, 109–14, 117, 201, 227
Pullus, Lucius Iunius, 117–21, 131, 137, 227
Pydna, 214, 219
Pyrrhus, 5–6, 8, 15, 21–2, 31–2, 51, 75, 207

Qart Hadasht, 23
quadriremes, 35, 37, 39–40, 108, 142, 164, 191, 196, 212
   meaning of word, 39
Quaestors, Treasury of the, 7
Quinctius, Decimus, 169
quinqueremes, 35–6, 39–40, 53–4, 58–9, 61, 65–6, 69–75, 77, 79–81, 86, 89–92, 108, 111, 115, 122–3, 143, 164, 171, 173, 177–8, 181, 183–4, 187, 191, 196, 204, 211–12, 217, 226
   arrangement of oarsmen, 61

construction, 62
crew size, 79–80
invention of, 39
meaning of word, 39

ram, 35, 37
raven *see* corvus
Regillus, Lucius Aemilius, 211–12
Regulus, Gaius, Atilius, 84–5, 105
Regulus, Marcus Atilius, 90–1, 93, 99, 102, 126
Rhegium, 51–2, 54–5, 146–7, 169
Rhodes/Rhodians, 40, 157, 210–12
Rhone River, 164, 166
Rome/Romans, 14–17
   allies, 17
   citizenship, 18
   consuls/consulship, 5, 8–9, 19, 24–5, 53–6, 58, 60, 63–5, 73, 80, 82–5, 88, 90–3, 95, 97, 100, 104–106, 109, 112–14, 117–18, 123–4, 143, 145, 163, 173, 175–6, 181, 190, 192, 202, 207–208, 211, 214, 216–20
   expansionism, 17
   fleet, subscription, 122
   marines, 6, 16, 26, 65–7, 69, 72–4, 76–7, 79, 86, 89–90, 101, 104, 108, 110–11, 114–15, 147, 189, 194–5
   seapower, 98, 133–7, 203–204
   Senate, 3–4, 18–19, 58, 88, 97, 102, 113, 134, 141–2, 165, 172–3, 184, 189–90, 192–3, 207, 216–17
   ship construction, 58–60, 70–1, 105, 122–3, 134–5, 191
   ships, 70–2
   soldiers 15–16
Roman-Carthaginian treaties, 7

Sack of Rome, 15, 21
Sacred Band (of Carthage), 26, 30
sacred chickens, 112–13, 133
Sacred Isle, 124
Saguntum, 162–3, 184, 203, 207, 225
Salamis, 37, 44
Salinator, Gaius Livius, 210–11
sambuca, 177
Samnium/Samnites 7, 81, 167, 170

Samos, 211
Sardinia/Sardinians, 23, 52, 83–4, 113, 153, 158–9, 164, 175, 181–2, 189, 201–202
Scipio Africanus, Publius Cornelius, 185–94, 196, 200, 208, 211, 213, 215, 219–20
Scipio, Gnaeus Cornelius (Asina), 63, 83–4
Scipio, Gnaeus Cornelius, 63, 104, 166, 183–5
Scipio, Lucius Cornelius, 83, 211, 213
Scipio, Publius Cornelius, (father of Scipio Africanus) 165, 183–5
Scipionic circle, 9
scutum, 16
Segesta, 29, 44, 82
Seleucids/Seleucid Empire, 159, 209–13
Selinus, 29, 44
Sempronius *see* Longus, Tiberius Sempronius
septireme, Hannibal's flagship at Mylae, 75
Shekelesh, 28
shipworm, 34
Sicans, 28
Sicca, 127, 148
Sicels, 28
Sicilian Expedition, 29, 44
Sicily, 28–32, 44–5, 88–9, 95, 107, 121, 12–18, 130–7, 149, 174
Sîde, Battle of, 157, 212
Sîde/Sidetans, 222
Sidon, 23
signal flags, 37
Solus, 31
Spain, 24, 52, 158, 162, 164, 201–203, 207
Spendius, 149–53
spolia opima, 176
storms, 101, 104
Straits of Gibraltar, 23
Sulci, 84, 137
Sybota, Battle of, 48
Syphax, 193
Syracuse, 28–9, 44–5, 51, 56, 64, 117–18, 152, 168, 172, 175, 179–80, 189, 199, 227
Syria, 209, 211

Tarentum, 31, 168–9, 172, 179, 198, 207
Tarentum, naval battle off, 169–70

Tarraco, 183–5
Tartessians, 159
Tauromenium, 56
Taurus Mountains, 213
tax farming, 224
taxes/taxation, 18, 103, 127, 150, 178, 181, 192, 209, 224
Tebessa *see* Hecatontapylus, 126
Telamon, 145
teredo see shipworm
Teuta, 141–4
Therma, 105
Thessaly, 208
Thucydides, 43–4, 48, 66
Thurii, 169–70
Tiber River, 7
tin, 23
Toledo, 185
Trafalgar, 21
treaties, 5, 7, 30, 52, 56, 162–3, 169, 171–2, 211, 217
Trebia River, Battle of, 166–7
trierarchs, 122
triremes, 33–6, 39–40, 42–7, 58, 66, 75–7, 79–80, 122, 164, 170, 197, 212, 221
　meaning of word, 33
　operational range, 38
　rowers, 42
　service life, 34
　speed, 33–4

triumphator, 19
triumphus, 19
Tunis, 95, 148–9, 152, 193
Tunisia, 22–3
Turdetani, 159–60
Tyndaris, Battle of, 34, 84–6, 92, 105, 114, 137
Tyre, 23
Tyre, Siege of, 61, 66

Utica, 22, 150–2, 180, 190, 193–4, 218, 220

Veii, 7
Velia, 169
Venice, Arsenal, 60
veterans, 20, 30, 52, 148–9, 208, 213
Vibo, 165
Vitulus, Quintus Mamilius, 56
Vulso, Lucius Manlius, 90–1, 93, 105

Xanthippus, 96–9
Xerxes, 28, 40

Zacynthus, 173
Zama, Battle of, 196–7, 219, 225
Zonaras, John, 13, 27, 54, 83–4, 120, 122, 128, 130, 159